Dr Joyce Brothers, a noted psychologist, broadcasts regularly on NBC radio and is a columnist for *Good Housekeeping*. Her books have been widely translated. A United Press International poll named her as one of the ten most influential American women, and a George Gallup survey named her as one of the 'Ten Most Admired Women'. Dr Brothers was for six years a member of the faculty of Hunter College and Columbia University in New York City and she is now a frequent guest lecturer at universities all over the United States. She is a graduate of Cornell University and received her PhD from Columbia University. She is married with one daughter.

DR JOYCE BROTHERS

What Every Woman Should Know About Men

GRANADA
London Toronto Sydney New York

Published in paperback by Granada Publishing Limited in 1983

ISBN 0 586 05772 2

First published in Great Britain by
Granada Publishing Limited 1982
Copyright © Joyce B. Enterprises, Inc. 1981
Originally published in the USA by
Simon & Schuster 1981

Granada Publishing Limited
Frogmore, St Albans, Herts AL2 2NF
and
36 Golden Square, London W1R 4AH
515 Madison Avenue, New York, NY 10022, USA
117 York Street, Sydney, NSW 2000, Australia
100 Skyway Avenue, Rexdale, Ontario, M9W 3A6, Canada
61 Beach Road, Auckland, New Zealand

Printed and bound in Great Britain by
Cox & Wyman Ltd, Reading
Set in Baskerville

Granada ®
Granada Publishing ®

Contents

To my sustaining, loving husband, Milt, whom I love with all my heart, and to all of my family I hold so dear: Estelle, Morris, Lisa, Amir, Micah, Tillie, Maurice, Elaine, Richard, Margery, Perry, Stephen, Cindy, Tom, Patricia, Bruce, Nancy, Robert.

PART ONE
The Fragile Sex

1

Women know precious little about the men in their lives. They live with them, work with them, love them, fear them, fight them, seek their advice, resent their attitudes, watch their diets, bear their children – but they do not really understand them as well as they should.

Every week I get dozens of letters from women seeking advice on problems they have with their husbands, dates, employers, elderly fathers, sons. And most of the questions I am asked after lectures and television appearances are about men. If I have heard it once, I have heard it a thousand and one times, that half-humorous, half-furious plaint, 'I just don't understand that man.' I hear it from gloriously attractive film stars and models and from grand-mothers, from young magazine editors, from new mothers and from wives who have celebrated their twenty-fifth wedding anniversaries, from corporation executives, bank tellers, waitresses, college students – from women every-where I go.

But what is there to understand? Are men and women really so different?

They are.

They really are. I spent months talking to biologists, neurologists, geneticists, research psychiatrists, and psy-chologists – the scientists who are opening new frontiers in the study of humankind – in preparation for this book. Much of what I learned from them is so new that it has not reached the textbook stage yet. It is only beginning to appear in the professional journals in bits and pieces.

What I discovered was that men are even more different

from women than I had thought. Their bodies are different and their minds are different. Men are different from the very composition of their blood to the way their brains develop, which means that they think and experience life differently from women.

It is not that one sex is better or worse than the other. It is simply that the sexes are different. If we can understand these differences and learn to use them creatively, all of us, men and women alike, will be happier with ourselves and with each other.

It has become almost an article of faith in recent years to maintain that there are no significant differences between the sexes apart from the most obvious and cherished differences. The fact is that there are other, and probably more important, differences between the sexes than the male and female reproductive organs.

I am talking about differences here – not about equality and inequality. Some people confuse the two ideas. I like the way sociologist Alice Rossi put it once. 'As far as male and female are concerned,' she said, 'difference is a biological fact, whereas equality is a political, ethical and social concept. No rule of nature or of social organization says that the sexes have to be the same or do the same things in order to be social, political and economic equals.'

Some of the differences between men and women are culturally determined, others genetically. And sometimes we do not know quite which, since science has not yet concluded whether many differences – such as the fact that more men than women stutter, for instance, or that girl babies smile more than boy babies – are imposed by their genes or their environment. Or perhaps by both. But we do know that:

Men change their minds more often than women do.
They snore more,

Fight more,
Masturbate more.

Men have thicker skins and longer vocal cords.
Their blood is redder,
Their daylight vision better,
And their metabolic rate higher.
And more of them are left-handed.

Men feel pain less than women do.
They age earlier,
But they wrinkle later.
They lose weight more easily,
But rich men are fatter than rich women.

Men's immunity against disease is weaker.
They talk about themselves less,
But they worry about themselves more.
And they are not as sensitive to others as women are.

Men *are* different. In countless ways. But if they are, so what? Men, it seems, have always been different. Does it really matter?

It matters.

It matters very much. More than it ever has before. Women's relationships with men are in transition along with life-styles, values, and aspirations in this era of technical and cultural dislocation. Just about every second marriage ends in divorce these days. Both at home and at work outside the home, women are rebelling against what they see as male dominance, male chauvinism, male exploitation, and male harassment.

Men do not see it the same way. What men see is that their power base is eroding. They are no longer undisputed lords and masters. And many of them do not quite understand why. All they know is that at work women are no longer those nine-to-five ministering angels who were as willing to sew on a button or make coffee as to do the filing and take dictation. They are competitors now, rivals for salary increases and promotions.

And things are not much better at home. Wives are insisting that husbands take a more active role in caring for the children and share the domestic chores more equitably. Taking out the rubbish is not enough any more.

It is unsettling at the very least. Even those men who believe strongly in equality for women find it disturbing. No one likes to lose age-old comforts and privileges.

I myself have been well aware of how ingrained this sense of male prerogative and privilege is ever since I had to fight practically tooth and claw to study for my master's degree and then my doctorate in psychology at Columbia University. Tooth and claw may be a bit of an exaggeration, but I had to fight.

The whole thing was completely unexpected. I had graduated from Cornell that spring at the age of nineteen (I had started college when I was fifteen) and a few weeks after graduation, I received my letter of acceptance from Columbia. Life could not have been rosier. I had just become engaged to Milt, so both romantically and academically my life was full of promise. Then I received a summons to meet the head of the psychology department at Columbia. I naively assumed he wanted to discuss my plan of study.

I can see his office, just as if I had left it this morning. It was enormous, lined with bookshelves. Books were everywhere. I can also remember almost every word he said.

'Miss Bauer,' he began in a cold and rather distant tone (I was Joyce Diane Bauer then), 'I asked you to come here because I think I owe it to you to discourage you from coming to Columbia.' My eyes opened wide and my stomach practically turned over. What was this all about?

What had I done?

'We accepted your application because we had no choice,' he said grudgingly. 'You had the highest qualifying examinations of any applicant. And you were an excellent student, it seems, at Cornell.'

Yes, I had been. There was no 'seems' about it. I had made three honour societies while I was at Cornell. And I had majored in two fields – home economics and psychology. I had always known I wanted to be a wife and a mother and a psychologist. I had wanted to prepare myself as well as possible for all three roles.

'So we could not refuse you,' he continued. 'But we would like you to know that we feel you are standing in the way of some man who can really use this education.'

My heart stopped. I was only nineteen, remember, and by now I was a very scared young woman.

'We have more applications than we can accept. We think it would be far better if you would cede your place to a man who will make psychology his lifetime career.'

My mouth was open to tell him that this was exactly what I planned to do. I was not planning to work for my master's degree and then for my doctorate on a whim or just to pass the time. It was going to be hard work, demanding the best I had to give. I planned to use the knowledge I would gain.

He went on, not giving me a chance to speak. 'In the past, we have occasionally accepted women. And almost without exception, they have married, had babies, and quit. That was the end of them. All the time, effort, and energy we had spent on them was wasted. Absolutely wasted,' he emphasized. 'We expect that you will follow the pattern. You are an attractive young woman.

'I put it to you,' he concluded, 'that you are standing in the way of a man who could really benefit from the training we have to offer.' And he leaned back in his chair behind the desk that seemed as big as an aircraft carrier.

Today I am not quite sure how I mustered the courage. I remember how scared I was. But I managed to smile and I said, 'I understand the point you are making, but I want to be a psychologist. Columbia offers the best training that can be obtained and I'm enormously pleased that I have been accepted. This is what I want. And this is what I am going to do. I promise you that I will do as good a job as any man.'

It was so quiet in that office after I stopped speaking that you could almost feel it.

After a moment he stood up. 'If this is your decision, I respect it,' he said. Never in my life had I felt such disapproval. 'But I want you to know,' he told me, 'that we will make life very difficult for you.'

And they did. The psychology department was practically 99·9 per cent pure male and some of those men made the six years of my graduate study difficult in unnecessary ways. I had to convince each new professor in each new course that I was serious and that I could do the work, even though I was younger than the other students – and the wrong sex.

I still flush with belated anger when I think about that episode, that imperturbably male assumption that I should cede my hard-earned place to a man. But today I understand the head of the psychology department. He was experiencing a kind of future shock.

This could not happen today, not in quite the same blatant way. It is an indication of how much things have changed since mid-century – and how fast men have had to change their attitudes and expectations. That man, the highly respected head of the psychology department, never felt kindly towards me, although I happen to know that he took a certain pride in pointing to me as an example of the high calibre of students attracted by the prestige of his department. But our relationship was always distant, always strained. That encounter stood between us.

This kind of exacerbated tension is present in very few male-female relationships today. We have all come a long way, both men and women. But there are strains. And they seem to be intensifying. They are not confined to the heads of university departments and determined female students. They exist on every level – in offices and factories, in police departments, hospitals, the armed services, in politics, in law firms and in the media, in the home and in marriages.

If women want to, they can ameliorate these strains – and without sacrificing any of the gains they have achieved.

In a way it is like being your own Secretary of State. If you are going to negotiate with another power, even a beloved power, for rights, privileges, and concessions that will make you happier, richer, more comfortable, more secure, and more equal, you must understand what those rights, privileges, and concessions mean to the other fellow. Information is the secret weapon of diplomacy. Once you have an insight into how the other power will react – and why – then you know how to go about getting what you want. You also know when it will not be worth the effort, when you will only be banging your head against a stone wall.

A woman can improve her relationship with almost any man – husband, lover, son, colleague, employer, friend – if she understands more about the sources of men's behaviour, their secret fears, the long-term effects of male fragility, their idealism, their hunger for love, their inability to see things the way women do. There are always exceptions, of course. When I talk about men in this book, I am talking about the broad spectrum of the male sex, not the individual. It is important to remember that no matter how great the differences are between men and women, the differences among members of the same sex are usually equally great if not greater. For instance, it is an accepted fact that women have more manual dexterity than men. They can type faster and more accurately. But there are men who can type faster and more accurately than women. And there are women who are true klutzes and can barely tie their running shoes.

Why can't men try to understand more about women? They do try, but not very hard. I told you – men are different. It seems to be more difficult for them to empathize with the feelings of others. The fact is that men do not know all that much about themselves. Nor do they seem to want to. A striking illustration of this is the difference between the popular men's and women's magazines.

The traditional magazines directed primarily at women who have chosen marriage and motherhood as a career offer 'job-oriented' articles on sex, child care, marriage, food, fashions, furnishings, money management, medicine, and psychology. Particularly psychology. In almost every category from sex to money to food, the articles tend to have some psychological content. There is a strong emphasis on understanding oneself, one's children, one's mate. The fiction tends to explore problems wives and mothers face in their daily lives.

The newer magazines addressed to women working outside the home are equally service-oriented, offering advice on how to succeed in what has been until recently a predominantly masculine preserve, the middle and upper echelons of business. Again, there is an emphasis on psychology, on insights into oneself, one's male and female colleagues and superiors.

Men's magazines, on the other hand, tend to stress performance – sexual, business, sports – rather than insight. The fiction is characterized by action and adventure. Women appear – both in the fiction and in the photographs and drawings that are the mainstay of these periodicals – as sex objects. The non-fiction tends to be of high calibre, but rarely treats such topics as male insecurities, health problems, relationships with colleagues at work, feelings towards women, dissatisfactions with the quality of life, roles as fathers and sons. There is little introspection in these magazines.

Women seem to feel that the proper study of woman is woman and that the more a woman knows about herself and others, the better she will function. Not only that, but she is willing to share her self-knowledge with the world.

If you want to know how an eleven-year-old felt the first time she menstruated or a fifty-year-old felt when she was fired from her job, how a woman felt when her son moved in with his girlfriend or when she learned that her husband was unfaithful, chances are that it is all there in black and white for the reading in some women's magazine.

But if you want to know how a man feels during orgasm or why and how he can stay slumped in front of the television set for hours on end every weekend during the football season or what went through his mind when he learned that the baby was a girl – forget it. Men don't talk about these things. And they are not interested in reading about how other men *think* and *feel* about such subjects.

This attitude also embraces factual matter. Dr Estelle Ramey, professor of physiology and biophysics at the Georgetown University School of Medicine and a leading endocrinologist, maintains that it extends into the world of research in some cases.

She cited as an example the discovery that the hormone testosterone seems to increase the likelihood of high blood pressure in men and thus contributes to their earlier deaths from heart attacks and strokes. 'I don't feel that there is significant research going on in this field,' she said, 'because the men who are doing the research don't want to know why they die earlier. They take the fact that they do with a kind of fatalism. It has taken a woman to bring the subject up. We have to find ways of protecting men from testosterone without interfering with their sexual function. I don't want to live in a world where you have blue-haired little ladies surviving their husbands by years and years.'

I will discuss just how hormones affect men in a later chapter, but this indicates the aversion men have to finding out about things that affect them personally – let alone sharing that knowledge with others.

This resistance, fortunately, is encountered only in certain areas of scientific research. There have been great leaps in our knowledge of human beings and especially of the differences between males and females. It is this knowledge that I want to share here. It is what I feel every woman should know about men – how they differ physically, mentally, and psychologically from women. It is in a woman's self-interest to be informed about these differences. There is nothing abstruse about most of the information. It can be translated into everyday terms and it explains many of the things that puzzle women about men. For instance:

Did you ever wonder why your husband or lover turns over and falls asleep within seconds after love-making, leaving you awake and lonely? See page 179.

Did you ever wonder why a man will say 'I'll call you tomorrow' at the end of a pleasant evening and then does not call? Page 235.

Did you ever wonder why your nine-year-old son, who can take the lawn mower apart and put it back together so that it works better than before, cannot read as well as his eight-year-old sister? Page 37.

Or why the man in your life falls on the couch after you

have both gone on an all-day hike and complains that he is pooped while you bustle around and do the laundry and get supper? Page 31

Did you know that scientists now suspect that love really is 'chemistry' and they have pinpointed the 'cupid chemical'? Page 247

When should you worry about your man's interest in pornography and when should you shrug it off? Page 222

Did you know that men fall in love faster than women? And why? Page 248

Did you ever wonder what single quality men value most in a woman? Page 231

Or why a man is more shaken by his wife's infidelity than a woman by her husband's? Page 277

Once a woman understands why men act and feel the way they do, she can put what she has learned to immediate use. It is like having a master key that unlocks the mysteries of masculine thought and behaviour

2

And the rib, which the Lord God had taken from man, made he a woman, and brought her unto the man. And Adam said, 'This is now bone of my bones, and flesh of my flesh: she shall be called Woman, because she was taken out of Man.'
GENESIS 2:22-23

Adam may have been the first human being, but it was the last time the male was ever first. From the moment the sperm fertilizes the ovum, the resulting embryo is a potential Eve. Scientists call it the Eve Principle.

'Nature's programme in differentiating the embryo is to form Eve first, Adam second,' asserts Dr John Money, professor of medical psychology and director of the Psychohormonal Research Unit at the Johns Hopkins Medical Institutions in Baltimore.

'You can think of maleness as a type of birth defect,' adds immunologist Dr Stephen Wachtel of the Memorial Sloan-Kettering Cancer Center in New York. 'In the beginning,' he says, 'we are all headed toward femaleness.'

To understand men, it helps to understand how maleness is determined in the first place. And for that we have to go back and find out what goes on in the embryo in the weeks and months before birth.

You may remember from school biology that every cell in your body contains forty-six chromosomes, each of them packed with genes, and that the gene mix is different for everyone. The genes in your own set of forty-six chromosomes comprise a unique formula that produced a unique human being – you. All that concerns us here, however, are two chromosomes out of the forty-six, the sex chromosomes. The pair are called, rather unromantically, X and Y. Men have one of each, an X and a Y. The Y chromosome is the one that determines maleness. Women do not have a Y. They have two Xs instead.

Every ovum or egg contains twenty-three chromosomes, one of them an X chromosome. Male sperm also contains twenty-three chromosomes, and the sperm released during each ejaculation are divided into X-carrying sperm and Y-carrying sperm. If an X sperm fertilizes the egg, the embryo will have two X chromosomes and the baby will be a female. If a Y, the embryo will have an X and a Y chromosome and the baby will be a male – maybe.

For the first month or so after fertilization, the cells of the embryo divide and redivide at a dizzying rate until the tiny foetus is recognizably human with a head and body and arms and legs, but sexually it is neither one thing nor the other. It has what one might call dual controls, embryonic his-and-her sex potential, clusters of cells poised to develop into male or female sex organs.

In due course the healthy female embryo develops female sex organs and the potential for male sex organs disappears. Females are relentlessly, inevitably, stubbornly female. There is no fooling around with their sexual destination – unless the mother has been taking hormones or other medication that affects the embryo's hormonal mix, or there is some genetic defect that distorts the hormonal mix or the embryo's reaction to it. Females are destined to be female from the instant the X-carrying sperm unites with the ovum.

It is different with the male. All babies would be female, even those that result from the encounter of a Y-carrying sperm with the egg, unless something more happened.

That something more seems to be the prodding of a

recently discovered scrap of matter that clings to the outside of male cells. Scientists now believe this is the ultimate determinant of maleness. The microscopic scrap, which is called the H-Y antigen, spurs the Y chromosome into doing its job of starting the foetus on the road to masculinity. The first sign that the H-Y antigen has nudged the Y chromosome into action comes about six weeks after conception, when the embryo begins to develop testes.

But not even these embryonic testes are enough to ensure that the baby will be a boy. Again something more must happen. The hypothalamus, a part of the brain that is no bigger than an almond when fully developed but is immensely powerful (it regulates breathing, temperature, and blood pressure, among other functions), must release a substance that in a kind of domino effect eventually gets a message through to the testes that it is time to start producing sex hormones.

When they get the signal, the testes go to work. They put out large amounts of testosterone, the male hormone, and smaller amounts of oestrogen and progesterone, the female hormone and the 'pregnancy' hormone. (Both men and women have all three hormones, but in different proportions.) This hormonal blend encourages the further development of the male sex organs. And finally the embryo is demonstrably male.

What scientists have learned in the laboratory is just how persistent femaleness is.

For instance, if the testes are removed from a male rat embryo, the rat does not develop as a sterile male. It turns into a female. Genetically the rat is still a male, since it possesses both an X and a Y chromosome, but anatomically and behaviourally it looks and acts like a female.

Experiments have revealed that a male rat castrated immediately after birth will act like a female when mature, even to the point of exhibiting female sexual behaviour.

There is none of this dithering back and forth with the female. When the ovaries are removed from a female rat embryo, it still develops as a female – a sterile female, but definitely a female. When the ovaries are removed immediately after birth, the rat still develops as a female.

How much of this applies to human beings? It is impossible to say, but we do know that there are genetic males – individuals with both an X and a Y chromosome – who grow up to look and act like females; who, in fact, believe that they are female. These people inherited a sensitivity to the masculinizing hormones, testosterone and other androgens. This sensitivity immunized them while in the womb against the male hormones that their testes produced, with the result that there was no further development of the male sex organs and the babies *appeared to be female at birth*.

Dr Money, who has followed the development of a number of these deceptively sexed people, says that they 'never think of themselves as anything but girls'. There is no reason for them to. 'They marry,' he says, 'and function as sexually normal females, even though every cell in their bodies carries the male X-Y pair of sexual chromosomes.'

This handful of research findings – there are many, many more – illustrates the force of the thrust of femaleness and how vulnerable the male is during the process of sexual differentiation. There are a myriad of things that can go wrong – and do go wrong – for the male. Most foetuses lost in miscarriages are males.

Some eminent Catholic and Protestant theologians have had serious discussions in recent months about whether God might not be a female. It is true that in many cultures God is thought of as Mother. The very fact of the discussion is an interesting example of the force with which femaleness asserts itself.

But this is in the realm of philosophical speculation. Does

any of this affect us directly? Does the rather precarious sexual development of the male affect the relationship between men and women?

It does. For one thing, it establishes the fact of male fragility even before birth. Not only is the male hold on his sexual identity tenuous compared to that of the female, the male is more vulnerable from the word go. Even though nature tries to stack the deck in favour of males with about 5 per cent more male than female babies born each year, more boys than girls die during the first year of life. In 1978, the latest year for which figures are available, 15·3 out of every thousand male infants died, compared to 12·9 female infants. As the years go by, that initial 5 per cent advantage disappears until, in the late teens, the sexes are about equal in number. After that it is all downhill for the male. Their fragility becomes more and more evident, the ultimate heartbreaking proof coming when men die eight years earlier than women on the average.

More men than women die from fourteen out of the fifteen leading causes of death.* More women do die from diabetes, but not very many more, and men suffer far more kidney damage as a consequence of diabetes than women.

Women are practically immune to some diseases that afflict men. Males are more likely to contract certain types of cancer, especially lymphoma and leukaemia. They suffer more often and more severely from staphylococcus infections and respiratory illnesses, such as influenza and pneumonia. Three times as many men as women, for instance, fell victim to the recently pinpointed type of pneumonia known as Legionnaires' Disease. Men also contract central nervous system infections more often and

* Heart disease, cancer, cerebrovascular disease, accidents, influenza and pneumonia, conditions of early infancy, diabetes mellitus, arteriosclerosis, bronchitis and emphysema and asthma, cirrhosis, congenital anomalies, homicide, nephritis-nephrosis, peptic ulcer, suicide.

suffer from gastroenteritis more frequently. And this is just skimming the top. They are prey to many, many more infections than women.

Even when the tables are turned, men are more at risk. Take high blood pressure. Women tend to be more susceptible than men. For every four men with high blood pressure, there are five women. But more men die from it. 'Men don't tolerate it as well,' reports Dr John H. Laragh of the New York Hospital – Cornell Medical Center. 'The truth is that men don't tolerate anything as well as women.'

There is no mystery about why men are more vulnerable to infection and why they die younger. The villain is that Y chromosome. Or, to put it the other way around, it is the lack of the second X chromosome that women have. The X chromosome is not only a sex chromosome, it also carries the genes that protect us against many infections. Women with their two X chromosomes have double protection.

The two X chromosomes not only give women double protection, they also give them a second chance. Colour blindness, for instance, is an inherited trait carried on the X chromosome. Eight per cent of the male population suffers from colour perception problems, compared to less than half of one per cent of the females. This is an aggravating affliction and sometimes dangerous. Most people who are colour-blind have trouble distinguishing between red and green, so that green for go and red for stop look the same to them. Other people can see only shades of black and white and grey.

If a woman carries the gene for colour blindness on one X chromosome, there is a good chance that her second X chromosome will not carry it. If it does not, the colour-blind gene is, in effect, cancelled out.

Very little has been written about male fragility. It is one of those subjects that men do not like to read about, talk about, or think about. They are even 'reluctant to seek [medical] care or adopt behaviour that would diminish the risks of dying sooner from chronic diseases', reported Dr Charles Lewis and Mary Ann Lewis in the *New England Journal of Medicine*.

For example, women buy three-quarters of the vitamin pills sold in the USA. It can be argued that they buy them for their husbands and sons as well as for themselves, but according to the president of one drug company, their research shows that 61 per cent of the country's vitamin-swallowers are women. And women go to the doctor and the dentist more often than men – and they are certainly not taking their husband's gall-bladders or teeth with them.

There is nothing genetic about males' refusals to concern themselves with their health. They are taught that men are strong and that a real man does not give in to aches and pains. From the moment the baby boy takes his first step and promptly falls down, he is told 'Big boys don't cry.' All through childhood boys are told 'Don't act like a girl. Don't act like a sissy.' Television reinforces the message. Commercials show more women than men in need of and using the health products that are advertised. These sex-role teachings simply compound men's vulnerability. Not only are they genetically more susceptible to disease, they are also brainwashed into resisting the idea that they should take care of themselves.

The subject of male fragility is starting to surface now as people become aware of its far-reaching implications. Even so, the warnings tend to come from scientists in disciplines such as anthropology that encourage a longer perspective, or from women like endocrinologist Dr Ramey, and Dr Joan Ullyot.

Dr Ullyot, a prize-winning marathoner as well as a physiologist at San Francisco's Institute of Health Research, says, 'Physically and psychologically, women are tougher than men.' Taking an extreme example to make her point, she says that 'shipwrecked women survive better than shipwrecked men. It may have something to do with better insulation or better natural ability to metabolize fat.'

'I've always been amused that the astronauts have all been men,' Dr Ramey said when the first female astronauts were chosen. 'In our experiments, we found that females can take a hell of a lot more tumbling and disorientation in space than males can without showing signs of shock.'

'Woman is, on the whole, biologically superior to man,' maintains anthropologist Ashley Montagu. Women 'endure all sorts of devitalizing conditions better than men: starvation, exposure, fatigue, shock, illness and the like. The female is constitutionally stronger than the male and only muscularly less powerful. She has greater stamina and lives longer.'

Some researchers fear that the male is truly imperilled. 'Males may well be an evolutionary dead end,' says Fred Hapgood, author of the scholarly *Why Males Exist: An Inquiry into the Evolution of Sex*. Hapgood is taking the long view, of course, and he was referring specifically to the animal kingdom, but that is our biological kingdom too.

So there it is. Men are fragile creatures, at risk from the moment of conception. And, at the other end of the life span, the female lasts longer. Coming and going, women have the best of it. Biologically, that is.

3

Male fragility seems paradoxical when we consider that men have been regarded as the stronger sex throughout the centuries and certainly have been the dominant sex. No matter how many advances women have made, the world is still run largely by and for men. When push comes to shove, it is the men who are doing the pushing and the shoving. If men are so fragile, how is it that we live in a male-dominated world? The answer is that when one puts all the pieces together, it makes good biological and anthropological sense. It also becomes clear that we are coming to the end of an era that has lasted from the ice age to the present. Here are some of the significant pieces.

It is not only the sexual organs and systems that make men's and women's bodies different. We are different inside and out, from the places hair grows on our bodies to the construction of our skeletons to the way we breathe and the very consistency of our blood.

Men's blood is heavier. They have about 20 per cent more red corpuscles than women. These are the cells with haemoglobin, the substance that delivers oxygen wherever the body needs it. Oxygen goes to work to release the energy in the fats and carbohydrates stored in our bodies. The extra red corpuscles mean that men get more oxygen and have more energy.

They need this extra dose of red corpuscles for more than energy. Men cannot manufacture blood as efficiently as women can. This makes surgery riskier for men. Men also need more oxygen because they do not breathe as often as women and they breathe more deeply. This also exposes them to risk. When the air is polluted, they draw more of it into their lungs.

When ether was first used as an anaesthetic, doctors were horrified to discover that the mortality rate for men was twice as high as for women. After a certain amount of trial and error, they learned to adjust the amount of ether so that it would anaesthetize the deep-breathing men without killing them.

A more recent – and chilling – finding is the effect of exhaust fumes on children's intelligence. These exhaust fumes are the greatest source of lead pollution in cities. Researchers have found that the children with the highest concentrations of lead in their bodies have the lowest scores on intelligence tests, and that boys score lower than girls. It is possible that these low scores are connected to the deeper breathing that is typical of the male.

Men's bones are larger than women's and they are arranged somewhat differently. That feminine walk that evokes whistles is a matter of bone structure. Men have broader shoulders and a narrower pelvis, which enables them to stride out with no wasted motion. A woman's wider pelvis, designed for childbearing, forces her to put more movement into each step she takes, with the result that she displays a bit of jiggle and sway as she walks.

If you think that a man is brave because he climbs a ladder to clean out the roof gutters, don't forget that it is easier for him than for you. The angle at which a woman's thigh is joined to her knees makes climbing awkward for her, no matter whether she is tackling a ladder or stairs or a mountain.

While it is true that men are more fragile than women, it is also true that they are stronger. There is no contradiction here. Strength can go hand-in-hand with vulnerability. When West Point started admitting women in 1976, they ran a lot of tests to check the relative strength of the new women as compared to the men. They found that the young women had only one-third the upper body strength of their male classmates and two-thirds the strength in their legs. Their abdominal muscles were as strong as the men's.

Men's fat is distributed differently. And they do not have that layer of fat just underneath their skin that women do. In fact, they have considerably less fat than women and more lean mass.* Forty-one per cent of a man's body is muscle, compared to 35 per cent for women, which means that men have more muscle power. When it comes to strength, almost 90 per cent of a man's weight is strength, compared to about 50 per cent of a woman's weight.

This higher proportion of muscle to fat makes it easier for men to lose weight. Muscle burns up 5 more calories a pound than fat does just to maintain itself. When they are just sitting around doing nothing, men burn 3.7 calories an hour for each square foot of skin surface,† compared to 3.5 for women. So when a man goes on a diet, the pounds roll off much faster.

However, there is a plus to women's greater fat reserves. The subcutaneous layer of fat, that thin layer just under the skin, acts like an invisible fur coat to keep a woman warmer in the winter. It hardly seems fair, but women also stay cooler in summer. That fat layer helps insulate against the heat, but basically women owe their summer comfort to the fact that they sweat so much more efficiently. Their sweat glands are distributed more evenly over their bodies, which enables them to cool off faster.

---

* Among the rich, it is the other way around. Rich men are fatter than poor men – about 20 per cent fatter on the average. And rich men's wives are about 20 per cent thinner than the wives of poor men.

† Speaking of skin, men's skin is thicker than women's – and nowhere near as soft. The thickness prevents radiation from the sun from getting through, which is why men wrinkle less than women do.

The flip side of men's enviable muscular leanness is that they do not have the energy reserves women do. They have more start-up energy, but the fat tucked away in women's nooks and crannies provides a rich energy reserve that men lack.

Runners talk about 'hitting the wall'. This refers to the excruciating pain and weakness that suddenly hits them when they have used up all their glycogen. Glycogen is the form in which carbohydrates are stored in muscles. A runner who is putting out more than 80 per cent of his top effort will use up the glycogen stored in his muscles in about two hours. Sometimes sooner. At this point, he or she hits the wall. A man can go on for a while, but he slows down dramatically. A woman can go on much longer. She switches over to her fat reserves. Weight for weight, fat yields more than twice as much energy as glycogen. The female sex hormones help a woman's muscles to use this fat more easily than men can.

Not all of us are runners, although sometimes it seems that way, but the drama of 'hitting the wall' is played out in the lives of many couples. I have heard so many women complain about it that I have come to think of it as 'the weekend fizzle-out'. A typical fizzle-out scenario goes something like this:

Wendy and Charles start out one Saturday afternoon for a fifteen-mile run, which each has worked up to gradually. Charles completed the fifteen miles well before Wendy. He was six inches taller than her five feet six and had proportionately longer legs.

A couple of hours later, Wendy suggested that they go out for dinner. 'I'm kind of tired,' she said. 'I don't feel like cooking.'

'You're tired!' Charles exclaimed. 'I've had it. I'm not going to get dressed and go out.'

'Okay,' she sighed. 'What'll it be? Hamburgers or scrambled eggs?'

'Eggs,' he said. 'I'm too tired to chew.' Wendy scrambled eggs and made toast. Later she cleared the table, washed the dishes, tidied the kitchen. 'I'm tired too,' she muttered to herself as she put things away. 'Why do I have to do everything?'

In fact Wendy coped with the kitchen chores easily. What she resented was doing them alone. Or more precisely, doing them at all. She wanted to go out to eat and felt Charles's refusal to dress was selfish and lazy.

When she came back into the living room, she glared at Charles who was watching television. 'If you want anything else,' she said, 'you can get it yourself. I'm tired of waiting on you.' And that was the first round of a fight that lasted the rest of the weekend.

The weekend fizzle-out has a thousand variations. Elaine wants to go dancing after a day's riding and Jeff says that he is too beat. Linda wants to go to the movies after she and Doug have spent the day spading up a new garden. Doug wants to go to sleep.

Jill and Steven played tennis all afternoon. Then Jill needs help to rearrange the living room furniture; Steven says 'Forget it.'

These men are not being lazy. After putting out their maximum physical effort over a period of hours, they are at the end of their physical tether, in a state very close to that of the runner hitting the wall. Women have far more endurance. Over the long haul, they can stay in there and keep going longer than men.

And I really mean the long haul. Cardiologists at the University of Alabama who tested healthy women on treadmills discovered that over the years the female capacity for exercise far exceeds male capacity. A woman's capacity to exercise drops about 2 per cent for every ten years of age compared to a drop of 10 per cent for men.

A woman of sixty who is in good health can exercise up to 90 per cent of what she could do when she was twenty years old. A man of sixty has only 60 per cent of his twenty-year-old capacity left.

This greater muscular power, the ability to lift heavier weights and run faster and farther, is one of the significant differences between the sexes that has made males the dominant sex through all these centuries (the other is that men don't give birth).

If we put the male's greater strength together with what is known and what amounts to educated guesses by historians about the social structure of ice age civilization, it makes sense that the male should have dominated Men were stronger, taller, and heavier. They could run faster and throw straighter. These attributes cast them in the role of hunters, fighters, protectors, and leaders. The men went out into the forests, tracked and killed the bears and the wolves and the deer, and dragged them home for the women to cook. The women stayed close to home, bearing and caring for the children and probably gathering nuts and picking berries to add to their diet. It was a logical division of life's responsibilities. The pregnant woman could not face the hardships of the hunter's life without endangering the unborn child. Nor could the nursing mother join the hunt without endangering the suckling.*

---

* I must point out that there are other theories and other interpretations. Sociologist Martha Dobbins, for instance, suggests that in the earliest human groups the males may have been sent out to hunt not because they were the strongest, but because they were the most dispensable. 'In the very early pre-history, ninety-five thousand years ago, there may not have been any significant differences in size and strength between men and women,' she told the American Association for the Advancement of Science. 'But because women produced children and produced milk, which would have been the only reliable source of protein, and because of a survival advantage for a group that did not risk its reproductive, milk-producing members, men would have been encouraged and channelled into risk-taking activities.'

In the course of hundreds of generations, these physically based roles were culturally reinforced to the point where they seemed immutable even when men went out to the office or the factory in the morning instead of tracking prey through the forest. Men were leaders; women were nurturers and followers. That was the way things were, the way they always had been.

But nothing stays the same forever. That significant difference, the greater male strength that tipped the scales in ice-age days, is not significant in the nuclear age. As sociobiologist Edward O. Wilson of Harvard University says, 'Mankind's greatest problem is that it is caught in the twentieth century with a nature largely shaped by evolution to deal with ice-age problems. That nature is a hodgepodge of special genetic adaptations to an environment that has largely vanished.'

Evolution is a slow and uneven process. Right now we have nuclear-age minds trapped in ice-age bodies. Our ice-age bodies thrive on physical exertion. They are geared to ice-age needs. The result is that we have to find time to exercise our bodies in order to keep them functioning efficiently.

Can you imagine ice-age man doing sit-ups? Or leg lifts? Or dieting?

The significant difference that will determine dominance in the future will not be physical strength but mental. What is interesting is that the mind, like the body, is sexually differentiated.

4

Men and women do not think the same way. Their brains are almost as different as their sex organs. The very idea of male and female brains is startling. Until so recently that it seems like the day before yesterday, a brain was a brain was a brain. Now we discover that there are his brain and her brain.

His brain is not even shaped quite like hers. At least not if he is a canary or a thrush – or a rat. Birdsong is controlled by a cluster of cells in the bird's forebrain. Researchers have discovered that these clusters are larger in male songbirds than in the female. And male birds are lustier, more tuneful, and more persistent songsters than females. Those birds that warble their hearts out at dawn every spring are mostly male.

It is not only bird brains that show sexual differences. The part of the brain that controls sexual behaviour is larger in male rats than in females. And as someone who has spent her share of time doing laboratory experiments, I can testify that male rats are a whole lot more interested in sex than the females.

No one has fathomed the sexual mysteries of the human brain yet, but now that birds and rats have blazed the way, we know a lot more than we did just a few years ago. We know, for instance, that sex hormones play a leading role in the development of the brain.

This was shown clearly in one breakthrough discovery when slices of brain tissue from unborn mice were immersed in various growing mediums. The slices that were marinated in a bath of sex hormones showed significant

growth. The others did not. We also know that in the beginning, the foetal brain is what scientists describe as 'bi-
potential and undifferentiated'. What they mean is it can go
either way, male or female. The sex hormones eventually
dictate which fork it will take. When these hormones reach
the embryonic brain, it begins to develop the differences in
structure and then in function that characterize male or
female brains. This does not happen overnight, but extends
from prenatal days into adolescence.

A boy's brain develops at a different rate from a girl's, but
before I go into the significance of this, it is important to
understand a bit about how our brains work.

The brain is divided into a right and a left hemisphere,
which are connected by nerve fibres. These hemispheres of
our mind are as different as those of our planet, perhaps
even more so. The right hemisphere governs the left side of
the body and the left hemisphere governs the right. It works
like this:

1. *Wiggle the toes on your right foot.*
   It was the left side of your brain that gave the wiggle
   message to your toes.
2. *Wiggle the toes on your left foot.*
   It is the same motion, but different toes, and the wiggle
   order came from the other side of your brain.
3. *Simultaneously place your right hand on the left side of your
   head and your left hand on the right side.*
   Each hand now rests on the side of the brain that
   controls that hand. Both sides of your brain were
   involved in getting you into this yogalike position.

The right and the left hemispheres do more than control
our movements. They are responsible for the way we think.
And each has its own specialities. The left hemisphere is the
verbal brain. It controls language and reading skills. It

processes information logically, step by step. We use the left brain when we balance our chequebook, read a newspaper, sing a song, play bridge, write a letter, weigh the advantages of paying off the mortgage versus the benefits of the tax deduction it affords.

No one quite knew what the right hemisphere was good for, if anything, for a long time. Some neurologists speculated that it was just a spare part. We know better now. It is the centre of our spatial abilities. We use it when we consult a map, thread our way through a maze, work a jigsaw puzzle, design a house, plan a garden, recognize a face, when we paint a picture, possibly when we listen to music, definitely when we solve a problem in geometry.

If you think of the old adage that a picture is worth a thousand words, it gives you an idea of how the right half of the brain works. Instead of processing information step by step the way the left hemisphere does, it processes patterns of information. It links facts together to form a concept and links a series of concepts into a coherent whole. It is intuitive. Some believe that it is the dreamer.

As I said earlier, boys' and girls' brains develop at different rates. The male right brain develops earlier than the female; the female left brain develops earlier than the male. This difference in timing accounts for the fact that many little boys do not read and write as well as girls of the same age, a fact that upsets many parents.

I get letter after letter asking 'Why is it that my son who can build quite complicated model planes cannot write as well as the little girl next door who is a grade behind him in school?' Or 'Why is it that our boy cannot read as well as his younger sister? He is very bright. He taught himself how to play chess.' In most cases, the answer is that Johnny can't read as well as the girls because his left hemisphere is not as developed yet as theirs is. But his right hemisphere is doing fine.

In fact, all through his life, his right hemisphere will probably do better than his female peers' right hemispheres. Men are right-hemisphere–oriented and they use this side of their brain more efficiently than women do. Scores of studies have established that males have superior spatial abilities. One study involved rats who had to find their way out of a maze. The males found the exit faster than the females. When female rats were treated with male hormones they did just as well as the males.

In another experiment, boys and girls were given two different objects, one to be held in each hand. They were not allowed to see the objects. After a few minutes, the objects were taken away and placed on a table containing dozens of objects that were roughly the same size. Each youngster was asked to pick out the two objects he or she had held.

On the face of it, boys and girls did equally well. They identified almost the same number of objects. But when their scores were analysed, there was a significant difference. The girls did equally well in identifying objects held in their right and left hands. The boys did very poorly in identifying what they had held in their right hands, but did much, much better in picking out the object they had held in their left hands, a task performed by the right half of the brain.

Women are left-hemisphere–oriented, more verbally adroit. Their left hemisphere develops earlier, which gives them an edge in reading and writing. Men and women even use their brains differently.

Men use the right hemisphere more efficiently than women do. The converse is not true, however. Women do not use the left brain more efficiently than men. The male and female brains are by no means set up as mirror images of each other. What it adds up to is that we are blessed with two different ways of thinking and learning.

The male brain is specialized. Men use the right hemisphere when dealing with spatial problems and the left for verbal problems. A man may be putting together the backyard swing and climbing bars he bought for his little girl's birthday. While he is poring over the unassembled parts, consulting the instruction sheet, and fitting Pipe A into Slot XX, he may also be chatting with his wife about plans for the Rotary Club dinner. His right hemisphere is occupied with visualizing the way the backyard gym fits together, the left is carrying on the conversation.

The female brain is not specialized. Right and left hemisphere work together on a problem. This is possible because in the female brain left-hemisphere abilities are duplicated to some extent in the right hemisphere and right-hemisphere abilities in the left.

This gives women two important advantages. The ability to zero in on a problem with both hemispheres makes women much more perceptive about people. They are better at sensing the difference between what people say and what they mean and at picking up the nuances that reveal another person's true feelings.

The other advantage is that it makes them less vulnerable to accidents than men. If a man's left hemisphere is damaged by a stroke – and men are twice as liable to suffer these cerebrovascular accidents as women – he may be unable to speak or to read or to write, depending on how extensive the damage was, and he seldom regains his former fluency. If a woman's left hemisphere is damaged by a stroke or any other accident, the chances are very good that she will regain most of her abilities. The areas of verbal function in her right hemisphere can take over.

The specialization of the male brain may, like male strength, be a double-edged sword in the long run. It could spell the end of male dominance. Physical strength, the key to dominance in the past, is as vestigial as the appendix today. The key to survival in the nuclear age is going to be perception, the ability to sense how others feel about an event or an issue or a threat and what they are likely to do about it.

Everyone can think of episodes in our foreign policy that illustrate a serious lack of perception. As more women enter government and politics at the higher, policy-making levels, I am convinced there will be fewer such episodes. My only concern is the slowness of their entry. Politics is still a jealousy guarded male preserve for the most part. Sharon Percy Rockefeller summed it up very well when she said, 'Women are not the better half. They are the other half. But in government, they are the missing half.'

Women's greater sensitivity and their logical method of processing information may be seen by our descendants a few thousand years from now as the 'significant difference' that replaced male strength and gained women the dominant role. Or – if we are very fortunate – that 'significant difference' might bring about a society in which both sexes are equal, using their brains with their special functions for the benefit of all.

5

Men may be fragile and their life spans shorter, they may not be all that perceptive, but there is hardly a man who would choose to be a woman.* And why should they? Men have more privileges, more money, more power, and more independence than women. Who would give all this up? And yet, even with all these male advantages, there is something about women that makes many men uncomfortable and – deep down in their unconscious – even fearful.

This is the dark root of male chauvinism. We toss the term around, but few people understand its true significance. Nicolas Chauvin was a hero worshipper. The hero he worshipped was Napoleon, that man of small stature and vast ambition. After fighting valiantly in Napoleon's campaigns and suffering many wounds, Chauvin was retired on a small pension. To the day of his death, he was so passionate an admirer of Napoleon that his name came to be associated with inflated notions of military glory, and chauvinism came to mean a kind of superpatriotism, a blind allegiance. The meaning stuck for more than a century and a half. A current dictionary definition of chauvinism is 'invidious attachment or partiality for a group or place to which one belongs'.

In the 1960s, the women's movement adopted the term 'male chauvinist' to describe a man who refused to accept women as equals. 'Male chauvinism refers to a blind allegiance and simple-minded devotion to one's maleness,' says psychiatrist Sherwyn Woods of the University of

* With the exception of members of that tiny minority who feel that they are females wrongly imprisoned in a male body.

Southern California School of Medicine. 'It is mixed with open or disguised belligerence towards women, who engender anxiety in these men.'

Male chauvinism should be understood for what it is – a male defence against women. It is also an offence, but that is secondary. Many men actually dread women and feel equal to them only in their dreams. In everyday life, women make them feel inadequate.

It goes back to the first woman in a man's life, his first love – his mother. No matter how gentle, loving, and indulgent she was, he was in awe of her. She was all powerful, all knowing. Some of that awe stays with a man all his life and tinges his adult relationships with women. A man may be very rich, very powerful, very pleased with himself, but he will still have an unconscious primitive fear of women. Men are wary of a woman's power. It is different from theirs. More frightening.

Nevertheless, men do not want to change places with women. By and large, men are comfortably confident that male is better. And it seems that a high percentage of women also feel that male is better. Study after study shows that the majority of women want their first child to be a son. If they could have children of only one sex, they would choose to have boys. Even the most recent surveys made after two decades of the women's movement show that if they could choose, the majority still want their firstborn to be a boy.

This carries enormous social implications for the time when we are able to choose the sex of our children with little or no effort. It may not be all that far off. Researchers are working on dozens of sex-control techniques in laboratories all over the world.

At this writing, the only reliable method of sex control is abortion. The sex of the unborn child can be determined by amniocentesis, a procedure that entails relatively little risk.

If the embryo is the 'wrong' sex, the woman can choose to have an abortion.

Will doctors do this? Simply on the basis that the woman does not want a child of the sex she is carrying in her womb? Yes, some will. 'The final arbiters of what children should be born are the parents themselves,' claims one doctor in the United States. 'Only they know what is best for their marriage. I don't have any hesitation in cooperating with an abortion if both parents want only girls and the current pregnancy tests out by amniocentesis to be a boy.'

Less agonizing methods of sex control will soon be available. One approach being considered involves artificial insemination. The Y-chromosome sperm would be separated from the X-chromosome sperm. The Y chromosome, you remember, is the one that produces males. The husband would give a sperm sample in the laboratory. The Y-chromosome sperm would be isolated and then used to artificially inseminate the wife.

Another approach is the 'Boy Pill', which men might take to stop X-chromosome sperm from being produced. Still another possibility is a vaginal cream or jelly that would knock out the X sperm, but not affect the Y.

A Canadian physician claims to have obtained good results from a special diet. Dr Jacques Lorrain of Sacre-Coeur Hospital in Montreal prescribed high-salt foods and no dairy products at all for a group of patients who wanted sons. He reports that 80 per cent of the women who started his diet six weeks before conception and stayed on it until their pregnancy was confirmed gave birth to boys.

Other researchers are concentrating on the timing of the fertility cycle. In an Israeli study, women who wanted sons were instructed to abstain from intercourse from the beginning of their menstrual period until two days after ovulation, on the theory that the vagina and cervix are most hospitable to X sperm starting on that second day. Nearly two-thirds of the women gave birth to boys. The Israeli results boosted the 5 per cent advantage I mentioned in an earlier chapter to a healthy 16 per cent.

When these sex-control techniques are perfected and generally available, it may be like opening Pandora's box and letting loose a host of unpleasant consequences. Suppose, for instance, that you want a daughter and your husband wants a son. Without telling you, he starts taking 'Boy Pills'. What then?

There are cosmic consequences to such sex control and women who want sons should take time to think about them. It is generally agreed that a surplus of males could result in more crime, more wars; increases in male homosexuality, prostitution, and polygamy; and a loss of women's freedom, since females will be a rare commodity. One thoughtful psychologist points out that women might not even be able to go out to the shops alone, since male sexual tensions will be so high because of the scarcity. There might also be an increase in class tensions, because young men from lower socioeconomic groups will seek out young women from higher status groups, in competition with the young men in the higher socioeconomic groups.

A tangle of instincts and desires lies behind a woman's wanting her first-born to be a male. Tradition plays a part, the desire of a man to have an heir and his wife's desire to please him. A woman may hope for a son who will grow up to be like his father, and who will take care of her if something should happen to her husband.

There is also the desire of a woman to have the very best for her child, and she may believe that in most respects, men have better lives than women. There may also be a hint of a bleaker motive, a desire – possibly unconscious – for absolute power over a male.

Women do not usually talk or think much about why they want a son. They just do. When they are asked why, their answers are often confused and off target. In a recent sex-preference survey, one of the chief reasons women gave for wanting a son rather than a daughter was that it costs more to bring up a girl! (The latest figures for the cost of bringing up a boy, feeding him, clothing him, giving him the necessary medical and dental care, is $75,000. This takes him from birth to his twenty-first birthday. The latest figure for bringing up a girl from birth to twenty-one is . . . $75,000.)

The most important factor is rarely if ever considered – the enormous advantage enjoyed by the firstborn. Firstborn children are brighter and achieve a higher position in life than the children who come later. It is important to remember that I am speaking in terms of statistics. There are many successful men and women who were later-born children. And there are firstborns who never seem to amount to anything. But in general the firstborn is a privileged being.

His superiority is no recent discovery. At the turn of the century, the English psychologist Havelock Ellis explored the relationship between birth order and fame. He chose people who had been given three or more pages in the *Dictionary of National Biography*, a sixty-six-volume work. He left out members of the nobility as well as people whom he considered notorious rather than famous. He ended up with a list of 975 men and 55 women, more of whom were firstborns.

Around the same time, the American psychologist J. M. Cattell analysed the birth order of 855 American scientists. He found the same thing. There were more firstborns among these prestigious men than middle or youngest sons.

Over the past eight decades, there have been countless other surveys, all of them finding the same preponderance of firstborns among achievers. It is clear that the male firstborn tends to be brighter and more successful than his younger brothers and sisters.

Until a year or two ago, this was considered to be the result of the firstborn's enjoying his parents' undivided time and attention. This extra dose of stimulation and socialization, it was believed, got him off to an earlier and better start than his younger brothers and sisters.

Now we are discovering that the key to the superiority of the firstborn may not be the adult company he keeps, but the richer mix of sex hormones he is born with. A six-year study carried out at Stanford University under the direction of psychologists Eleanor Maccoby and Carol Jacklin is bound to be a landmark in this field.

The researchers started by measuring the hormone levels in blood taken from the umbilical cords of 218 newborns. They discovered that firstborn children of both sexes had more female hormones – more progesterone and oestrogen – than later-born children. It is suspected that there is a link between the amount of progesterone and later intellectual development. They also found that male firstborns have higher levels of testosterone, the male hormone, than their younger brothers.

The final stage of the investigation – correlating the relationship between hormone levels at birth with the child's development at age six – has not been completed yet, but preliminary findings indicate that there is a relationship between sex-hormone levels and the superiority of the eldest child.

The Stanford group has come up with something else that may turn out to be extremely significant. If several years have elapsed between the birth of the first son and his younger brother, the hormone levels seem to bounce back. The younger brother has the advantage of the same rich hormonal mix as the firstborn, a good argument for wider spacing between children.

Their early data, however, hint that this may not hold

true for girls. If the firstborn is a boy, the girl that follows will not have the benefit of her elder brother's high hormone levels, no matter how many years have elapsed between their births.

If this indication is confirmed, it means that when the day comes that sex selection techniques are available, women must weigh the firstborn advantage against the disadvantage of a second-born daughter. To me, this would be an overpowering argument for choosing first a girl for me – and then, much later, a boy for him.

It may be years before we know the whole story about hormone levels and birth order, but the effect of birth order on personality is no secret.

One weekend last summer Milt and I went to the county fair a few miles away from our farm with our friends Celia and Channing. Celia insisted on having her fortune told. She came out of the fortune teller's tent, her eyes wide.

'She knew all about Channing. She said I was married to a man who had a super-active conscience, a great deal of integrity, and was a hard worker. That's certainly all true. But what made me believe that she really had second sight or something was that she said he always demands too much of himself. And then gets upset if he doesn't do as well as he thinks he should.'

My husband laughed. Milt and Channing had played golf that morning and Channing had been furious with himself when he flubbed two easy putts. 'Maybe she was watching him on the golf course this morning,' Milt joked.

'It's no joke!' Celia was indignant. 'How could she know what he's like? She said that he's very conservative. How could she know that?'

'Tell me,' I asked Celia, 'did she want to know if your husband was the eldest in his family?'

'Why yes, she did. And I told her he was.'

I smiled. 'I bet she said something about his being

successful. And ambitious.'

'How did you know that?' Celia exclaimed.

'It's easy,' I told her. 'Birth order has a great deal to do with character and personality. The eldest child has certain traits that make him a little different. Your fortune teller probably has a degree in psychology.'

The eldest child is usually intelligent, ambitious and very hard working, just as she told Celia. He is a cooperative person and gets along with his business colleagues and neighbours and his in-laws, but he does tend to be stubborn. He makes a point of doing the right thing. He is not aggressive as a rule, but once his dander is up and he is convinced that the other fellow is wrong, anything can happen.

'I don't know if you'll like it,' I told Channing, 'but one psychiatrist took a look back in history and discovered that nearly all the wars that the United States has been involved in were started or escalated while an eldest son was president.'*

I made a mental note to finish telling Celia about the characteristics of firstborns later when Channing was not around. I knew she would be interested to know that it is normal for the eldest child to have problems in showing affection. Firstborn males are just not demonstrative. They want to be close to people, but they do not seem to know how to go about it. It is harder for them than for most men to make friends – and making friends is hard for all men.

No one knows exactly why it is harder for firstborns. I suspect that part of it – but only part – stems from their parents' lack of experience. Parents do their learning on the first child. Some worry too much and are too nervous. Others alternate between being too strict and too lenient.

* One exception is the Spanish American War, which was fought during the presidency of William McKinley, who was the seventh of nine children – and proof that you do not *have* to be a firstborn to get to the top.

Some take a long time to learn to respond to baby's cues, with the result that they do not feed or cuddle him or change him at the appropriate time. The baby, because of this, is not able to develop emotional confidence in them and as he grows older, he relies on himself for what he needs. This, of course, is a trait that makes for success. Whether it makes for happiness is something else again.

Male only children share the characteristics of firstborns, but they have one handicap all their own. They often grow up into neurotic men. In one study of 353 adults, male only children proved to be more neurotic than male firstborns. This stems from the almost inevitable competition that springs up between fathers and sons. The only child has no siblings to dilute the impact and he may exist in a constant state of anxiety, especially during adolescence, that shows up as neurosis in the adult.

Younger brothers have a different personality profile. They are more insecure than firstborns. Big brother – and to a lesser degree big sister – is always ahead of them, always being held up as an example. Teachers expect the younger boy to live up to his big brother's scholastic record, to work as hard and accomplish as much. So does the football coach. And so do his parents. But he rarely does. He is overwhelmed by their expectations and resentful of them. He tells himself that he can never be as good as his big brother and he believes it. It becomes a self-fulfilling prophecy.

If parents only knew that their actions and attitudes had the opposite effect from what they intended, I am sure they would try to change. The younger boy should be considered just as much of an individual as the elder. He should be encouraged to develop his own strengths, not to be a carbon copy of his big brother.

Little brother excels where big brother fails to shine – in relationships with others. Little brother is a congenial soul.

He tends to be a joiner, but rarely a leader. It is often difficult or impossible for people to believe that their friend who is so open and sharing and responsive is full of insecurities unless they understand the effect big brother's achievements have on little brother's ego.

When a woman is thinking about marriage, she should take these traits into consideration. Every woman who yearns for the trappings of success and wants to belong to the elite group of movers and doers should know that her best bet as a husband is a firstborn. He may be undemonstrative and inhibited in bed, but he has such a strict conscience that he will be more faithful than a later-born.

This may not be true of the only child. Since he has never had to take on the responsibilities of an older brother, he tends to feel that he should have whatever he wants. After all, he has *always* had just about everything he has wanted. He will want his wife's complete attention and devotion, as he has always had his mother's complete attention and devotion.

If a circle of good friends and a relaxed life mean more than financial success or power, a woman will be more likely to enjoy life married to a later-born. The wholehearted love and admiration of a wife will go a long way towards diminishing the later-born's feelings of insecurity. However, if his wife starts criticizing him and is openly envious of his elder brother's success, she may drive him into the arms of another woman. He needs approval.

Big brothers are certainly not villains, but they stand in the way of their younger sister's development even more than of their younger brother's. And this is another consideration that worries me when women say they hope their first child will be a boy.

A girl will complain that her elder brother gets all kinds of privileges just because he is a boy. He can go to the movies with his friends on Saturday afternoons and she cannot. 'You're too young,' her parents tell her. When she argues that her brother went to the movies with his friends when he was her age, they say 'But he's a boy.' Their daughter fusses and fumes, but mother and father are adamant. In incident after similar incident, little sister learns that girls are not as capable as boys. They cannot do what boys do, she is taught, because they cannot look after themselves.

When little sister is a teenager and starts going out with boys, she sees her elder brother as an asset. He brings his friends home so it is easy for her to meet boys. And he acts as a protector and adviser. Her girlfriends envy her.

But a few years later, she wonders how it is that these girlfriends are junior executives and she is still in the typing pool. Big brother had a lot to do with it. Successful women, studies show, usually do not have elder brothers.

Parents centre their hopes on the male firstborn who will carry on the family name. He may even grow up to be president. When his little sister comes along later, everyone is delighted, but no one thinks in terms of her being president, except possibly of the PTA. Her parents do not expect as much of her as they do of her brother. She is not encouraged to excel at school. She learns that femininity comes first and achievement second. By the time she starts working, she is conditioned to think of her job as a holding action, something to keep her busy between school and marriage. No wonder she wins no promotions.

This holds true even in families where one or both parents believe in sexual equality. They believe women should receive equal pay and equal opportunity, should have equal rights. But when it comes to letting their little girl develop a sense of independence and exploration, their belief weakens. They want to protect their little darling.

The female firstborn does not suffer from this overprotection. Parents seem to have higher expectations for the daughter who is their firstborn. She is pressured to do well in school. They discuss possible careers with her. She is more capable, more confident, and more successful whether she chooses marriage, a career, or both.

Many women are unconscious male chauvinists. They have that 'simpleminded devotion to maleness' that leads them to want their firstborn to be a boy. And the time is coming when every woman will be able to choose. If she wants both a son and a daughter, she should do some hard thinking about how to give both her children the best start in life. On the basis of what we know now, there is only one way to ensure that your daughter will have the same advantages as your son. And that is for her to be the firstborn.

PART TWO
The Stages of Man

6

'All men are children,' Chanel said once. 'If a woman understands that,' the shrewd French couturier declared, 'she understands everything.' I would not make quite so sweeping a statement, but if a woman is aware that there is a child hidden within every man, it is a giant step towards understanding the male mystique, because during his adult life, almost every man goes through a series of stages in which that child plays a role.

In recent decades so much attention has been lavished on the stages of childhood – from the terrible twos through the teenage tyrants – that the adult stages have been almost completely ignored. It was as if once a boy emerged from adolescence, he was a man and that was that and nothing much more happened until he began the inevitable descent into old age. True, every woman knew that a man in his forties was almost as unpredictable as an adolescent. But that was about it. No one paid much attention to the years between twenty and seventy-five.

Times have changed. Psychologists, anthropologists, sociologists, endocrinologists, neurologists – the whole spectrum of medical, social, and psychological researchers – have turned their attention to the adult male and discovered what Shakespeare knew so long ago – men go through a lifelong series of developmental changes.

Almost every man, be he oil rigger or accountant, politician or plumber, salesman or physician, goes through five stages as an adult, the first and third stages being the most crucial as well as the most difficult.

1. Onward and Upward: The tension-ridden years from twenty-one to about thirty-five, the age varying somewhat from man to man, when the male concentrates on establishing himself at work, marrying, and starting a family.
2. Consolidation: The years from about thirty-five to forty or possibly forty-three or forty-four, when he pulls together the accomplishments of the previous period.
3. The Pivotal Decade: It may be from forty to fifty, forty-five to fifty-five, or somewhere in between. It is the time when a man senses the arrival of middle age, and it is characterized by physical and psychological distress. The quality and character of the rest of a man's life are largely determined during this stage, hence its description as pivotal.
4. Equilibrium: The years from fifty or fifty-five until retirement. They can be very sweet. But if a man has not solved the problems of the Pivotal Decade, these years will be a bitter reprise of that stage.
5. Retirement: A time of satisfaction and serenity – or resentment, disappointment, and fear. It all depends on how a man emerged from the Pivotal Decade.

The woman who understands what a man is going through at these different times in his life will be able to deal more easily with the men she encounters at work and in the community and also smooth her husband's passage through these stages – or at the very least cope more easily with his moods and behaviour.

In the following three chapters, I will take these stages one by one and explain just how men change from stage to stage, how they feel, and how it affects their actions and their attitudes towards others – especially towards the women in their lives.

But before that, just a few words about women. Do they

stay the same, forever frozen in time and space, as they were at twenty-one? Of course not. Every woman knows that her life has its own series of stages, but women's lives are in such a state of flux and there is such diversity in their life patterns – wife, mother, working woman, and all the combinations of these – that the present social and sexual revolution will have to shake down a bit before women's lives can be analysed and codified.

And there is something else. As Yale psychologist Daniel Levinson, who has studied the shifting developmental stages of the adult male, admitted, 'I chose to concentrate on men, because I wanted to deeply to understand my own adult development.' Women must keep in mind that the majority of studies are still led and controlled by men.

7

Most men in their fifties and sixties claim that the years between twenty-one and thirty-five were the unhappiest of their lives. This seems hardly credible. These are the years when a young man starts out to conquer the world, when he is brimming with ambition and hope, the years when he falls in love and marries and starts his family, the years when he decides on his personal and career goals. More than that, studies have shown that the early years when money is tight and the children are young are the happiest years of marriage.

What is going on here? Are the studies at fault? Or the men's recollections? Neither. There is no contradiction. The Onward and Upward stage is the happiest of times – and the unhappiest.

A few years ago I ran into a man I had known very well at one time. Ben and his wife Nancy had lived on the same rundown block on New York's West Side as Milt and I did when we first got married. They had their first baby a few months before we had Lisa. We saw quite a lot of them until they bought a large house in the suburbs and moved away.

'Nancy and I are divorced now, you know,' Ben told me.

I hadn't known. I was surprised. They had seemed every bit as happy as Milt and I. And that was extremely happy. 'What happened?' I asked.

He shrugged. 'Who knows? For one thing we had four babies in five years. Nancy was always pregnant. And exhausted. Neither of us had a full night's sleep for almost six years.

'I'd just been taken on by a big advertising agency. I was

working my tail off. I brought work home every night, every weekend. I had to do a lot of travelling. It wasn't easy.

'Then we bought the house. It was much too large for us, but great for the entertaining that we would be doing when I moved up the ladder. It was way more than I could afford, but we both fell in love with it. We lived with bare floors and moving-crate furniture for a few years. It didn't bother us. We knew it wasn't forever.'

'You were a good team,' I said. 'I always thought of you and Nancy as working towards your goals together.'

'Yeah, I guess so. We had a pretty good time, to tell the truth. The only entertaining we did for years was spaghetti at the kitchen table and cheap jug wine. But we used to laugh a lot. Just the same, when I look back and think of all the nights I lay awake trying to figure out what was going on at the office, who had the inside track on this account and that — and how I could squeeze him out, I wouldn't relive those years for all the tea in China.

'Then I got a couple of promotions, one right after another. That was the big breakthrough. By the time I was thirty-two, I was making real money. Nancy bought a lot of new clothes. We started buying furniture and fixing the house up. But once we got over the excitement, something was missing.

'I found myself getting impatient with Nancy. She wasn't the woman I had married. We never talked about anything except the kids. It struck me one day that she was actually a very dull woman. Then she told me that she wanted a divorce. I had been seeing a woman I'd met on a business trip and Nancy found out about it. Audrey was everything that Nancy was not. Better dressed. Had more to talk about. A little come-hither in her eyes. I wasn't really serious about her. But Nancy was plenty serious. She insisted on the divorce. And that was it.'

Like Ben, most men find that marriage does not live up to

their rosy expectations. Unlike Ben, most successful men stay married. The most successful men marry before the age of twenty-eight and are still married to the same woman thirty years later, although paradoxically men are more liable to be disappointed in their wives than women are in their husbands. This cannot be blamed on the women. It is a direct result of that male lack of sensitivity, their relative inability to fathom what people are really like – and that stems from the way the male brain works. As we learned, women are far more perceptive.

A young bride has a pretty good idea of what her groom is really like and what she can expect in marriage, but most men go into marriage with a startlingly starry-eyed naiveté. There is not much a woman can do about this. Of course, if you consciously play a part during courtship, you are asking for trouble later on. But if you are yourself and he persists in seeing you as a combination of his mother, Elizabeth Taylor, and Joan of Arc, all I can say is enjoy it while it lasts. And be aware that he is going to be a little let down when he finds out that you are just your own adorable self. He will get over it.

Women should know that there comes a day early in almost every marriage when a man realizes, for instance, that his wife is not the housekeeper his mother was. Her underwear is heaped on a chair in the bedroom. There is a ring around the bathtub. And the ice-cube trays are empty.

On top of that, sex is not as abundantly available as he had expected. The working wife may bring home a briefcase full of work two or three nights a week that absorbs her attention until midnight. And so may he. Or she may protest that she is too tired after a day at the office and an after-supper session at the local laundromat. Instead of lazily delightful Sundays in bed, he finds himself vacuuming the living room and scrubbing the bathroom while she prepares dinner for guests.

Then the financial facts of life become clear. Even though his wife may work, he discovers that two cannot live anywhere near as cheaply as one. He worries about how he will manage if his wife gets pregnant.

This is all perfectly normal. They are good and loving husbands, but all the time there is this thing in the back of their heads: this is not the way they imagined married life was going to be. Most men envision themselves in the role of a superchild and their wives as a combination of adoring, selfless mother and erotic, exotic mistress or, as the saying goes, a lady in the drawing room and a whore in bed. Caught up in this blissful dream, a man is hardly more aware that his wife has needs and fantasies of her own than he was of his mother's needs when he was a child.

Most men look forward to having children. These days a woman may agonize over the decision. Should I wait another couple of years? Or will it be too late then? Should I have a baby at all? Will I regret choosing career and freedom over motherhood and a child? How will my husband really feel if I say I don't want to have a baby?

A man does not go through this kind of agonizing. He wants a child, especially a son. He has visions of a rosy-cheeked, gurgling infant like those in the baby-food ads. Colic, teething, the diaper pail in the bathroom and all the rest never cross his mind.

Men rarely have any idea of the enormous impact a baby will have on their way of life and their marriage. Nor do most men enjoy being fathers as much as most women enjoy being mothers. In a way they feel as if they are being pushed out of the nest, much as a child feels when a younger brother or sister is born. Given a chance to express their feelings in strict confidence, young fathers acknowledge that their ideas about life with baby were way off target.

Eighty per cent of a group of college-educated men from twenty-five to thirty-five said that baby had created a major crisis in their marriage. The other 20 per cent admitted that baby had created problems, but did not describe them as taking on crisis proportions.

The crisis group complained of constant fatigue. If baby did not keep them awake at night, money worries did, especially if the wife had stopped working to stay home with the child. And they worried that their wives would get pregnant again before they could afford it. Between the loss of the second income and the expense of the baby, their standard of living had gone way down.

These new fathers resented their loss of freedom. They could no longer go out with their wives on the spur of the moment. Most of all they resented the fact that their wives were less interested in sex than they used to be. 'Disenchantment' was the word the researchers used to describe the mood of these first-time fathers.

Fatherhood is not the all-important role in a man's life. His starring role as he sees it during the Onward and Upward years is that of the promising young man on his way up. He has important tasks to accomplish. He is driven by the need for achievement.

'If I'm not executive vice president by the time I'm thirty-five, I've had it,' he worries in the predawn hours. 'If I don't own a house by the time I'm thirty . . . if I don't have a four-figure balance in my current account . . . if I don't have an office of my own . . . if I'm not elected to the club . . . if I'm not . . .' He is driven by goals that he sets himself, one after another.

This is sometimes hard for women to understand. Margaret Mead, the anthropologist, explained it with her usual insight when speaking to a group of executives' wives several years before her death. 'Women can enjoy an irreversible achievement,' she told them, 'by giving birth to a child. Men have nothing like that. The only way men can realize themselves is through their work.'

These are the years when young men run hard. Their chief interests are their families and getting ahead on the job. They push themselves to win promotions and salary increases. This singleminded dedication takes its toll. One of the most significant studies of successful men followed a group of college men from their sophomore year until middle age. 'Men who at nineteen had radiated charm.' wrote Dr George Vaillant in his report on the study, at twenty-nine and thirty 'seemed colourless, hard-working bland young men in grey flannel suits' who pitched in at home to change the baby's diapers and at work were constantly looking over their shoulders to see if the competition was gaining on them.

No wonder men look back at these years and tell themselves 'I'm glad I'm not young any more.' Not only do they have to push themselves towards success, they have to make up their minds about where success lies for them. This is not the easiest of tasks. A man may spend a lot of time and energy exploring his options, daydreaming about this style of life and that style of life and their relative rewards. The daydreaming is not lost time, but an efficient way of trying a career and a life-style on for size, a process that women do not always understand because it often seems childishly capricious.

'My husband is a nut,' a young woman told me after I lectured before a group in Omaha. 'He'll sit around after supper and talk about how we should get up and move to Alaska. If we both work, he'll say, we will have a real stake in the future in five or six years. We will spend all night talking about it and figuring out how we will manage. Will he go up there first and look for a job and a place to live? Or should we both go and hope for the best?

'A week later he'll be sitting around talking about how he ought to be taking a couple of courses at the university towards his master's degree. It would make a big difference in his chances for getting ahead, he says.

'It seems to me he comes home with a different crazy scheme every week,' she complained. 'I used to take him seriously, but now I know it's all talk. What do you do with a man like that?' she asked.

'You listen to him,' I told her. 'He's paying you a big compliment. He's daydreaming out loud, trying to figure out just what kind of a future he should aim for. And he's sharing it with you, because you matter a lot to him. He wants to know how you feel about his various ideas.

'Don't forget,' I told her, 'that you can do the same thing yourself. What is it that *you* want out of life? Dream a little. And share your dreaming with your husband. That way you have a good chance of finding a way of life that will satisfy both of you.'

Not every man in the Onward and Upward stage is open and sharing about his hopes and plans for the future. Many of them assume that their wives are going to like whatever it is they choose to do. They automatically assume that their job, their career, their needs come first. You can't really blame them. It is the way they have been brought up.

All a woman can do is recognize this and let the man in her life know that she has her own set of dreams and ambitions. With good will, she and her husband can figure out how both of them can achieve their desires. I can tell you right now, however, that if your career should entail your having to move across the country, your husband will have a hard time adjusting to it if he is doing well in his own career. You will be putting your marriage at risk. After all, these are *his* Onward and Upward years, when he has to establish himself and start working towards his goals.

If Nancy and Ben had spent time talking about the kind of life they both wanted, their marriage might not have come unglued. But they took the traditional path. This was in the 1950s, remember. Nancy had the babies and Ben had his career, and for years, neither of them dreamed that they were running on separate tracks. Not until they found themselves light years apart.

'Ben thought a wife should concentrate on being a mother and a hostess. And so did I at first,' Nancy told me when we met unexpectedly on the plane from Chicago to New York.

'We bought this enormous white elephant of a house because Ben wanted to be able to entertain in style,' she said. 'It was ridiculous for a young couple to saddle themselves with such a debt.

'I used to feel dowdy and resentful at the obligatory company dinners. All the executives' wives would be talking about their tennis games and their hairdressers and clothes, clothes, clothes. I'd be wearing the same long skirt I'd worn to the last dinner and a top I'd found in a thrift shop. I hated it!

'When Ben got his big promotion, things got easier. It was a real luxury to be able to take a winter vacation and get my hair done every week and have my own car. But Ben wanted to change our whole life. He completely dropped our old friends. When I'd suggest asking one of the women who carpooled the kids to school over for dinner, he'd say "Yuck. We don't want to waste time with that couple. He's on his way to nowhere. Let's ask the Densons over. I'd like to get to know him better." Ben did everything in his power to suck up to the top men in the firm.

'Then he took up with Sandy. He seemed nice. He was very helpful to Ben. Gave him all sorts of tips about what was going on behind the scenes. And he spent a lot of time with him – dinner, drinks, duck shooting. It turned out that they were after some pretty strange ducks. And it was just like Ben fell in love with him.

'I don't know exactly what it was, but I just knew Ben was seeing some woman. Then I found out that he was seeing a woman Sandy had introduced him to. That was it as far as I was concerned.

'I'd done my bit. I'd taken care of the kids and the house. I'd done without a lot of things because I had faith in Ben. I was sure the time would come when we'd have a very comfortable life. And it would be all the sweeter because we'd worked so hard for it. And here he was going around with this woman!

'I thought about it for a long time. And then I decided to get a divorce. Ben was not at all upset. He was quite generous with child support and alimony. I went back to college and studied business administration. I have a good job now. And a good life.'

I was sure Nancy was telling the truth. She had an air of well-being, and attractive self-assurance. I had listened carefully to her version of those difficult and frustrating years, especially her feelings about two aspects of the Onward and Upward stage that have distressed and infuriated many women – the shedding of old friends and the acquiring of a mentor.

Most ambitious young men acquire a mentor towards the end of the Onward and Upward stage. 'The mentor is ordinarily eight to fifteen years older,' says psychologist Daniel Levinson. 'He is enough older to represent greater wisdom, authority, and paternal qualities, but near enough in age or attitude to be in some respects a peer or an elder brother. He takes the younger man under his wing, invites him into a new occupational world, shows him around, imparts his wisdom, sponsors, criticizes, and bestows his blessing.'

Ben was unfortunate in finding a mentor who had unresolved problems of his own, a mentor who thoughtlessly encouraged him in his extramarital fling. Nancy was not far off the mark when she said that it was as if Ben had fallen in love with Sandy. There is no homosexual connotation here; rather there is a tendency of the young man to idealize the older one, adopt his ways and accept his values. The younger man may start dressing like his mentor, switching from sports jackets and grey flannels to pin-stripes. If his mentor has a martini at lunch, the younger man will have a martini, too. If his mentor plays golf, pretty soon the younger man is out on the links every weekend.

Most wives, like Nancy, resent the mentor, but he is a key figure in the life of the Onward and Upward man. Studies show that the man who does not have a mentor seems to miss out on a significant stage of emotional development. His life is harder – first during his thirties and then in his late forties and fifties when he himself should be acting as a mentor. It is almost as if the mentorless man had skipped an important grade in school. So no matter how fed up a woman may get when her husband is under the spell of his mentor, she would do well to bite her tongue. This is a necessary stage in her husband's development. She can remind herself that this too will pass.

Because of its very intensity, the relationship is usually shortlived, a matter of approximately three years. The breakup more often than not is sudden and unpleasant, also because of the intensity of the relationship. The young man rebels at the older man's rule. He wants to assert his own authority, be his own man. Breaking with his mentor is a pale repetition of his earlier adolescent break with his father. This second break with a father figure leaves him feeling free and confident, ready to take on the world. It also marks the approaching end of the Onward and Upward stage.

An easier, more tranquil period follows, the Consolidation stage. This is when a man pulls together all he has achieved in the past fifteen or so years. Things fall into place. He feels sure of his skills, his potential, his knowledge. Everything meshes. He has a certain maturity and authority. Life goes smoothly both at home and in the world at large. If he complained of nervous stomach or tension headaches during the Onward and Upward period, these seem to disappear. His health is usually excellent, although he may be just a bit heavier than he should be. The Consolidation stage man has finally hit his stride as a satisfactory lover, tender and inventive. All in all, he is the most delightful of men.

This seems to be true whether a man is intensely ambitious or rather placid about life, content to earn a living doing something he finds rewarding, but not feeling compelled to push his way to the top. This stage is all too brief. It is the blessed calm before the storms he faces in the Pivotal Decade.

8

After the tranquillity of the Consolidation period come the rough seas of the Pivotal Decade, the dangerous years of passage through the midlife crisis and the male menopause into the harbour of Equilibrium.

If a man ever needs an understanding wife, it is during this decade. Suddenly men are seized by rash compulsions to change their lives – and burn their bridges behind them As one midlife counsellor put it, 'Drowning one's sorrows in booze is a common escape, although mistresses, motor-cycles, and expensive foreign sports cars are not uncommon.' What is even more common is divorce. This is the time of the well-known 'twenty year fractures' when marriages that had seemed solid enough suddenly collapse and end in divorce.

The compulsion to escape is probably the most common manifestation of the pivotal years. Escape from what? Middle age. This is what the midlife crisis is all about. 'I don't feel middle aged,' the forty-five-year-old will protest. But he is. And he knows it. Otherwise he would not be protesting.

We enter middle age somewhat later than previous generations because of our longer life expectancy. Middle age is not a state of mind or physical condition. It is the time when a man has lived half of his probable life span. It arrives almost four years earlier for men than women, because of the fragile male's shorter life expectancy. The fortieth birthday is what psychologists call a 'psycho-social marker' in a man's life. Until then he thinks about the number of years he has lived. After forty, he thinks about the number of years he has left. Forty is the psychological watershed.

'I'll probably retire in twenty-five years,' a man thinks on his fortieth birthday. 'Take my Social Security and my pension. I'll have twenty, maybe twenty-five years for myself. Travel a little, go fishing, maybe I'll take a couple of courses or maybe try my hand at painting. And then – who knows? After that I guess I'll be glad to take it easy.'

But then he reads a newspaper report that according to the latest figures, the average forty-year-old white male can expect to live another 33.4 years. 'My God!' He catches his breath. 'In thirty-three years, I'll be dead!' Suddenly his life is more than half over.

The transition from thinking 'if I die' to 'when I die' is traumatic, especially when a man thinks of how much he had hoped from life and how little he feels he has accomplished. By the time a man turns forty, he has just about reached the top of his career ladder. If he has not achieved the partnership or the professorship or the key to the executive washroom, if he has not been given his own sales territory or his own secretary or a desk by the window, chances are that he never will. This holds even more true for men of lesser ambition or lesser opportunity. The less educated and less privileged a man is, the earlier his chance to prove himself in the working world is cut off.

There are exceptions, many exceptions. Some men are late bloomers and achieve their successes in their fifties. And there are those men, a small minority, who will continue to leap from peak to peak of success into their sixties. Sometimes even beyond.

While the fortieth birthday is a psycho-social marker for a man, it is not necessarily the time when he realizes he is middle-aged. A man fights that knowledge as long as he can. But it is a losing battle. Middle age can creep up on a man or it can arrive in a flash as it did for James.

James, forty-two, was sitting in the dentist's chair when in the space of thirty seconds, he realized that he was middle-aged. He had been aware that the years were going by. That very morning when he shaved he had turned his head from side to side and scrutinized himself. Was he developing jowls? He had read in the *Wall Street Journal* that men were going in for cosmetic surgery these days.* He put down his razor and with his fingertips lifted the sagging skin under his jaw towards his ears. It was a distinct improvement. But a face lift? He scowled and shook his head. He slapped the sagging flesh just a little harder than usual when he splashed on the aftershave lotion.

There was no denying that he was getting grey. The hair on his chest was not the badge of virility he used to consider it now that it was sprinkled with grey. And lower down, it was the same. He had heard that women dyed themselves down there. After all, those bottle blondes had to be consistent, didn't they?

Sitting in the dentist's chair, James sighed. It was one of those things that he guessed he'd never know now. This was the moment of truth. The dentist had just said, 'There's no saving this tooth. It's got to go and so has this one. I'll give you a nice little bridge.'

The dentist tapped the tooth and James winced. Not with pain – the nerve was long dead – but something that was almost panic. False teeth! The beginning of the end. James had always been a faithful husband, but he had his share of sexual fantasies. And one of them was that some time the fantasies might come true. But not now. Not with false teeth.

As it happened, he became involved in his first extramarital affair very shortly after his expensive bridge

* Men represent from 20 to 30 per cent of plastic surgeons' practice in large cities, and there is even a recently published medical textbook devoted to male plastic surgery.

was in. Even before it was paid for.

Men in their forties are men who have affairs – more in fantasy perhaps than in reality. Some men are too scared. Some men have no opportunity. Some consider it sinful. A handful never consider it. But most men, as a 'high public official' once put it, 'lust in their hearts' after women who are not their wives. And a good number of them manage to satisfy that lust.

What women need to understand is that most of these men are devoted to their marriages. They love their wives, although they may find marital ex a little boring after all these years. Or – and this is very often the case – not all that available.

Why does this urge to philander hit a man now? The urge has always been there. It is not peculiar to the Pivotal Decade. What is new is that men like James who have previously suppressed that urge now give in to it. It is a way for a man to avoid the knowledge that he has passed the watershed of his life. The desperation he feels when he realizes this, and that he has about reached his limit in his chosen field, can deepen into a depression. To combat the depression he seeks conquest – sexual conquest of a younger woman. And for a while this makes him feel young and vital again.

It is a form of regression to the little boy within, very similar to the way he regressed to bedwetting when his little sister was born. Now he regresses to chasing after girls. A man also unconsciously equates his wife with his mother, his first love, just as getting married marks a young man's emancipation from his mother in the pivotal years, a love affair is another symbolic breaking loose from the apron strings – this time from his wife. The little boy in the man, however, expects his wife, like his mother, to keep on loving him and caring for him and turning a blind eye on his escapades.

But these affairs are like aspirin. They provide only temporary relief. Eventually a man has to face up to the causes of his depression and come to terms with middle age. This is the only way he can pull himself out of the midlife crisis. If he cannot get himself squared away during the Pivotal Decade, he will keep floundering in this miasma of desperation and depression for the rest of his life.

He has to cope with this himself, but a wife can help. The most important thing she can do is involve him as much as possible in the life of the family, make him a key member of the household. The man who retreats behind his newspaper every night to brood or who sits staring at television until he is semi-stupefied will sink deeper into depression, feel more alone, more ineffectual.

Sometimes a man will dearly want to be with his family, but finds it impossible. No one responds to his silent calls for help. Bob, for instance, could not seem to make contact. He had concentrated on his job and his upward climb for years. He had gone through all the motions of being a good father – attending parents' nights at school, going to his daughter's debating contest and his son's clarinet recital. But he spent very little time talking with them. He brought work home most nights and retreated to his attic office after supper.

When Bob turned to his family in his midlife crisis, they were simply not there. His son and daughter were completely involved in their own lives, their school activities, and their friends. His wife, Ann Louise, was on a dozen committees and spent her days dashing from meeting to meeting and her evenings working on reports or doing research. There seemed to be no room for Bob in their lives.

He made a few fumbling efforts to reach out to them, but they were so fumbling and so unexpected that they were not recognized for what they were. And after that, he made no further effort to involve himself. His inability to reach out to his children and wife was in part a result of his depression and in part the act of a child – 'If they don't want to play with me, I don't want to play with them.' A woman should never underestimate the power of the child in the man. Sometimes the child seems to be in the driver's seat at the very moment when all a man's adult judgement and insight is needed.

Ann Louise was busy, but she was also a loving and sensitive woman. She understood that Bob was depressed, although she did not understand why. One night she suggested that he might want to get some help. He had seemed so unhappy lately, she said. He might want to see a therapist.

Bob reacted furiously. 'What's wrong with me? Do you think I'm crazy or something?'

There was nothing to be gained by insisting. She decided to do the next best thing, to see a therapist herself.

A week later she was sitting in the office of a psychologist who specialized in midlife counselling, telling him how edgy her husband was. How very sad he seemed.

'The more you can involve him with the family the better. You have to try to appeal to something inside him,' suggested the psychologist. 'How about a weekend trip for the two of you?'

Ann Louise thought for a moment. 'He likes to fish,' she said. 'He used to collect old coins, but he hasn't bought any lately. And he used to like to play blackjack.'

'What about a weekend in Vegas?' asked the psychologist. 'He can play blackjack. From your description he's not an addictive personality. And you could take in some of the shows there. It would be a real escape for forty-eight hours.

'Or you might try reawakening his interest in his coin

collection,' the psychologist went on. 'If there's an auction someplace where you can stay in a good hotel or a resort, you could make a weekend out of it. He might like to talk to other collectors. And for that matter,' he added, 'there's nothing wrong with a fishing weekend. Why don't you think along those lines?

'One more thing,' he said, 'you might suggest that he have a physical check-up. Try to be casual about it. Make an appointment for yourself and tell him. Then ask him if he wants you to make one for him, too.'

Ann Louise went into action. She liked the idea of a weekend trip, but she worried that if Bob were in a really bad mood, the weekend might be a real flop, no matter how carefully she planned it. Instead she decided to enlist his help in arranging a surprise birthday party for their daughter. He resisted at first, but despite himself he ended up getting involved in the preparations. And the night of the party when he saw the delighted surprise on his daughter's face, he smiled a smile that brought tears to Ann Louise's eyes. He was happy. She could tell.

After that she went ahead with the weekend. It took some coaxing, but she finally persuaded him to sign up for a cheap charter flight to Vegas. They both had a wonderful time and Bob won enough at blackjack to put him in a jovial mood.

But most of what Ann Louise did to help Bob out of his depression was less spectacular and sometimes very discouraging. He was withdrawn and grumpy a great deal of the time. But she persevered. Bob understood what she was doing, although he never admitted it, and it made him feel good. Ann Louise did all the giving and he did the taking, but marriage — in fact, all close relationships — go through periods like this. And the times when Bob was his old warm and outgoing self were more than enough reward for Ann Louise. (Sometimes it doesn't seem fair for the woman to do all the giving; but usually, when you put it in perspective, there have been times when you were on the taking end, too.)

It takes the better part of the decade to cope with the emotions stirred up by the onset of middle age. This does not mean that all ten years are spent in a state of crisis or depression or domestic upheaval. The moods ebb and flow. There are periods of intense happiness. But there is one time of deep crisis, both physical and psychological. How intense it is depends upon the man and his temperament.

This is the male menopause. It is not, as some people believe, just a catchall term for the various manifestations of the midlife crisis. The name admittedly is ridiculous. For women, the menopause means just that – the cessation of menstruation. They lose their ability to reproduce. But men continue to produce sperm up to the age of ninety and perhaps beyond. The male menopause has very little to do with reproduction. It is a definite male syndrome with definite symptoms. And there is nothing imaginary about it.

One of my husband's medical colleagues told him that he felt out of sorts and was going to have a check-up.

'What's the problem?' Milt asked.

The other physician shrugged. 'Nothing and everything,' he said. 'All of a sudden I can't sleep nights. I lie awake and worry. I worry about money. I worry about when I'm going to find time to have the car greased. I worry about what my daughter's doing with her boyfriend. I worry about having a heart attack.

'And I'm driving my wife crazy,' he said. 'I'm absolutely impossible and I know it, so I decided to make an appointment with Sam, my old college roommate, for a physical.'

'Good idea,' Milt said. 'Let me know what you find out.'

A couple of days later the orthopaedist telephoned. 'Male menopause,' he announced.

'What?' my husband asked.

'That's what's wrong with me. Male menopause, a middle-aged man's syndrome. That's what Sam said.'

'Do you feel better now that you know what's ailing you?'

'Yeah, sort of. I felt a lot better when he reeled off a list of the symptoms and I realized that I didn't have all of them Just enough to make me feel lousy — insomnia, anxiety, smoking too much, hypochondria. At least I don't have hypertension. And I'm not impotent, thank God. He told me that some men just fall apart. Can't work. Don't do anything. They're not even interested in sex!'*

'Did he prescribe anything?'

'I'm to cut out the cigarettes and get some exercise four times a week. Jogging, tennis, swimming. But the most important thing he told me was just to hang in there. It won't last, he said. Another six or eight months and it should be behind me.'

Milt's colleague was fortunate. Only those medical men who keep up with the latest medical journals know it exists. Many older medical men do not believe there is such a thing as the male menopause, even when they experience it themselves. They ascribe their symptoms to tension or overwork or marital problems. Even now that the male menopause has been recognized as an actual group of physical and psychological symptoms that affect men in their forties and early fifties, it is still not mentioned in most medical textbooks.

The silver lining to this particular cloud is that, just like the mentor in the Onward and Upward stage, the male menopause is a short-term affliction. During this period, however, the impulsiveness that characterizes the pivotal years is intensified. A man may insist that he is going to sell their house, give up his job, cash in his insurance, retreat to

---

* In almost every case the impotence and lack of interest in sex are purely temporary, unless they are caused by some underlying physical condition.

an island where he will write the great American novel, spend a year in Rio, join an ashram and spend the rest of his life contemplating.

The wife who can restrain these impulses in her husband is worth far more than her weight in gold. This is no time to make far-reaching decisions if they can possibly be avoided. As the physician told Milt's friend, the thing to do is just 'hang in there'. A man will almost certainly regret any drastic change he makes in his life during these months. Not that a change may not be in order. But it should be thought through – coldly and carefully.

Another problem is that many men seem to be afflicted with a kind of tunnel vision at this period. They see nothing but what they want to see. They think of nothing but themselves. Colin was one of these. The midlife crisis hit him hard. He went around in a dark cloud of self-absorption for months.

Colin was a successful man. Kim and the children had everything they wanted. And he had nothing, he told himself. He was full of self-pity as he thought how hard he worked. He completely ignored the fact that he had been having a grand and glorious time, and that he thrived on competition and relished every iota of his success. But now he had convinced himself that he had been foolishly self-sacrificing all these years. In a spurt of indignation, he decided that enough was enough. He was going to change his life. Think of himself for a change. Do what he wanted. And he knew just what he wanted to do.

When he started to tell Kim this one night as they were getting ready for bed, she offered to take his temperature. 'You must have a fever,' she said. He insisted that he had never been more coldly rational. 'Then let's talk about it tomorrow,' she said, 'when I'm not half asleep.'

The following evening he began to outline his plan for the future. Kim listened quietly. And suddenly, Colin realized that he had not considered Kim or the children in any of his planning. He had not even thought about how Kim might react. Now he was appalled. Not until this very instant when he started putting his plan into words had he understood how unrealistic it was. And yet – there was a lot about it that appealed to him. As sanity replaced selfishness, he fell silent.

'What's the matter?' his wife asked.

'What I've been thinking about is quitting my job and looking for a seasonal resort to buy and run. Work hard half the year and goof off the rest of the time. Somewhere in the Rockies, I thought. Somewhere where there's spectacular scenery. How does that grab you?'

'I don't like it,' Kim said. 'I can't see myself as the inn-keeper's wife. And I don't want to leave Philadelphia. I like it here. Our friends are here. The children's school is here. We can't uproot them and plunk them down in some school thousands of miles away.

'And what about your work with the handicapped?' she asked. 'I can't believe that you are going to give that up. You organized the whole volunteer group. You did all that lobbying.'

Colin sighed. 'You won't believe it. It just never crossed my mind.'

'I think that what you need is a vacation,' his wife said. 'What about taking some time off soon and going to a resort in the mountains? As guests,' she added hastily.

'Not a bad idea,' he said. 'In fact, you've given me an idea. Maybe what I ought to be thinking about is some kind of resort for the handicapped. With someone else running it.'

'That sounds more like you,' Kim said. 'Let's think about it.'

Colin and Kim took that vacation and observed how the resorts were run. Colin made copious notes of the changes that would be needed to turn them into vacation havens for the handicapped. When they got back home, he and Kim spent hours talking about the ideal resort for the handicapped. It was an idea they both liked.

By that time, Colin was well on his way out of the midlife crisis and steering a straight course for the next stage, Equilibrium. His passage through the Pivotal Decade had been much less stormy than Bob's. And much more productive. Bob's wife had helped him through this crucial decade, but Bob had never really faced up to middle age and all that it implied. Colin, on the other hand, had turned his escapist desires into an asset. He had begun to make plans for the future while coming to terms with the present. These years are harder for some men than others. Some get ulcers and divorces. Others go sailing through with only the mildest spells of turbulence.

Is there any way a man can make these years easier on himself? Or that a woman can help him make them easier? Not really. A difficult childhood helps. So does a deep sense of caring. And an utter lack of ambition. But none of these are conditions that can be manufactured on demand at the onset of middle age.

The men who go through the troubled decade with the least strain are those who had unhappy childhoods. One survey of thousands of men found that a difficult childhood turned out to be an asset in later life. These men knew how bad things can get – emotionally, financially, physically. They were in touch with reality. And they were not frightened by it. They were able to tolerate stress and disappointment more easily than men with more idyllic childhoods. This was particularly true of the generation that grew up during the Depression and were then plunged into the Second World War. They knew the value of stability, a home, a family.

Men with a strong sense of responsibility for others also

weather these years fairly easily. These are the men whom people turn to for advice and comfort, the men who contribute to charity, work on community projects, and care passionately about making the world a better place.

With both these groups, it is the old-fashioned virtues that seem to keep them on a steady course – altruism, hard work, courage, perseverance, compassion, responsibility, a deep sense of duty.

The third group is somewhat different. Several years ago two enterprising researchers drew up a balance sheet for happiness. Optimism, competence, self-satisfaction, cooperativeness, and other positive qualities were considered assets. Anxiety, hostility, dissatisfaction, emotional problems, and so on were considered liabilities. They discovered that the men who are happiest throughout the Pivotal Decade are those who have few liabilities – and few assets. In other words, the less a man has going for him, the happier he is. These men do not aspire to much and thus they never regret not achieving.

It is man's reaching for the stars that tends to make him unhappy and dissatisfied during these troubled years. When he realizes that he is middle aged and probably never will reach those stars, it is a hard blow at a vulnerable time. But I feel it is better to expand your horizons by reaching for the stars – even if you fail – than never to reach at all.

Towards the end of the Pivotal Decade, most men have adapted to the reality of middle age and they pull themselves together. They resolve their conflicts and concentrate on the future. By his early fifties, a man has usually laid the foundation for the rest of his life. 'There is nothing more beautiful in the world than the man who resolves his midlife crisis,' Dr Peter Brill of the Center for the Study of Adult Development, University of Pennsylvania, told a medical audience. 'He feels himself valuable and potent. He feels an emotional depth that has not been there for twenty years.'

9

The last two stages of a man's life – Equilibrium and Retirement – can be sweet. The Equilibrium Stage, from the early fifties to sixty-five or whenever a man retires, is the calm after the storm. It is like a rerun of the Consolidation Stage – only better. Life is in balance. A man no longer has to strive the way he used to. He has arrived. He is respected for his accomplishments and experiences. These are the second-honeymoon years, a time of renewed intimacy, of well-deserved indulgence. But calm does not mean stagnation, and the Equilibrium Stage is one of growth. A man still has what psychologists call 'developmental work' to do. He has to prepare for the rest of his life.

Retirement is a relatively new concept. Until very recently men did not retire. They simply dropped dead at ages that we would now consider heartbreakingly young. Social Security in the USA only dates from the 1930s. We have no long tradition of life in retirement, no time-tested patterns to follow. Each man has to shape his retirement years for himself. And most men do not know themselves well enough to do this until they reach the Equilibrium Stage.

If you ask a man what he plans to do when he retires, eight out of ten will reply that they are going to garden, play a lot of golf, catch up on their reading, spend time with the family, pursue a favourite hobby or whatever. These are often the men who take early retirement because they can hardly wait to enjoy their leisure. For the first time in their lives they are going to devote themselves to play. I think it is a lovely plan. Men who have worked all their lives have earned the right to play. But something strange happens.

A man plants an ambitious garden. More flowers than his wife can cut, more vegetables than the family can eat. He keeps track of the money spent on seeds, on fertilizing and spraying. And soon he starts negotiating to sell his raspberries to the local store. It is the same with golf. He spends grim hours practising on the putting green. He keeps charts and analyses each round as if he were plotting the gyrations of the stock market. Within months, sometimes even weeks, play is transformed into work.

His pastimes turn sour, because that is all they are to him – ways of passing the time, substitutes for the work that gave his life meaning, gave him his very identity. It is sad, but play for play's sake makes most men uncomfortable. All their lives they have been trained to believe that the only thing that is valuable is work. And so they work. They work at their golf game. They work at bringing up their children. They work at making their marriages work. They even work at making love. To most men sexual foreplay is a chore, a duty rather than a pleasure.

If you ask one man about another, he will say, 'Oh, Bill's in real estate . . . he's a mechanic . . . a computer programmer . . . an upholsterer . . . a dentist' and leave it at that. He will not go on to say that Bill lives in the little ranch house at the corner of Main and Maple and his wife used to teach first grade and Bill is a good jazz pianist. It would never occur to him. Men identify themselves and each other by their occupation.

So when a man retires, unless he has prepared himself for this state, he often has the feeling that he has lost his identity and status. At first, he is eager to relax and play, but he begins to feel nostalgic about the time when he was 'somebody'. Like Ernie. I don't know if Ernie ever existed, but three medical men from different parts of the country have told me this story.

Ernie had never thought about planning for retirement. He expected to enjoy it. He looked forward to being home and just pottering around.

A few months after Ernie retired, an acquaintance ran into him in the post office. He was studying the photographs of the ten most-wanted criminals posted on the bulletin board.

'Anyone there you know?' the man asked jokingly.

'No,' Ernie said. 'I was just thinking how nice it must be to be wanted.'

There are some men who do not plan for retirement because they do not plan to retire. My dad was one of these. He practised law almost up to the day he died. And he was one of the happiest, most fulfilled men I have ever known. But not every man has a profession or a job that permits him to work as long as he feels up to it. Nor does every man want to work all his life.

Then there are those men who refuse even to think about retirement. It frightens them. Bob was one of these. Remember him? The man who was so furious when his wife suggested he see a psychologist because he was depressed and withdrawn during the Pivotal Decade? Bob had had a great deal of trouble in accepting middle age. The prospect of old age was intolerable.

The Equilibrium years should have been good for him. Their children were married. Their mortgage was paid up. They were able to splurge a bit. When their first grandchild was born, it seemed to his wife, Ann Louise, that life had never been more blissful. But Bob panicked. He hated being a grandfather. It was like a nail in his coffin. A few nights after the baby was born, Ann Louise snuggled up to him in bed. Bob recoiled. 'Who wants to fuck a grandmother?' he said nastily.

Bob had never worked through the conflicts and anxieties of the Pivotal Decade. They pursued him and poisoned his

Equilibrium Stage. He was depressed and bitter. He felt he had been cheated by life. When his wife tried to get him to plan for retirement, he snarled, 'For God's sake, stop borrowing trouble. Let's enjoy ourselves while we can. When I retire, all I want is to be let alone. I'm just going to sit back and take it easy.'

That is exactly what he did. Bob died a little less than two years after he retired. In a way, he was the perfect statistic. There is a proven correlation between death and retirement. Analysts have discovered that there is a peak in the male death rate about two years after retirement. The men just seem to rust out.

It does not have to be that way. And that brings us back to the Equilibrium Stage. If a man will take a good look at himself during this time – financially, physically, emotionally – and do some solid thinking about how he wants to spend the rest of his life, he will not rust out. It takes courage to face the fact that in a decade or so he will be entering the last stage of his life, and that the life expectancy of the average American male at age sixty is about seventy-seven years.* But – if a man wants to, he has a good chance of breaking through these longevity averages.

First, he ought to improve his health habits. Next, he ought to use the Pivotal years to plan for the Retirement Stage. Men who have something to wake up for every morning live longer.

The next step is to make friends, preferably younger ones. Friends are far more effective than apples when it comes to keeping the doctor away. The important difference pinpointed by one study of retirees between those who were happy and those who were not was that the happy ones all had at least one close friend in whom they could confide.

* The reader may remember that earlier I wrote that the age expectancy of the average forty-year-old male was 73.4 years. There is no discrepancy here. The longer a man lives, the longer his life expectancy is.

The unhappy retirees did not. Most retired men who commit suicide have no friends.

There has always been a great myth about men and friendship. Male friendships are considered strong and noble, bonding men even closer than brothers. Don't believe it. Most men are scared to death of being friends with another male. First, because they are so competitive that it is hard for them to trust another man and second, because they might be considered homosexual. What American men 'have been taught about emotion is destructive to them,' Dr Peter Brill has written. 'It ruins friendships with other men.' He is absolutely right.

While men by and large prefer the company of other men to that of women (there are exceptions, thank goodness), prefer drinking with men, working with men, playing cards, talking politics, goofing off with men, they rarely have a male friend. Companions, yes. Pals. Acquaintances. But not friends.

It is usually not until a man reaches his fifties that it dawns on him that there is only one person in the world in whom he can confide. When the chips are down, it turns out that a man's best friend is not his dog, but his wife. It is sad but once a man outgrows or loses his boyhood friends, he rarely establishes a lasting friendship as an adult.

When women ask me how they can help their fiftyish husbands prepare for retirement, I tell them that the best thing they can do is provide an active social life for him so that he will come in contact with people in other lines of work than his own. It is easier for a man who is a building contractor, for instance, to make friends with a teacher or a pharmacist than with someone in an allied trade who would bring out his defensive and competitive instincts. Sometimes the mentor relationship helps a man make friends with a younger male. These relationships do not *always* disintegrate painfully.

Anything a woman can do to encourage her husband to become active in the church or the community, to enrol in a language or photography class, to join the local bird watchers or whale savers, to sign up for a callisthenics or swimming programme is on the plus side. Local politics, amateur music groups, volunteer work at the hospital are all good ways for a man to meet like-minded souls.

Even if a woman's best efforts do not succeed in finding her husband a friend or two, she has still done something vitally important. She has established an active social life for him. And this will also help him live longer. One study that covered nine years of close observation found that men with active social lives were happier and healthier than the stay-at-homes.

If a man completes the Equilibrium Stage with a good idea of how he will spend his time in retirement, with a friend or two and an established social life, he has accomplished the developmental tasks of this stage. His harvest years will be rewarding and he will probably outlive the longevity tables.

But sometimes plans go wrong. Even careful ones. What then? And what about the men who planned to spend their retirement years on a perpetual vacation and then discovered that having a good time was not all that much fun? Some, like Lionel, can adapt quite easily.

Lionel discovered he had retired on the wrong side of the continent. And he had planned so carefully! The family had always spent vacations at the lake in New Hampshire and loved it. For years Lionel had planned to retire there. It had everything – swimming, boating, fishing in the summer, skating and skiing in the winter. And if they tired of the rural life, Boston with its cultural resources was only an hour's drive away. He and his wife knew people in the vicinity and Grace was just as enthusiastic about it as he was.

They were happy as clams for the first couple of years. Then their daughter, a nurse at a Boston hospital, married and moved to Los Angeles. Their son who worked in New York was transferred to Scottsdale, Arizona. Practically overnight there were thousands of miles between Lionel and Grace and their children.

Lionel did not want to spend the rest of his life looking forward to a once-a-year visit from his son and daughter, so one night he got out his road maps. 'Ocean or desert? What do you think?' he asked Grace. And three months later they were tucked away in a small house surrounded by groves of walnut and avocado trees just far enough north of Los Angeles to be free of the smog. They were close enough to both of their children to be able to see them whenever they wanted – and far enough away so that their son and daughter did not have to feel they had to see them every Sunday.

Bruno had a much more difficult time. He was a widower. His wife had died shortly before he retired and he was full of grief. He came home from work every night and sat slumped in front of the television until he finally pulled himself up and went to bed. He managed all right while he was working. His job as quality inspector for a shoe manufacturer provided a structure for his life. But when he retired, he seemed to age overnight. Widowers have devastatingly lonely lives. It is almost always the wife who takes care of the social life of the couple. When she is not there to ask people over for dinner or to play cards or whatever, nothing happens.

Bruno's telephone seldom rang. People seemed to forget that he existed. His daughter was alarmed. It seemed impossible to rouse him to any interest in life. And he was only sixty-five. He had been vigorous and virile while her mother was still alive. One Saturday she showed up with a bag of groceries and a gift-wrapped rectangular package.

'What's that?' her father asked. 'It's not my birthday.'

'It's for you,' she said. 'I worry about the way you eat. All that junk food. You're not getting a balanced diet.'

He opened the package. 'A cook book?'

'It's for beginners,' she said. 'It has all the things you like – meatloaf and spaghetti and stew.'

After she left, Bruno leafed through the cookbook, then started reading it carefully. A little while later, he went out to buy more groceries. His first experiment, a meatloaf, was successful. Cooking turned out to be a challenge. Pretty soon the only time he turned on television was for the news and the Julia Child reruns. But cooking for one was frustrating. He was so proud of his new skill that he had to show off. He started inviting his neighbours for dinner. They returned the invitations and he met new people. Bruno bought another cookbook and then another. He was busy almost every evening.

Cooking changed Bruno's life. I have always thought of him as a wonderful example of the ripple effect. Any change you make in your life, no matter how trifling, affects the rest of your life in much the same way that a stone dropped in a pond creates ripples that spread out to the very edge. Cooking was the tool that enabled Bruno to pry himself out of his grief and loneliness and make a new life for himself with new friends and new interests.

The fortunate men are those like Colin, who emerge from the Pivotal Decade with an idea or a project that enchants and tantalizes them so much that they mull it over, talk about it with their wives, research it, and devote much of the fourth stage to working out ways to turn the idea into reality.

During his Equilibrium years, Colin, who had wanted to quit his job and run a resort in the Rockies six months of the year, spent many evenings turning his plan into a precisely detailed blueprint for a chain of vacation resorts for the handicapped. His wife Kim was an enthusiastic collaborator. Even before he retired, Colin had bought the land for his first resort and started blazing nature trails that could be navigated by wheelchairs.

Rick was another fortunate man, although there was a time when he considered himself anything-but. I met him and Diana after a lecture in Houston during which I had described how the irresponsible escapist ideas of the Pivotal Decade often turn into guidelines for the Retirement Stage.

'For a while I would have sworn that you were talking about me,' Rick said. In his forties, he had come to detest his job, partly because he realized that he had gone as far as he ever would and partly because it no longer offered a challenge. 'I was bored stiff and going round with a chip on my shoulder.'

He began to drink too much. One night when he came home, bloody and his shirt torn, after a brawl that had ended with his being thrown out of a bar, his wife, Diana, packed up and went to stay with her sister.

When Rick sobered up, he begged her to come home. Diana said she would, on one condition – that he promised to stop drinking.

He had been so shaken by her walking out that he would have agreed to anything. His macho reserve crumbled and everything he had been bottling up over the years came spilling out. How much of a failure he felt he was. How he hated his job. 'Even thinking about it makes my stomach turn, but I don't know where to go,' he told Diana, 'or what to do. I'm fifty-one now. Too young to retire and too old to get another job.'

'That's nonsense,' she said briskly. 'There's a big world out there. You can find something. But you won't if you don't look.'

It was not that easy. He looked. He looked hard. He answered ads, sent off résumés, went to a recruiting firm.

Nothing. There were jobs, but none of them as good as the one he had.

The solution came when Rick least expected it. They had driven to their little house on the Gulf for the weekend. 'I was walking around the place, looking at it real careful,' Rick told me. 'I was thinking of making the deck bigger. And then all of a sudden I thought "Golly damn! That's it!" And I shouted for Di.'

He asked if she remembered his crazy idea about selling 'room kits' that people could add onto their houses themselves. He had spent months drawing plans for prefabricated rooms that could be erected with very little effort. But when he had gone to the bank for a start-up loan, they had punctured his dream abruptly. 'No market,' they had said, turning down his application.

But that weekend he told Diana, 'What people need are houses. Not just rooms. Young people need small houses to start off with. Ones they can add on to later. And older people need small houses that are easy to take care of. There's a real housing shortage around Houston. And there's always going to be one unless the economy stands on its ear. I built this house. I can build others just like it.'

There was a gleam in Rick's eye that Diana had not seen for a long time. 'I don't quite know how to start,' he told her. 'We'd have to buy some land. Maybe just build one house at a time. It's something I can do. I know I can.'

It was an exciting weekend. They talked. They calculated. And they started planning. The planning stage lasted for years.

'I was lucky,' Rick told me. 'I had a job. I could take my time. Find out just what I would be getting into. There was a lot I had to learn. More than I thought.'

Now that he had something to look forward to, his old job was suddenly more attractive. He needed it. He stayed on until he was sixty-five and eligible for his pension. Rick was sixty-three when he broke ground for the first house, and he and Diana were almost as excited as they had been on their wedding day.

'It's a great life,' Rick reported. 'I'm my own boss. I have a terrific crew. I'm not cooped up in an office. And I don't have to make an enormous profit. I've learned so much about land usage and energy and water conservation that I figure when the time comes that I don't have so much get-up-and-go, I can always be a consultant.'

Rick was sixty-seven when I met him that night in Houston. Tanned and lean, he looked fifteen years younger. He had found a way of retirement life that suited him right down to the ground. It was hard work. But for him it was play.

I do not want to give the idea that the only happy and viable retirement is one in which a man pursues a new career or spends his days working hard. For many men, that is the optimum solution. But others truly want to take life a little easier, but without stagnating. They may study archaeology or learn how to make pottery or help teach Vietnamese refugees English or build and furnish Victorian dolls' houses.

I know a man in his seventies who lives for swimming. He is in the Masters swimming competitions where people compete against their own age groups. He is happy as a lark – or perhaps a shark would be a better analogy. The main thing is for a man to have or develop interests, to try this and that and the other thing until he finds a pursuit that fascinates him. This is the main task of the Equilibrium Stage and possibly the most rewarding of all the developmental tasks.

The success of a man's retirement depends in part on his wife's adjustment to having him at home every day. Women look upon their homes as their castles where they have reigned unchallenged for years. They are not ready to abdicate just because their husband has retired. But at the beginning, it is almost inevitable that her decades-old, cherished routines will be upset. She tends to resent his suggestions for different ways of doing things. She gets impatient when he goes shopping with her. And having another person in the house twenty-four hours a day can be irritating. 'Feather ruffling' is the way one of my mother's friends described it.

Every person has his or her own intimacy quotient. He or she can take only so much togetherness in any twenty-four-hour period. The best solution is for the wife to make her own retirement plans and discuss them freely with her husband. She should plan to get out by herself several afternoons a week. This is not the time for her to sacrifice the interests she has cultivated over the years. By the same token, she should encourage her husband to get out on his own.

What women should know is that they have more influence during the retirement years than at any time since courtship days. Men who tended to disregard their wife's advice in earlier years are now astonishingly ready to listen and act upon it. And they will go along with most decisions or suggestions she makes about everyday activities. This marital role reversal means that a woman should not hesitate to suggest certain rules or routines. For instance, I have heard woman after woman declare, 'I married him for better or worse – but not for lunch.' There is no reason why you should not make it clear that you prefer to have a cup of soup and a sandwich when the mood is upon you and that you expect him to take care of his own lunch.

It takes time to settle down in the new routines. Husbands tend to expect that life will go on just as it did every weekend, but the idea of a perpetual weekend dismays their wives. After all, they too have reached an age where they want to take it a bit easier, but often they find that overnight the demands on their energies are multiplied.

Again routines and rules have to be set up. Household

chores should be divided so that the wife does not feel put upon. But once the division of chores is made, hands off. Let him do things his own way. If you can't stand having someone else stack the dishwasher, don't delegate that task. Ask him to do the vacuuming instead. It is a bit like a new car. Perhaps the idling has to be adjusted. Or the glove compartment light doesn't work. But with a little work, everything should soon run smoothly.

A man does not change much in the Retirement Stage. He is about the same as he was during the Equilibrium years. If he was even-tempered and cheerful then, he will be the same now. If he was bitter and fearful, these traits may become somewhat more marked. There is nothing a woman can do if her husband falls in the latter group except try to make her own life as satisfying as possible. She will not be able to change him. And she has to realize that he needs her more than he ever has. She is wife and mother to him now. He needs her love and her kindness. This may come hard at times, but the fact is, as many widows discover, it is very good to be needed. So do not stint on your affection towards this man you have spent so many years with. You should not underestimate the psychic rewards of knowing that you are the most important person in the world to your spouse.

And one more thing. I have emphasized the husband-wife relationship throughout this description of the five adult male stages, but women can and should put this knowledge to work in any relationship with a man. I have seen too many women look up to their immediate superiors in business or the laboratory or the television studio or the magazine as if they were some sort of demigods. They are not. They are simply men who are working their way through a series of emotional and psychological stages. Women who understand the stresses and the growth inherent in each stage can profit by this knowledge – and men can profit by women's understanding.

PART THREE

The Men You Work With – and For

10

Some nights a man comes dragging home from work at eight or nine or even later. There are circles under his eyes. His whole body spells fatigue. Something came up at the office. He had to finish a presentation for a potential investor. He had to work an extra shift to fill a rush order. The client meeting ran longer than expected. A delivery was late and everyone had to work overtime.

His wife sputters with sympathetic indignation. 'They're working you to death!' she exclaims. He nods wearily and lets her get him a drink. What his wife may not realize is that he is as gratified as he is tired. Only the woman who knows what work means to a man understands that these occasions catapult him into an ego high that is as addictive as any drug. Most men find this kind of above-and-beyond-the-call-of-duty demand exhilarating. It means they are needed. It confirms their importance.

Men have two basic needs. Neither of them, no matter what they say, is sex. They need love and they need work. And work takes priority over love. If a woman could know only one fact about men and work, it should be that work is the most seductive mistress most men ever have.

I know a house painter whose cheeks grow pink with excitement when he talks about the proper way to prepare weatherbeaten clapboards for a fresh coat of paint. He has been painting houses for more than thirty years. Men are seldom that excited about a woman after thirty years. But work! That is different.

In his remarkable book *Working*, Studs Terkel told the story of a dentist who visited a famous actress backstage. 'I was sitting in the front row and looking up,' the dentist told the actress, 'studying the fillings in your mouth. Who's been doing your dental work?' As the author commented, 'It was not that he loved the theatre less, but that he loved dentistry more.'

And then there was the dentist who confessed 'I insulted a beautiful girl last night. I noticed that the corners of her mouth turned down a little and I asked if I could see her teeth. I wanted to see what kind of work she had.'

Some men are unaware of how much their job means to them. 'If I didn't have the wife and kids, I wouldn't be knocking myself out this way selling mutual funds,' a man will say. He may even believe it. But the truth is that the satisfaction he gets each time he makes a big sale is really what he is knocking himself out for. Not the wife and kids.

Work is not only the means by which a man earns money to provide for himself and his family; work, as I explained earlier, gives him his identity, gives him status. This is true whether he is a piano tuner or a supermarket manager, a bill collector or a college president. He counts because of his work.

'Last year the insurance industry gave a testimonial dinner in my honour,' a patient told Dr Jay B. Rohrlich, a psychiatrist who has written about work and love. 'They all made speeches about me. But they were not really about me. They were about my work.

'When I come home at night,' he went on, 'it's me they are looking at. Me they are talking to. Not my work. But my presence in the house doesn't mean a tenth as much as it means in the office.'

Nor does his home mean a tenth as much to him as his office. He is typical of more men than you might suspect. They may be good enough husbands, satisfactory lovers, dutiful fathers, but these are secondary roles in their lives.

Take Thornton, for instance. When he comes home at

night and Cathy tells him that young Christopher got a D in maths and that the septic tank has to be pumped out and that his mother has this funny little pain that comes and goes and that she has made an appointment for her to see the doctor, Thornton says, 'Jesus, I wish just one night I could come home and relax.' When he is good and ready, he lays down the homework law to Christopher and – maybe – he telephones his mother.

But you should see Thornton at the office when Mr Big tells him that the Widget deal may fall through. Suddenly all systems are go. There is fire in his eyes. Within seconds the Widget file is in front of him, a conference call has been placed to Widget Central, and Thornton is all competent charm as he zeroes in on his job of convincing the Widget management that they will be heading for bankruptcy or worse if they back out on the deal.

This is where it's at. Home is a back-up operation, a pit stop for rest and recuperation – a little sex to dispel the day's tensions, a good night's sleep, a clean shirt and back to the fun.

This is not a unique American phenomenon. When the Japanese government decided to study the quality of national life, they found that men were literally working themselves to death – from the lowliest worker right up to the head of the largest conglomerate. Eighty per cent of them had never taken vacations. Never! They preferred to work. What little free time they had was not spent at home, but devoted to acquiring or perfecting skills that would make them more valuable on the job.

The Japanese are far more caught up in their work than Americans. For instance, if your husband were driving home from work and there was a freak tornado that tore up the highway but left telephone wires intact, whom would he call first? You? His mother? The next-door neighbour? His boss? His brother?

All things being equal, he would probably call you and say he would be late for supper, but not to worry. He is safe and sound. This is just one woman's opinion. I have not run a study on this. But the Japanese have. Not about a tornado, but an earthquake.

Japanese men were asked whom they would telephone first if there were an earthquake while they were on the way home. Nearly 40 per cent said they would try to reach their boss first. Only 9 per cent indicated that they would try to get in touch with their wives.

American men are not *that* devoted to their jobs or bosses. A good 20 per cent of them absolutely detest their jobs. Some of them are miscast, but most of them are working at the drudge jobs – the dead-end clerical jobs, the repetitive assembly-line jobs, the jobs that require brute force and little else, the bottom-of-scale, mind-numbing jobs.

Edward is one of these men. He runs a hot-stamping machine that puts the emblems on hubcaps. His days are filled with noise and monotony. And constant pressure. 'They want more all the time,' he complains. 'They keep turning up the speed on the machines. It's not human. I hate the place.' And then he added, 'But it's not so bad. I'm lucky to be there.'

It is not just the money that makes Edward and others like him feel lucky to have these jobs they hate. The pay envelope is vital, but there is more to it. No matter how much a man dislikes his job, it gives him a sense of belonging. As Freud said a long time ago, 'Work gives a man a secure place in a portion of reality, in the human community.'

He is part of a group. He tells his pals that the transmission is shot on his car. They talk about putting up storm windows. They beef about the boss, about the new deductions from their paycheques. They rehash the fight they watched on television last night. There are dozens of strands that knit men together at work, even though they may seldom see each other outside. A man often feels more comfortable with his co-workers than he does at home.

When I was going through my files pulling out studies and papers on the subject of work and what it means to men, I was struck by the fact that more than half the material in my happiness file (and it fills two huge file drawers) had to do with work in one way or another. Men's happiness, their physical and mental well-being is so dependent upon their work that more men commit suicide when they are fired than when their wife or child dies. Getting fired shakes a man to his very foundation.

When Willis Reed was fired as coach of the Knicks a few years ago, he told a friend, 'It's the same with every coach. You get the job knowing that eventually you'll get fired. It happens to everyone. But you always think you're going to win.'

'Did it hurt?' his friend asked.

Reed shook his head. 'You listen to me,' he said fiercely, 'whatever happens to me in my life, I'm a man about it.'

It hurt. You could tell by his eyes that it hurt. By the huskiness of his voice. It hurt even though he had known it was on the cards.

Most men do not think they are going to be fired. They expect to work hard, to clamber right up the success ladder. Or at least remain at their level of capability until retirement. But when something happens and they get fired or laid off, many of them fall apart.

When a plant in Detroit closed down not so long ago, at least half the men who were laid off – normally healthy men – fell victim to diseases that are associated with stress. Ulcers, high blood pressure, migraine headaches. They developed arthritis. Some showed signs of severe depression. It was not that they had loved their work. Most of them did routine factory tasks. Nor were they in immediate financial distress. There were union benefits and there was unemployment insurance. But long before the benefits ran out, a significant number of the men were practically basket cases, in serious physical or emotional trouble.

One woman told me she had tried to cheer her husband. 'It isn't your fault that they had to close down,' she said. 'You're bound to find another place before your redundancy pay runs out. We should think of this as a kind of vacation.

'All he did was growl at me,' she said.

'If he hadn't growled, he might have cried,' I said. 'And that would have made him feel even worse.'

'I know,' she sighed. 'Men don't think they're allowed to cry.'

Men don't like to talk about being fired. They can talk about death, illness, divorce, but not this. It is shameful. It is taboo. And it is too bad. They deny themselves the relief that expressing their shock and anxiety would give. It is impossible, however, to repress these feelings. They come out in other ways.

In a Wisconsin city where several factories had closed down, psychologists and therapists reported that it was like being under siege. Suddenly they were confronted with marriage problems, drinking problems, drug problems, child abuse, wife abuse, rape, all kinds of violence, all surfacing at once. They had to set up emergency consulting groups.

A sociologist at Johns Hopkins University who studied the effects of the 1970 recession, when there was a 1.4 per cent increase in unemployment, found that there was a nearly 6 per cent increase in suicides as well as significant increases in admissions to mental hospitals and in deaths from alcoholism and heart disease in the years that followed. 'The 1970 increase in joblessness,' Dr M. Harvey Brenner reported, 'led to fifty-one thousand people dying or being institutionalized.' The 1980-81 slowdown in automobile manufacturing, which hit Michigan and especially Detroit very heavily, is expected to have an even more devastating long-range effect on the normal death and illness rates in Michigan.

When I cited these statistics to a women's group recently, one woman in the audience said, 'I don't believe it. Losing a job isn't that big a deal. Those men must have had something wrong with them.'

'No,' I told her, 'the only thing that was wrong with them was that they had lost their jobs.'

I went on to explain how doctors and psychologists have drawn up stress ratings for such life events as marriage, moving, mortgages, illness, the birth of a child and so on. Just recently researchers at the University of Chicago and the National Institute of Mental Health pinpointed ten 'life strains' that cause men serious or significant anxiety and depression. Three of these life strains were related to marriage, two to parenthood — and the other half were linked directly to a man's work. They included being fired, demoted, or forced to leave a job because of ill health.

When one group of recently fired executives were promised anonymity, they agreed to talk about how they felt. 'The whole thing was devastating,' one man said. 'One day I was told to report to my boss. I remember the look on his face. He told me they didn't need me any longer. After twelve years! I cleaned out my desk, picked up my briefcase and walked out.'

They were hag-ridden by all kinds of anxieties. 'Maybe it was all in my head,' an executive said, 'but I believed that my wife was looking at all those other men out there with jobs. And there I was. I wondered if she thought something was wrong with me.'

'I remember walking along Michigan Avenue and envying everyone,' another said. 'They all looked so busy. They were going someplace. They all had jobs. I was convinced of that. I never wondered how come they were walking down Michigan Avenue in the middle of the morning. Just like me. I felt like an abysmal failure. I wanted to cry. But I didn't. I stopped at a bar and knocked back a couple. I remember thinking, "Next stop Skid Row." '

Women rarely react so dramatically. Being fired is no picnic for a woman, but neither does she see it as the end of the world. Most women have a secure sense of themselves as human beings. Their identities are not derived from a job, but from a rich mosaic of roles, abilities, and characteristics. This diversity makes women's retirement years more fulfilling than most men's.

When people ask me what I will do when I retire, I laugh. There are so many things I want to do. If the time comes when I decide to stop appearing on television and to stop the constant travel involved in keeping my lecture commitments, I plan to use some of my time to do more writing.

I will certainly spend more time on our farm. And my husband and I dearly want to spend more time with our daughter, Lisa, and her husband Amir, and take whatever grandchildren we will have to exotic countries. For years I have had a hankering to take an active part in politics, even if I have to start out running for substitute dog catcher. And I have cartons full of recipes that I have clipped from newspapers and magazines over the years waiting to be tried out.

Some of my plans revolve around the family, others around the house, my profession, and some around exploring new fields.

Most working women have a similar range of interests and commitments. Work is often a man's mistress, but it is rarely a woman's lover.

With what we know about how most men draw their identity from their work, their panic when fired is understandable. It is as traumatic for the men at the low end of the salary range as for those who pull down six-figure salaries, but finding a comparable position is far more difficult for the executive.

It takes six months on the average for an executive to find another position in his field. One man went on thirty interviews in two months without getting a single offer. Another, after being interviewed by seventy-five different firms, was finally offered two jobs, neither of them nearly as well paid or prestigious as the one he had lost.

What can a woman do? How can she help a husband or a lover or friend who has lost his job?

What you have to realize is that inside that man there is a little boy who is scared to death. Whether he admits it or not, he needs his mother. Or, more correctly, he needs you at your most tender and caring. This is a time to put your own needs aside. Be warm. Be loving. And try not to be too hurt when you are rebuffed. When they are miserable and insecure and feeling like failures, some men have to lash out. Remind yourself that this will not go on forever. And above all, do not panic. That will tear whatever self-confidence he has left to shreds.

One constructive thing you can do is encourage him to get some exercise. A brisk two or three-mile walk will do more to lower his stress levels than two or three drinks. And it will help keep him in shape. Appearance is all-important on those job interviews.

A woman has to understand that the job-hunting period is horrendously traumatic for a man. More so than for most women. The psychic rewards a man used to get from his work no longer exist. He gets a lot of negative feedback. His former colleagues and co-workers feel uncomfortable in his company. They think 'There but for the grace of God go I.' And he feels uncomfortable with them, an outsider. Inside he is crying, 'Stop the world! I want to get back on!'

And yet that world he wants to rejoin is a rather inhuman place. This is what Dr Fernando Bartolomé, a French consultant on business administration, concluded after studying forty American executives and their wives. They were not what he called human beings, nor did their world have a human dimension. Not that he saw them as science fiction computeroids, simply as people lacking the ability to show warmth or sadness or even delight.

They had schooled themselves never to feel dependent on another person. Thirty-six of the forty insisted that they hardly ever felt dependent. Thirty-two of them said that when they did, they would not let anyone know they felt that way.

'Feelings of dependence,' said one man, 'are signs of weakness.' As for showing warmth or affection, forget it. One man said that he had been terribly embarrassed at a dinner party when his wife described another man as being his best friend. It was true, but it was something he preferred to keep to himself. He did not want anyone thinking of him as a man who needed friends.

Tenderness was permissible – within strict bounds. Parents admitted to feeling tender towards their young children, but they rarely showed it. 'I'm trying to make my children stand on their own feet,' one of the wives told Dr Bartolomé. 'I would never express my affection for them openly, because I don't want to smother them. I'm quite cold.'

Her husband approved. 'Doing things is more important than people,' he said. 'I want my children to learn to ski well. In skiing one only needs man and hill.'

These were not old dinosaurs or fuddyduddies. Their average age was thirty-seven. But they all felt that tenderness, dependence, openness, and similar traits were dangerous. They were certainly not traits conducive to success.

'I group my friends in two ways,' one of these men said, 'those who have made it and those who have not. Only the latter spend time talking to their wives about their problems and how bad their boss is and all that. The ones who concentrate more on communicating with their wives and families are those who have realized that they are not going to make it and therefore they have changed the focus of their attention.'*

There was general agreement among the forty men that their jobs came first. 'A lot of executives are seduced by their jobs,' said one. 'They become fanatical about them, because they like the work and because their companies reward their fanaticism.' That man's wife was both angry and hurt about being relegated to second place. 'When he goes away because of his job,' she said, 'I'm left alone to take care of everything. When he comes back, I resent him for abandoning me.'

Most of the marriages had burned out long ago. The myth is that executives' marriages are happier than most. The proof of the myth is supposed to be the fact that fewer men at the top get divorced in comparison to the rest of the population. Some 84 per cent of this country's top executives are married to their first wives. The figure for the total male population is only 53 per cent. But all this proves is that they have a lower rate of divorce, not that their marriages are happier.

There is a reason why fewer top executives get divorced. And it is not love. 'If your needs are not satisfied,' an executive explained, 'if the other person doesn't accept what you

---

* He was right. Making it requires total devotion. In the USA top male executives work sixty to seventy hours a week on the average. But they are not doing it for peanuts. Their average salary, according to a 1980 survey, is $134,500 – without counting fringe benefits and other corporate perquisites. Women in comparable positions also work an average of sixty to seventy hours a week, but only 8 per cent of them make more than $100,000 a year.

have to give or does not fulfil your needs or doesn't understand you, there is very little you can do about it. You can't
abandon the boat that you share with the other person.'

The shipwreck analogy is apt. These men are indeed
embarked on treacherous corporate seas. In some companies, even in these liberated times, a divorce can block
advancement forever.*

What is interesting, Dr Bartolomé says, is that these
businessmen seemed to be well aware that they were mising
something important in life. 'Many of the men I interviewed
said they would like to be able to express affection more
fully, but none of them showed any intention of exploring
ways of establishing more open relationships or new ways of
expressing their feelings. I found that in the corporate world
feelings are to be controlled, channelled, repressed,' he
summed up dismally. 'Not only are men told how they
should express their feelings – big boys don't cry – they are
also told what and how to feel.'

These uptight attitudes at the top are beginning to
change. People now understand that repressing feelings
completely is like cutting off an arm or a leg. It hurts and
you do not function as well without them. Corporations
have discovered that many executives have trouble dealing
with people because they cannot relate to them with
warmth and understanding.

Some firms now send executives to school to learn how to
express their feelings. Vice-presidents in charge of this and
that, comptrollers and treasurers, heads of personnel,
mortgage officers and production managers are being sent
to places like the Menninger Clinic, Outward Bound

---

*But what holds the wives in these burnt-out marriages where they take
second place to their husband's job? Why do these women who admit
feeling angry and resentful stay married to these men? Like tends to attract
like. The executive wife is usually as desirous of success and status as her
husband. As long as he is a success and provides her with the trappings of
success, she considers that she has made a satisfactory bargain.

wilderness camps, and college campuses for two- to seven-day seminars designed to help them learn how to behave like human beings.

The seminar leaders often start by trying to help their executive 'students' realize that there is more in life than work. It is not an easy task. One man, when advised that he would be better off if he 'diversified his emotional portfolio', frowned. 'You're trying to tell me that I work too much. I love my work. Why should I stop doing something I like so much?'

'No reason,' he was told. 'But what else do you do that you enjoy?'

'Well,' he started and then he stopped. He thought for a moment. 'Well,' he started again, 'there's .. I ... ' and he fell silent.

'If something happens and you can't work, what then?'

The man did not answer. His face darkened.

The greatest value of these seminars is that they start men thinking along new lines. Certainly the people who pick up the tab for these weeks or weekends consider them worthwhile. 'Since much of management is a matter of dealing with people,' a New York banker said, 'even a five per cent improvement in interpersonal abilities can be very worthwhile to the company in terms of managerial effectiveness.'

Not all men have to enrol in crash courses to learn how to express their feelings. Nor do all men put their work ahead of their families. Again, not all men are executives. But when it comes to what women should know about men and work, it is useful to put the top executive under the microscope. You may never have met the man who controls the company or institution where you work. You may not even know his name. But he holds the ultimate power. He controls your working environment – physical, social, and psychological – and that of the men in your life. It is vital to know how he thinks, feels and reacts.

What every woman should know is that he is not all that different from other men. It is a matter of degree. The top man puts work first, last and always. It is truly his mistress, the only thing in his life that evokes lasting passion.

11

Now that we know how men feel about their work, how do they feel about the women they work with? What do they think of them? Less than you might expect. The truth is that men take a dim view of the female work force.

Oh, their secretary is one in a million. And that curvaceous little receptionist is all right. And the office would not be the same without the fiftyish office manager who mothers the girls in the typing pool and stays late to get the work out. Still, girls will be girls – emotional, irrational, and downright cantankerous at that time of the month. But as long as they know their place, no problem. This about sums up men's feelings about their secretaries, receptionists, and the clerical staff.

What really gets men's goats are the others, all those women who suddenly have an inflated – that's the male view of it – idea of their own importance. 'Ballsy broads', the men call them. 'Castrating bitches,' they mutter to themselves. 'Frustrated witches.' It is not their assertiveness that turns men off, not their aggressiveness, nor their abrasiveness. What men have against these women, studies show, is one thing and one thing only – their sex. They are women. Pushing in where they don't belong. Once you realize that the male equivalent of a 'ballsy broad' is a 'go-getter', you start to get the idea. And what a woman must know is that this attitude exists at all levels, although not all men at all levels share it.

Remember, I am speaking of male attitudes in general. There are always exceptions. But these patterns represent the broad truth about the great majority of men.

It is a man's world at the top, at the bottom, and in the middle. Men are in the catbird seat as far as income, opportunity, status, and power are concerned. This is the way it always has been and, as far as men are concerned, it is the way it always should be.

But it is not going to be. Not for long. There have been changes already and there will be more. It is still a man's world, but with a difference. A man is no longer a man among men. Increasingly he is a man among women. And the women are not those meek office handmaidens of yesteryear. These women consider themselves his peers. He sees them as competitors, sometimes as threats. He wants as little to do with them as possible. They make him uncomfortable.

Most men do not know how to relate to the woman department head, sales manager, account executive, boss. Even men who have hired them for managerial positions find the relationship awkward.

'A woman is two people to me,' says John Emery, president of Emery Air Freight. 'She is an equal in ability, brain power, and thinking-through power. But she is also a woman. I would like to show her the same deference that I would show my wife or my mother. It still makes me uncomfortable,' he confessed, 'when my manager in Memphis, who works directly with the Teamsters, picks me up in the airport in her car. I always want to say, "Please move over. I'll drive." '

Few middle-aged men look on the female invasion of office and factory, bank and boardroom with John Emery's degree of equanimity. When I lecture outside New York and make even the most fleeting mention of the women's movement, there is invariably a handful of men in their forties and fifties who come up to me afterwards and ask, 'You really don't think there's anything to Women's Lib, do you?' They are scared to death of it.

'But not the young men. The young men are different,' a student protested when I was lecturing at her college. I had spoken of how difficult it was for men to accept women in the new roles they were claiming for themselves.

'Young men talk a different game,' I agreed, 'but I have seen nothing to make me think they are different.'

'But they are,' she insisted. 'You just don't know. None of the men I know would ever stand in a woman's way.'

She was so vulnerable. She made me think of myself at the same age when I had believed that all I had to do was work hard and prove myself and the whole world, male and female, would accept me. Then I encountered reality when Columbia University tried to talk me into ceding my place in graduate school to a man.

'You remind me of something Suzanne Keller of Princeton said once,' I told her. 'She is a sociologist. I don't remember her exact words, but she said something like, "In teaching young people, I have found that young women are starry-eyed. They think they will have it all. But I have found that while the young men talk a very liberated line, when it comes to behaviour, they are not willing to do things any differently from past male generations."'

'This fits in with my own observations,' I said. 'Studies show that most younger men champion equal rights for women. They also consider women who work to be far more alluring and desirable than housewives. But when it comes to themselves, they want a wife just like the girl who married dear old dad. A woman who will put him and his interests ahead of hers. They also would prefer her to be a virgin, but that's another subject.

'When it comes to life after college, the majority of these young men will be no more egalitarian than their elder brothers or fathers or grandfathers. When what people say does not coincide with their own self-interest,' I told the student, 'their actions rarely reflect their words.'

'What do you mean?' she asked. 'I don't understand.'

'It is simple,' I said. 'The young men who are now in or about to enter the Onward and Upward stage are facing a tremendously competitive world. The impact of the baby boom is beginning to be felt. That little population explosion has created what one economic historian describes as "a dense clot of people destined to fight with each other all their lives for the good jobs". Women who are embarking on a business or professional career are going to discover that they will seldom be treated as equals unless they fight for it.' Most studies show this to be true.

One study was carried out at a well-known school of business administration. The participants were 340 graduate students who were taking courses in management and organizational behaviour. They were divided into 85 teams, Red Teams and Blue Teams. Each Red Team was composed of three men and a woman; each Blue Team of three women and a man. Each team was assigned a project to complete during the semester. At the end of the semester each student was asked who had been the leader of his or her team and how the student felt about the team experience.

On each Red Team, a male student considered himself the leader. None of the women did. On each Blue Team, the lone man considered himself the leader. Thirteen per cent of the Blue Team women also considered that they had been leaders.

When it came to evaluating how they felt about the experience, there were significant differences. The woman on each Red Team reported that it had been a good experience. The man on each Blue Team reported that it had been terrible.

The Red Team men were almost as satisfied as the Red Team women. The Blue Team women were almost as disgruntled as the Blue Team men. The Blue Team women were critical of their teammates, both male and female. The Red Teams reported no dissension.

This study shows that men automatically assume leadership. That women seldom compete with them for leadership. That men feel acutely uncomfortable when they are outnumbered by women who are their equals. That women have difficulty in establishing good working relationships. It reinforces the studies about male attitudes that I mentioned earlier.

'If we analyse the findings,' I said, 'it seems most unlikely that there was not at least one young woman qualified to lead one of the Red Teams. I suspect that there were several. And I also suspect that these women did not compete for the leading role because it was easier to go along with the male majority. I am sure the Red Team women enjoyed the social fringe benefits of being the only woman on the team, benefits they would probably have forfeited if they had cast themselves as competitors instead of collaborators.'

'But you don't know that,' the student objected.

'No,' I agreed. 'And I don't really know that the sun will rise tomorrow morning either. But I'm willing to bet on it. We know that the Red Team men were almost as happy with the group experience as the women. They obviously felt comfortable. I think it is safe to say that the women on these teams did not make waves.'

She nodded. 'Yes, I guess so.'

'The Red Teams,' I pointed out, 'reflect the traditional male-female working relationship.'

'And the Blue Teams?' she asked. 'Are they the wave of the future?'

'I hope not,' I said. 'For women's sake, I really hope not. They demonstrated another facet of men's attitudes towards women. The lone man on each Blue Team considered himself the team leader, but he did not find it a rewarding experience. Being the only man made him acutely uncomfortable.

'Men can accept being in the sexual minority only when they are definitely in control. The male boss of thirty-five female clerical workers is in the catbird seat, for instance, as is the supermarket manager who has eighteen female checkout cashiers on his payroll. But when a man is out-numbered by women who are his equals in intelligence and capabilities, he hates it.

'What women should know about men is that men do not mind working with women – as long as they are the boss,' I concluded.

The fourth significant finding of the study was the inability of the Blue Teams to establish harmonious working relationships.

Men start learning how to work with each other very early. Expert after expert has pointed out that men conduct their working lives by a set of rules they have been learning ever since they were little boys playing football. In hockey and basketball and football, all the team sports that boys and their fathers and coaches take so seriously, boys learn to work together to win.

Arnold may not be able to stand Tony. And Josh may detest Joe. But if Tony is the best quarterback in the school team and if Joe shoots baskets more consistently than anyone else on the team, Arnold and Josh are going to put their personal feelings aside. By the time men enter the Onward and Upward stage, this is second nature to them. It is the basis of a male characteristic that I call The Big Switch.

The Big Switch mystifies women. Faith had never been able to understand Stefan's relationship with Hunter. Stefan works in one of those large accounting firms that hire a group of bright young men every year. They compete for the attention of their superiors in the hope of being assigned to one of the big accounts where there is more exposure, more opportunity – and more money.

Stefan hated Hunter with a passion. 'That guy is underhanded!' he raged to his wife. 'You can't trust him.' Almost every night Stefan came home with another story about how rotten Hunter was. Faith hated him as much as Stefan did. 'How can he do such things?' she would ask. 'Doesn't anyone understand what he's up to?'

Stefan would shrug. 'The guy's smart,' he would say. 'He covers his tracks. And you should see how he sucks up to management.'

One night Stefan came home exuberant. He kissed Faith and whirled her around the kitchen. 'We did it!' he crowed. 'We pulled it off. Good old Hunter and I got the brass ring.'

'Good old who?'

'Good old Hunter!'

'Hunter? I thought you despised him.'

Stefan disregarded this. 'We pulled it off,' he said again. 'They are giving us the Donnell account. That means money, baby.'

'You're going to be working with Hunter?' Faith was incredulous. 'How will you stand him?'

'Stand him?' Stefan was puzzled. 'Hunter's a prince. A great guy.'

'A prince?' Faith echoed. 'Just last week you told me he was a shit.'

Hunter was neither a shit nor a prince. He was Stefan's closest competitor in the office. Now that they had been chosen to work together on an important account, Stefan had already adjusted his feelings towards his former rival. He had made The Big Switch.

The Big Switch is alien to most women. But it is one of the rules men play by and a woman must be aware of it. The rule? To get ahead, you must get along. There is no point in looking on it as good or bad. It is the result of society's indoctrination of the male. What is important is to understand that The Big Switch is as easy for a man as turning over in bed. A woman who works with men must always be aware of this, otherwise she may find herself on the outside, the way Luisa did.

Luisa worked very closely with Will, a famous New York dress designer. She had started as a receptionist in the show-room. Now she was in charge of handling the department store orders for each season's new designs. It was a responsible position and Luisa found it challenging. Will rewarded her devotion with annual raises and bonuses.

Ever since Luisa had been working there, Will had been carrying on about Norman, another designer. He was sure that Norman had a spy in his workroom and was copying his designs. Luisa shared Will's indignation. On the occasions when she ran into Norman, she looked through him as if he did not exist.

To Luisa's shock and bewilderment, a day came when the two firms merged. Luisa had heard rumours, but since Will had said nothing, she dismissed them. When Will finally told her that he and Norman were forming a new design firm, she was stunned. And there was another shock on top of that. Will told her that there was no place for her in the new organization.

It had been one of Norman's conditions for the merger that Luisa be fired. 'She's always been so hostile to me,' he told Will. 'I don't want someone like that on the payroll.' Luisa was told that she would be given a good reference and her severance pay would continue until she found another position, but that she should start looking immediately.

To Luisa's way of thinking, she was being punished for being loyal to her boss. His enemy had been her enemy. What she did not realize was that today's enemy may be tomorrow's ally. And it had never registered with her that much as Will had complained about Norman in private, he had always been friendly and courteous in public.

Men feud with each other, fight tooth and nail for business, resort to various stratagems, but they seldom burn their business bridges. They maintain an air of civility in public. This enables them to take advantage of opportunities that might otherwise be forfeited. 'Business is business,' Will told Luisa, when he explained why she was being fired.

'That's so insincere,' Luisa said to me later. 'How can people be that way?'

'It may be insincere,' I told her, 'but it is the way things often are. The Big Switch exists. It is part of the male business mentality. If you had learned this, you would still have your job.'

'No,' she said, 'I would have had a better job. My job was upgraded with the merger. The man they hired to take my place is vice-president of marketing. That could have been me.'

I sympathized with her. It was a hard way to learn about The Big Switch.

Luisa is not an isolated instance. Many women have come a cropper from not understanding the rules of corporate life – or academic or professional or political life. There are not enough women in the middle and upper reaches who can share their knowledge with women who are starting out. And while some men are willing to impart their knowledge, many do not comprehend that women do not know these things. It all seems so obvious to them. But men have been playing by these rules for centuries. No wonder it is second nature to them now.

Some women have cut themselves off from advancement simply because they did not know enough about the male corporate environment and the real meaning of what people say.

This brings up a question. What about the keen perception women are supposed to have? The perception that is the result of both left and right brains coming to bear on a single subject or person or statement? What about the female ability to pick up unspoken thoughts? To understand how another person really feels? Why can't women put their perceptions to work in the corporate environment?

The answer is that they can. Very definitely. But in order to perceive, one first has to be familiar with the environment. Just as one cannot sail without charts, one cannot navigate the corporate waters without knowing where the reefs and shoals are. By and large women do not know enough yet about the corporate environment or that of the top echelons in banking, politics, law, or whatever to perceive correctly.

This was made heartbreakingly clear by Margaret Hennig and Anne Jardim, authors of the landmark book *The Managerial Woman*. They told the story of Helen, a $28,000-a-year middle-level executive in a large corporation. Helen had been assigned to develop career advancement programmes for women within the organization.

One Monday afternoon Helen's boss called her into his office to discuss her progress. Hennig and Jardim sat in on the conference. After Helen had outlined what she had accomplished and what she thought could be done in the future, the boss said, 'Great! I think we now have enough to justify a presidential policy statement to the organization. If you give me a draft by Friday, I can discuss it with the president when I see him this weekend.'

'But I won't be in on Friday,' Helen objected. 'I'm going to a conference out of town.'

He smiled. 'I won't mind if you give me the report on Thursday.' Helen protested that she would be busy all week preparing for the conference.

The boss lost his smile. 'I don't care what you have to do,' he said stiffly. 'I want the report by Friday.'

Later that afternoon, Hennig and Jardim met Helen who sputtered about what she considered the boss's impossible demands. 'We asked Helen,' they wrote, 'if she had any idea what she had just been offered. And had not heard. She had just been told in effect that her work had been good enough to merit a stamp of approval by the company's president. Translated into official corporate policy, what she had set out to achieve would now become a stated objective for every company manager. She might even become a recognizable face and name for the president, one associated with competent performance. Wasn't that worth some extra work?

'Helen looked stunned. "My God," she replied. "I never saw it." '

Helen endangered her relationship with her boss at the very moment he was opening doors for her advancement. It is impossible to gauge how far this set her career back. The boss was going to think twice before giving additional responsibilities to someone reluctant to put in extra work to take advantage of them.

It takes time and experience to be able to read the cues in the corporate environment. Men recognize them instinctively. Women have to learn them. I think of this as the fatal difference between the sexes that women will have to overcome before they achieve equality at the top.

Sometimes women have to make their own rules. To give just one example, women tend to be isolated in many office situations. They are shrewd, capable, and valued, but they just cannot seem to get on the inside track. They miss out on the office gossip and the speculation about who will get K.S.'s job and what the guys in Cincinnati said about the new sales quota. Men fill each other in on these items in the men's room or when they have lunch with each other. But the last thing that would cross their minds is to ask a female colleague to join them at lunch.

Even if they considered it, most men are too uptight to ask a woman to lunch. My advice to women is – Don't wait for them to ask you. You'll be drawing your Social Security before they get around to it. Go ahead and ask *them*.

'What about going out to lunch when we finish this report?' you might say, or 'Let's grab a bite before we tackle the rest of this job. We need a break.'

If you are a little uptight yourself, ask two men instead of one. Then you won't have to worry about your motives being misunderstood. You might just tell one man, 'I've got a yen for Chinese food today. How about you? I thought I'd ask Perry too. He's been taking Chinese cooking lessons and he'll know what to order.' All you have to do is make it clear that you enjoy their company on a friendly – not flirtatious – basis.

Another good way of breaking the ice is to ask for assistance. Not as the little woman who cannot get the hang of things, but as a co-worker who needs more information on a certain point. You might, for instance, pick up the telephone and ask Malcolm in the next office, 'If you have a free lunch one day this week, I wonder if you'd be willing to fill me in on the Tweedle and Doom negotiations. I still don't have the whole picture. Has Irving analysed the tax implications yet? Maybe he'd join us.'

The main thing is to get started on establishing those lines of communications that are so useful. Constance worked hard at it. Week after week, she asked one or another man in the office to have lunch. She understood very well that it was up to her to take the initiative in her all-male office. Finally it drifted into an informal arrangement where she and the six men in the office lunched together most Fridays.

'It's made all the difference in the world,' Constance says. 'The whole atmosphere has changed. It's easier for me to work with them. And it's a whole lot easier for them to work with me.'

Lunches usually do not create waves, but dinner, drinks, and out-of-town trips do. Not with the men involved, but with their wives. Stay-at-home wives have even more to learn about the world their husbands inhabit from eight to ten hours a day than working women do. And the most important thing they have to learn is to trust their husbands. Ruth had not learned this. Leah had.

Ruth's husband, Aaron, had to go to the home office in St Louis for a two-day meeting. Anita, Aaron's counterpart in St Louis, called him up. 'Let's have dinner the night you get here,' she suggested. 'I can fill you in on the new computer set-up.' The company had recently installed a sophisticated computer system that was scheduled to go into operation shortly.

'Fine,' Aaron said. 'I'd appreciate that. Where shall we meet?'

'Let's have drinks at my place first,' Anita said. 'It's easier to talk there.'

It was all businesslike and aboveboard. But Ruth did not like it one bit. 'If you want to talk business with her,' she told her husband, 'do it during business hours. I see no reason why you have to leave early just to have dinner with Anita. I thought these meetings were set up so you would all have a chance to talk business with each other.'

It was difficult for Aaron to explain that Anita was doing him a favour. Her offer to brief him on the new computer installation would give him an edge on the other branch managers.

Aaron was truly caught between a rock and a hard place. If he took the early plane to have dinner with Anita, he would have a domestic crisis on his hands. If he broke the date, not only would he lose the briefing she had so generously offered, but he would be forced to lie. And he resented that. But how could he tell Anita that he was breaking their dinner engagement because his wife insisted on it?

'If only I had told Ruth that I was having dinner with one of the guys, this would never have come up,' he thought. 'Next time I'll be a little smarter.'

Leah handled her feelings about the women in her husband's working world better than Ruth. 'I'm jealous of the women in my husband's office,' Leah told me. 'They share a lot of things with him all day long, things that interest him and that I don't know much about. One of the women in his office is a widow. She has two little girls. They're awfully cute. Nelson thinks she's great. He's always telling me some smart thing she's done or something she said. I just can't tell you how that makes me feel. Sometimes I hate her. But I know she's a very decent woman. And look at her life. She has to work all day and then go home to the children at night. She must have to pay most of her salary to the woman who stays with them during the day.'

Leah sighed. 'If I ever said anything about how I feel, it would make Nelson self-conscious. He would stop talking about her. And maybe I'd be putting ideas in his head.

'I keep reminding myself that she has more high-quality time with him than I do. I only have an hour or two in the evening after the kids are in bed – and we're both beat by then. And on weekends, the lawn has to be mowed or the leaves raked or something. And it's his only time with the kids.' She sighed again. 'I keep telling myself that if she is as great as Nelson says she is, she'll be leaving for a better job one of these days.'

She probably will leave for a better job and Nelson will probably help her. He is not the typical male executive, but a representative of a small, but growing, minority of men who are as willing to help a woman advance as they are to help a man. These are men who want their wives and daughters and sisters to have every chance to succeed in what-ever field they choose, whether it be as a wife and mother – or as a wife, mother, and chairwoman of the board.

One such liberated man who happens to be one of the top men in a textile firm makes a practice of putting the responsibility for a woman's success squarely on her direct superior. He will tell the man, 'This young woman we have just hired strikes me as capable and ambitious. If she does not do well, I will consider it your fault, not hers.' What he has done is to provide his new employee with a mentor. No small gift.

'Whether in academia, politics, or business, the mentor system is a tough and informal way of making sure the best insiders keep on the fastest track,' says sociologist Rosabeth Moss Kanter, who spent several years studying one of the Fortune 500 companies, a conglomerate with more than forty thousand employees. 'It has been almost impossible for a woman to succeed without sponsorship. If mentors are important for men, they are absolutely essential for women.'

They are extremely hard to come by, however. As one executive explained, 'Boy wonders are recognized by a power person in the company because they are very much like him. He sees a younger version of himself. But who can look at a woman,' he demanded, 'and see himself?'

The textile man who makes sure that promising young women have a mentor is one in a million. If a man is told by his superior that he is responsible for a young woman's success, that makes it easier for him. He is only obeying orders. At the same time, he may find it difficult to relate to the woman. She certainly will not remind him very much of himself at her age, although she may be just as ambitious as he was and have many of the same attitudes.

Many men are unable to recognize the feelings, attitudes and ambitions that men and women have in common. They are captives of sex-role stereotypes. They find it difficult to share their expertise with a woman. They feel women are better suited to such 'service' slots as personnel or advertis-

ing where their 'way with people' will be useful – and where
decision-making, which is the real power, is at a minimum.
They do not see that this 'way with people' is an extra asset,
not the sum total of a woman's qualifications.

The solution might seem to be for 'girl wonders' to have
female mentors. But there are not enough women at the top
to go around.*

Precious few women belong to the nuclear group in their
organization that holds the real clout. Even if a woman is
part of that inner group, she is usually on the outer fringes.
There are exceptions, of course, but consciously or unconsciously men tend to exclude women from the power scene.

The hardworking and extremely effective vice-president
of a manufacturing company was coldly angry about a
dinner party she had attended. 'The guest of honour,' she
told me, 'was the head of a European firm that wanted an
American supplier. We wanted the business. I had been
going over figures and production schedules with him all
week.

'The dinner was beautifully served, the wines superb, the
conversation light and amusing. But after dessert, my boss
suggested that the men have their coffee and brandy in the
library. "We have a little business to discuss," he said. I
stood up to go with them, but he shook his head. "Stay with
the girls, Libby," he said, "and enjoy yourself."

'I should have been part of those negotiations that night,'
she said. 'I could have been useful. But what was I to do?'

Ella Grasso used to tell how she lost out on an important

---

* Of the top eight hundred business leaders in the United States, a figure
that includes the executive officers of the five hundred largest industries
and three hundred heads of banking, insurance, retailing, transportation,
and utilities companies, only one is a woman – Katherine Graham of the
Washington Post Company. In connection with this, I asked the head of
one of New York's most prestigious executive search firms if any company
had indicated an interest in a woman as chief executive officer. The answer
was no. Not a single one.

committee seat when she was in the Connecticut State Assembly. 'I was clearly the best qualified for the opening,' she said, 'but the men caucused in the men's room. What was I to do?'

This did not stop her from going on to become Governor of Connecticut, but both incidents illustrate how very easy it is for men to exclude women from the decision-making arena. As more women become part of the power scene, this will change. But right now, the fact is that a woman will usually advance faster and higher under the wing of a male mentor.

The relationship of a woman with a male mentor is different from a man's with his mentor in important ways. For a young man, it is a growth process, a second run-through of the adolescent separation from the father, as well as an on-the-job learning process. For a woman, her mentor is simply a guide through the corporate maze. He gives her a kind of stamp of approval, lets it be known that she 'belongs'. The relationship is different for the mentor, too. He does not relive his youth through her as a man's mentor often does. He sponsors her because it will be in his own best interests as well as those of the company.

The mentor relationship presents a woman with problems that her male counterparts do not face. Problems that can be summed up in that familiar three-letter word – sex. The male mentor/female protégée relationship is sexually booby-trapped. A woman embarking on it must understand that she is taking a gamble. The stakes are high. And she may very well lose.

The story of Mary Cunningham – whose appointment as vice-president in charge of strategic planning for the Bendix Corporation by her mentor, William Agee, the chairman and president of that corporation, unleashed a firestorm of innuendo and malice – will undoubtedly go down in male corporate folklore as the classic example of why a man should be wary of assuming the role of mentor to a brilliant and ambitious and attractive young woman. And in female corporate folklore as the classic example of why a brilliant and ambitious and attractive young woman should be wary of her male mentor's high regard for her.

To quiet the gossip triggered by his promoting Mary Cunningham, William Agee went public with a statement that while he and his protégée were good friends, her promotion was based solely on merit. This turned out to be a mistake. Instead of pouring oil on troubled waters, he had added fuel to the flames. The upshot was that Mary Cunningham resigned.

She came out of it as a heroine and somewhat of a martyr. Everyone agreed that her behaviour had been impeccable. But still, she was out of a job. And it was a good four months before she was back on a payroll. One columnist summed it up with an old proverb. 'Whether the rock hits the pitcher or the pitcher hits the rock,' wrote Ellen Goodman, 'it's going to be bad for the pitcher. In this sort of corporate collision, it is the less powerful person who gets shattered. Mary Cunningham was just another pitcher.' And William Agee was still president and chairman of the board.

The moral of this tale, if it has one, is that a woman's relationship with a male mentor can never be as close or as productive as that of a 'boy wonder' with his male mentor. Earlier I told how exasperated Ben's wife used to get about her husband's devotion to his mentor. 'It was almost as if he were in love,' she said. That closeness is typical of the male mentor relationship, but the very suspicion of emotional closeness can spell death to the relationship between a woman and her male mentor. And it is almost impossible to avoid.

When a man and woman are seen constantly in each other's company, tongues start wagging. And more male

tongues than female. Contrary to what most people believe
– and what men would like to have you believe – men gossip
more than women. And if the young woman gets a promotion, it seems to be much easier for men to believe that she
got it because she slept with the right man than because she
was the right person for the job.

I find this attitude amusing – when I'm not infuriated by
it. It makes men seem like such idiots. Would any of the
men who tell each other that the only reason Mary got the
new sales territory was because she put out for the boss,
promote a woman themselves on that basis? Promote her to
an important and highly visible position? You can bet your
custom-made Gucci boots they would not.

What women have to understand is that this male gossip
is a weapon, a pretty deadly one. It is easier for a man to
believe that a woman got a promotion in return for a little
sexual hankypanky than because she was better qualified
than any man in the establishment. This is when equality
strikes home to men – and some of them feel that they have
to strike back. Gossip is one weapon. Do men game-plan
this out? Of course not. It is an almost automatic reaction,
based on a combination of present insecurity and past
centuries of regarding women as lesser creatures.

What can a woman do about this?

The single most important thing is to be aware of it, to
know that she is a target for gossip. A woman should not kid
herself that she is immune. You may have taken a vow of
lifelong chastity, but if you have a male mentor and you are
getting ahead in your company or institution or profession,
there will be gossip, I promise you.

It is, however, possible to defuse the gossip. Marilyn did.
Philip, one of the top men in the company where she
worked, had been impressed by a financial analysis she had
prepared for his department.

'I've seldom seen anything like it,' he told a colleague.

'It's very sophisticated. And imaginative. She practically made those figures sit up and talk. There's a real financial brain under those curls. She could be a tremendous asset. Somebody ought to see that she gets the attention of the right people.' After a minute, Philip said, 'You know, I think I'm going to make it my business to see that she does.'

And he did. He gave Marilyn an informal but intensive course in corporate politics and management; took her step by step through the maze of personalities, conflicts, and relationships in the company; made sure she met not only people in the organization, but people in the outside business community, too.

'The more people you know, the better,' he instructed her. 'When a man needs information about something, he'll say, "I'll call Baxter. He knows this field inside out." And within minutes he's got the information he needs. But a woman rarely has these contacts. She has to go to the library and spend hours on research. So it's important to build up your people bank.'

Day after day he shared his knowledge with her. They were together in the office, at lunch, and often after work. Inevitably there was talk. When Marilyn became aware of it, her first reaction was anger, then hurt. How could people have such low minds? She admired Philip and was deeply grateful to him. She knew how lucky she was to have his guidance and support. But that was as far as it went. She also knew that if the gossip continued, it could wreck her chances of advancement.

She was wise enough not to discuss the gossip with her mentor. Instead she invited him and his wife, Ellen, to dinner one night. She made sure that a couple of people in the office knew about it and also knew that her special date for the evening was a man she had been seeing quite often.

'Ellen and I hit it off immediately,' Marilyn said. 'But even if I hadn't liked her as much as I did, I was determined to be on good terms with her. I figured that if we were good friends, it would scotch the gossip about Philip and me.'

The next weekend Ellen invited Marilyn and her date to a barbecue. And a couple of weeks later Ellen dropped in at the office to pick Marilyn up for lunch.

Marilyn's boyfriend did his part too. He began meeting her at the office instead of her apartment those evenings when they went out together.

It worked. The gossip did not go away, but it subsided to the point that it was no longer a threat. Some months later Philip told her that he and Ellen had understood exactly what she was trying to do and respected her for it.

'I liked the way you tackled the problem on your own,' he said. 'I liked it because your solution worked.' What he did not say was that he was even more pleased that he had not had to get involved in any confrontation or to defend the relationship to his colleagues.

Marilyn has had two promotions in three years and no longer needs a mentor. Her strategy worked well for her. Another woman might devise a different approach depending on the situation and the people involved. The thing to remember is that it can be done. The gossip inspired by malice and jealousy can be rendered relatively ineffective. And the most important step, as I said before, is the first one – accepting the knowledge that the relationship can and probably will be misinterpreted. Once you have accepted this, you can go on to handle it.

Not every woman has the temperament, ability, or desire to go to the top in her field, but most women, no matter what level of achievement they find most fulfilling, have someone in their working lives who plays the role of mentor.

Margery, who sold stockings in a department store, wanted desperately to move from her low-commission department to one of the high-commission departments like furniture or household appliances. It seemed almost impossible. Both those departments employed salesmen, despite the fact that it is women who use the appliances and women who generally choose the furniture.

One afternoon on her coffee break in the store cafeteria she mentioned how much better coffeee tasted when it was made in an automatic drip machine. 'And it's more economical,' she told the man sitting next to her. 'You use less coffee.'

The man was the new merchandise manager. He quizzed Margery about what she knew of the merits of other kitchen appliances. After that, he made a point of chatting with her whenever he ran into her. He was impressed with her interest in household appliances and her knowledge. 'We could use someone like you in that department,' he said once. And she jumped at the opening. 'That's where I want to be,' she told him. A few months later she was transferred. The new merchandise manager had acted very much like a mentor.

Professors often act as mentors to college students, steering those they consider promising to scholarships and opportunities that other students may never hear of. The loan officer may act as mentor to one of the bank tellers.

The relationship exists on almost every working level and they are often as sexually booby-trapped at the low end of the pay scale as they are on levels where the salaries and the power are greater. There is the same vulnerability to gossip and misunderstanding.

It seems a little ridiculous that sex should play such a make-or-break role in the world of work. It is certainly inappropriate. And it does not make sense to most women, because they would scorn to use sex for advancement. But it is part of the mythology that men cling to, possibly because they themselves use sex during working hours in a most destructive manner. And I will tell you what you should know about these men and how to deal with them in the next chapter.

12

Margaret cried all the way home on the bus. She could not take it any longer. It had been going on practically since the day she started work. She was eighteen and this was her first job.

'Communications clerk,' they called her. What she did was wheel the mail trolley from office to office, dropping mail and memos in the In boxes and emptying the Out boxes. She liked it. She was getting to know everyone. 'I know who's getting promoted and who's leaving to have a baby,' she told her roommate. 'When there's an opening for a receptionist or a typist, I'll be able to get my bid in first.'

There was only one thing wrong. Every time she went into Mr Hopkins's office, he made those cracks. He would whistle and say, 'Look at those tits!' Or 'Maggie, baby, shake them for me.' It got so Margaret hunched her shoulders when she delivered his mail. And today – today when she went in, he had got up from behind his desk and grabbed her breasts. Margaret had twisted away and run out of the office. What was she going to do? She could not go back into his office again. She would not.

Gloria is putting herself through college working summers and weekends in a cocktail lounge. 'I hate it,' she told me, 'but the money's good. It's just that you can't tell a guy "Get your crummy hands off me" and expect him to leave a tip. And tips are what it's all about. If I made a fuss, they'd fire me. They want girls who will go along with the fanny pinching.'

Jennifer had a good job in the public relations department of a large drug company. Her new boss asked her to attend a conference with him in San Francisco. Jennifer was flattered. She worked late nights preparing press releases on the company's new products. She set up a schedule of newspaper interviews for her boss. She thought that she had finally found herself a mentor, someone who would help her advance.

When they arrived in San Francisco, he told her, 'I cancelled the room my secretary reserved for you. I've got a double one. It will be easier that way.'

She could hardly believe it. 'I'm not interested in sharing your room,' she told him coldly. It was impossible to book another room in the convention-jammed hotel at that point. She finally found a motel room some distance away.

When they got back to the office, her boss called Jennifer in. 'I don't think we are going to work well together,' he said. 'I suggest you resign, so I won't have to find reasons to fire you.'

Jennifer resigned.

No one talked openly about sexual harassment until a few years ago, but now it is being taken seriously as a crime against women. 'It is fundamentally a man's problem,' *Newsweek* reported in 1980, 'an exercise of power almost analogous to rape, for which women pay with their jobs and sometimes their health. It is as traditional as underpaying women.' The magazine went on to describe it as 'the boss's dirty little fringe benefit'.

It is not only the boss who indulges in it, as women well know. A woman's male co-workers are possibly even more guilty than the boss. The only difference is that they do not have the boss's power to fire her if she resists their advances. But they can make a woman's life miserable. Whether it is her boss or her partner on the assembly line or the man at the next desk, a woman is damned if she does and damned if she doesn't. Statistics are hard to come by, but the most accurate figures I can find indicate that at least three-quarters of the female working population have experienced some kind of sexual harassment.

It takes many forms. Leering . . .making suggestive sexual remarks . . .telling dirty jokes . . .using obscene language . . . purposely brushing against a woman's body . . . fondling a woman against her wishes . . . threatening to fire her if she does not agree to sexual relations . . . rape.

Men do not see it in quite these terms. They scoff at complaints about suggestive remarks, the leering, the pinching, and all the rest. They insist these are nothing to get excited about. 'It's all in fun,' they say. 'Women like it. They provoke it. Bring it on themselves.' To most men, sexual harassment only occurs when a boss says 'If you don't go to bed with me, you're fired.' They agree that taking advantage of a woman in this way is wrong. But for the most part, they feel that anything else that happens is the woman's fault.

Sexual harassment is not confined to office situations. It takes place on college campuses when professors seduce female students with the promise of higher marks or the threat of lower ones. It happens in the army, in sports, in government. It happens in television and films.

In the last year or so, a number of major corporations have made it clear that any male employee found guilty of sexual harassment can be fired. This is encouraging, but it is no guarantee that this 'fringe benefit' will disappear from the workplace.

Women themselves are going to have to deal with it. The first thing a woman has to know is why men do it. Sex is not the object. Not at all. It is power. Dominance. Nothing else. The purpose of sexual harassment is to put a woman in her place, make her feel inferior. This, of course, makes the harasser feel superior.

One would think that men – especially on the managerial level – have enough going for them and do not have to resort to these sexual tactics to feel superior. And the truth is that not all men are like this. Many men, those who are secure in their own individuality, are absolutely wonderful. They put themselves out as employers and co-workers to treat women as equals. I cannot speak highly enough of them. But women do not need to be told how to get along with these men. It is the others who cause them problems.

The men who leer and ogle, who pat and pinch, who grab and squeeze, the men who threaten are men with fragile self-esteem. They continually have to prove to themselves that they are strong and superior.

We know that men are born insecure. Remember the Eve Principle? Every embryo would be born a female unless a number of connections were made at exactly the right moment. 'Male insecurity begins in the womb,' says Dr Walter J. Ong, professor of humanities in psychiatry at St Louis University. 'The embryo has to fight to be masculine. He is conceived in an environment in which he is totally dependent, yet which is partly hostile because it is feminine. The male embryo has to start quickly secreting his own male hormones. In order to be a man, he must in the beginning have his life dominated by a woman. And he spends the rest of his life proving himself – asserting the masculinity he fought so hard for at the outset. And because of this,' says Dr Ong, 'males are always ready to fight. Contest is the pattern of his life. It is different for the female. The female does not have to battle to assert her femininity. That is why females are fundamentally stable.'

It is not only psychiatrists who affirm this. A novelist insists that he can always tell whether a book is written by a man or a woman. 'Men's books,' says Charles Simmons, author of *Wrinkles*, 'have a sense of combat to them, a terrible sense of danger, an all-or-nothing mentality. You don't get that in women's books. There you feel ease. Women are there. Steady. Staying on. Men are succeeding or failing.'

But even so, how can men be insecure when since the dawn of civilization male children have been brought up to believe they are superior to female children? Men have always seen themselves as gallant knights galloping up on a white charger to rescue the beautiful maiden. And a girl dreamed of the Prince Charming who would carry her away with him. The hero to whom she will succumb. Happily ever after, of course. This sufficed to bolster men's fragile self-esteem for generation after generation. They knew that women were dependent on them.

But things have changed. There has not only been talk of women's rights, but legal steps have been taken to help women attain these rights. How much real impact this will have in the long run is something we will not know for at least another couple of generations, but the immediate effect has been to make a great number of men feel threatened and insecure. They have to prove themselves over and over.

And how better for a man to prove himself than to attack those persons who are threatening him?

The reasoning that goes on in a man's mind is not this specific, not this logical. I have known men to deny these feelings with all the honest indignation at their command. Decent men. Intelligent men. And because they were decent and intelligent, they have admitted after some pointed questioning and heated discussion that, yes, they do feel that way. A little. Sometimes. Quite often, in fact. They are surprised to discover these feelings in themselves. Men who face up to their feelings in this way will probably never harass women. As the cliché goes, their consciousness has been raised.

So we know what sexual harassment is. We know why men engage in it. But how does a woman handle it? That is the $64,000 question. And there is no easy answer.

Men get away with the milder forms of harassment – the suggestive remarks, the leers, the pats on the bottom – because women do not want to make an issue of it. They are afraid of looking foolish. Some women even worry that they may be misinterpreting innocuous gestures or words. There is an easy rule of thumb here. If it makes you feel uncomfortable, you are not misinterpreting it. It is sexual harassment.*

The problem is how to handle it without making life worse for yourself. The easiest way is to nip it in the bud. The first time it happens say 'I don't like that kind of talk . . . Please keep your hands off me . . . I dislike dirty jokes.' And refuse to be drawn into any discussion of what you don't like about it or why. A straightforward 'cut it out' will often do wonders without making a big issue of it.

Where women get in trouble is in being shy or fearful and not saying anything until it finally gets too much for them. Then they often tend to overreact.

Take Margaret, the young communications clerk. She was too unsophisticated to know how to stand up for herself. And Mr Hopkins knew it. He undoubtedly got as much of a charge from her obvious distress as from his sexually loaded remarks. If Margaret had known enough to speak up at the beginning and say something like 'I'm very embarrassed by that kind of remark, Mr Hopkins', that probably would have stopped him.

---

*Not every pat on the bottom is harassment. Nor every hug in the hallway. When an interviewer asked Patricia Harris, who was Secretary of Housing and Urban Development during the Carter Administration, if she felt she was treated any differently from the male Cabinet members, she smiled and said, 'Well, the President doesn't kiss the male Cabinet members when he sees them.'

If he persisted, and some men might because their pride would be at stake, she could have taken it one step further. 'I asked you not to make any more remarks like that, Mr Hopkins. I don't like them. If you talk that way again, I will have to tell the boss about it.'

If that did not shut him up, my suggestion would be for Margaret to borrow or rent a small tape recorder and take it up with her when she delivered Mr Hopkins's mail. If he made another remark, then she could say, 'I just recorded what you said. I'm going to play this tape for the boss.'

That should do it. He would probably get angry and say something to the effect that 'You don't need to make a court case out of it', but he would clam up. If he did not, then Margaret has the evidence. She can play the tape for the boss and I am sure it will get results.

Gloria, the cocktail waitress, is not as helpless as she thinks. She could quit her job, of course, but she would probably run into the same situation in any cocktail lounge. Her problem is to maintain her self-respect and get her tips without alienating customers or the boss. It does not need to be a matter of submit or quit. When a man gets too familiar, she can go over to the boss and say, 'Listen, that guy's too much. He's all over me. I can't handle him. Could one of the other girls take that table?'

Now it is the boss's problem. He may ask the customer to leave if he is conspicuously obnoxious. Or he may assign another waitress to the table. She will probably be willing to take over, because she will know that Gloria will do the same for her when necessary. And besides she will get the tip. The customer will probably get the message and keep his hands to himself.

I told Gloria that if she handled each incident as it came up, she would probably be able to avoid the pinchers and the patters without making a scene or losing her job. After all, not every man feels that he is entitled to pinch and pat for the price of a couple of drinks.

Jennifer had more to lose than the other two women. She had worked hard to reach her position in the public relations department. She was making a good salary. And she saw the job as a stepping stone to a management position – vice-president in charge of public relations was the spot she was aiming for.

How can she handle a man like the new boss who made it clear that he considered sex part of her job? Faced with his threat to manufacture a reason to fire her, she handled it by resigning.

This was poor judgement. It was not going to be easy for her to find an equivalent job. Nor was it going to be easy to explain why she had left such a good job without any definite prospects in view. If she told the truth, she might not be believed. If a future employer checked on her story, it would almost certainly be denied.

If she had not been so shocked, she would have realized that she had other choices. I would have advised her to say 'I'm afraid that you leave me no alternative except to write a memorandum about what happened in San Francisco and what you have just told me. I will make sure that copies of the memo go to your boss, the president of the company, the chairman of the board of directors, and the United States Equal Employment Opportunity Commission. I will, of course, give you a copy of the memo as well.' (Victims of sexual harassment in Great Britain could copy in the Equal Opportunities Commission.)

What would happen then?

It depends.

In all probability, her boss will apologize and ask her not to send the memo to the top brass. He may be very convincing.

What should she do?

A lot depends upon her personal assessment of the man,

but my advice would be for her to say 'I'm sorry. This has gone too far. You threatened me.' It is very likely that if she agreed to let him off the hook, she would soon discover that he was making her life quite unpleasant. That he was, in fact, doing just what he had threatened – manufacturing excuses to fire her. In a case like this, you have to bring up your big guns right at the beginning and use them.

What would the memo accomplish?

Again it depends.

The new boss might be told to 'cool it' and Jennifer might be given a token raise and promised that everything was all straightened out and she had nothing to worry about. In these circumstances, she would be able to look for another position while she was still employed. But given the climate of the times and the fact that no company wants the publicity spotlight turned on an instance of sexual harassment, the company might very well fire her new boss.

In that case, Jennifer could probably look forward to a successful future with the company. Top management is not going to hold such assertiveness against a competent female employee. Not today. Not when it is still difficult to find women qualified for management level jobs.

The woman who is a victim of sexual harassment should neither try to ignore it the way Margaret did, nor act in emotional haste the way Jennifer did. Once you understand how insecure these men are, it is easier to put a stop to this nonsense. These 'macho' types usually have a core of pure marshmallow. In most cases, a clearcut statement to the effect that you do not care for their behaviour is usually all it takes.

Not always. This would not have worked for Jennifer. In cases like this, a woman must be ready to counterattack in strength. She can complain to the man's superior. She can register a complaint with the Equal Employment Opportunity Commission (Equal Opportunities Commission in

Great Britain). But the most important thing a woman should know about sexual harassment is that she does not have to put up with it. And she should not. It is a kind of blackmail and the only way to put an end to it is to stand up for your rights as a human being. The more publicity that is given to this crime against women, the sooner it will disappear.

PART FOUR
Men and Sex

13

It has been going on practically since the beginning of time in one way or another. In popularity, if not in frequency, it is right up there with eating and drinking and watching TV. It is definitely democratic, for as Cole Porter reported, 'Birds do it, bees do it, Even educated fleas do it.' I admit I do it. Elizabeth Taylor Hilton Wilding Todd Fisher Burton Warner has certainly done it, to say nothing of Hilton and Wilding and Todd and Fisher and Burton and Warner. Even Queen Victoria did. And Albert Einstein. And sooner than most of us expect, the neighbourhood tots are going to be doing it.*

I am talking about sex, of course. The surprising thing in view of how long the human race has been doing it is how relatively little we know about it. Sometimes when men and women ask me questions like how long should it last† and how often should we do it‡ and would it be even better if I were circumcised§, I think that the birds and the bees have an easier time. They just go ahead and do what comes naturally without worrying about whether they are doing it right.

People are not birds and bees, however, and sex is different for us. For one thing, we call it 'making love' and most of the time it is. For another, sex is rarely for the sake of

---

* No matter what their parents may think, recent studies that have come across my desk reveal that more than a third of the girls in the United States and almost half of the boys have done it before they were sixteen years old.
† As long as it takes.
‡ As often as you want.
§ Probably not.

reproduction with us the way it is with the birds and the bees and the elephants and the fruit flies. Not with our average 2.2 children per nuclear family.

At its most wonderful, the sex act is a physical and emotional communion that enhances and deepens love. But this is the peak experience. In the valleys between the peak experiences, what we seek in sex is pleasure . . . closeness . . . reassurance . . . comfort . . . release from tension . . . escape. Some men even use it as a sleeping pill. And there is a dark side to sex when it is used to dominate or degrade or hurt.

No two people experience sex or think about it in exactly the same way. Certainly no man and woman. There is one thing, though. Whatever a man thinks about sex, you can be sure that he thinks about sex almost constantly. The woman who complains 'All you think about is sex' is usually absolutely right.

Women are sexual, but men are extremely sexual. They appraise almost every woman they see sexually. They note her legs, her behind, the way she walks. They speculate about how she would be in bed. Women also look at men with appreciation. But their appreciation is more romantic than sexual. They admire a man's broad shoulders, his manly stride, his firm jaw. But a woman rarely looks at a man's crotch, for instance, in the sexually speculative way that a man looks at a woman's breasts.

Men think about sex, dream about sex, and daydream about sex far more than women suspect. Researchers have discovered that up to somewhere between the ages of thirty-five and forty, the average man thinks about sex almost six times an hour. What this means is that sex thoughts are darting about in men's heads all day long. 'I really feel horny . . . I bet Miss Stacked is really something in a bikini . . . I wonder if the old man's secretary does it on the first date . . . I'd really like to get that girl in a dark corner.'

In his forties a man's interest slackens a bit. Sex only crosses his mind every half hour or so. And after the mid-fifties, few men think about sex more than once an hour.

You might want to keep a record of your own sex thoughts for a few days and see how you compare. If you think about sex half as often as the average man, you have sex on your mind a whole lot more than the average woman.

Men dream about sex at least three times as often as women. Researchers believe it is because they think more about it while they are awake. 'Women tend to dream more about family,' reports Dr Milton Kramer, director of the Dream Sleep Research Laboratory at the Veterans Administration Hospital in Cincinnati. And this, he says, undoubtedly reflects their preoccupation with the family during their waking hours.

When women do have sex dreams, they tend to dream about men they know. The sexual content of their dreams usually stops at kissing and caressing. They are passive. Things are done to them, not by them. There is a strong element of romance.

Men usually dream about fantasy women and specific acts of intercourse. They are active and take the initiative. When a man does dream of a real woman, that woman is hardly ever his wife. Not if it is a sex dream.

Men also daydream or fantasize more about sex than women do.* Their sex daydreams tend to be lengthy and very detailed. A man may grow bored with marital sex, but never with his fantasies. In a fantasy, sex is everything he ever wanted it to be. There are no disappointments. Nothing is forbidden. Incidentally, the men who daydream most about sex tend to be most successful with women – and also the most disappointed in sex.

---

* With one exception. Between the ages of thirty and thirty-four, women seem to daydream more about sex than men do.

This is not as contradictory as it may seem. One psychiatrist explains it this way. 'Think of a child with a banana split. Perhaps to a young child, a banana split actually tastes as good as the fantasy of it. But before long it doesn't live up to the fantasy. This is basically true of many of life's experiences, including sex experiences. Few things can match fantasy, because the mind can create the ultimate experience.'

Despite our thoughts and fantasies, despite all the books about sex that make the best-seller lists, we know a lot less about sex than one might expect.

Women should know about men's sexual capabilities, their secret fears and secret desires, about the reasons why men are so often out of sexual touch with women, about how men think about sex and experience it – before, during, and after. But most women do not.

One reason for this is that men seldom share their feelings, especially about sex. It makes them acutely uncomfortable. Another reason is that they do not really understand that women do not know these things. They have never grasped how very different men and women are – not just physically, but mentally and emotionally.

It may help if you think of it this way. Half the world is populated with strangers. They are imaginary people, people who exist only in our own minds. We see them and we impute to them feelings and thoughts that we think they have. But we do not really know. These people are the men in our lives. No wonder we are surprised when they do not act the way we think they should. No wonder *they* are surprised when we do not act the way they think *we* should.

There is no reason to feel embarrassed about this ignorance. Even the most sophisticated sex researchers often do not understand the opposite sex. It is extremely difficult.

If you doubt this, just try for the next two or three

minutes to pretend that you are a man making love to a woman. Close your eyes and think about how you would feel, what you want your partner to do, what you would do, how you feel about her response, how you move your body, how you caress her, how you feel when ejaculation is imminent, how you feel when you ejaculate, how you feel ten seconds later – and how you feel about your partner.

When a group of sex therapists tried a version of this experiment at the annual conference of the American Association for Marriage and Family Therapy, they were startled by their own responses. They were asked to relax and close their eyes and visualize how they would feel and act in certain situations if they were a member of the opposite sex. How they would feel and act if they were feeding a small child, visiting their parents, going out on a date – and finally, how they would feel making love.

The women were enthusiastic about the sexual exercise. 'I felt like I didn't have to passively wait for a man to do it,' one reported happily. 'I was the man.'

Another said, 'I just felt so – well, so tall.' And another said, 'I could do all the things I wanted to do.' All the women who participated had positive reactions.

For the men it was something else again. 'I just couldn't visualize it,' said one. 'I didn't want to.' Most of the men had resisted the exercise.

'When I finally did make the effort,' one man said, 'I felt that I was sure having a lot more fun.' A third man, who also had had to force himself to visualize himself as a woman in a sexual situation, said, 'It was the first time I ever thought I'd want to be a woman. I sensed that it would make me feel closer to people.'

The therapists were shocked when the leader of the group pointed out that all their fantasies had reflected sexist stereotypes, such as men take the initiative and women have more fun. The leader explained that their reactions had showed very little insight into how the opposite sex really felt in the various situations. The experiment had been a form of consciousness raising, designed to help the therapists have more empathy with patients of the opposite sex.

If your responses were similar to those of the sex therapists, the following chapters will help you understand how men really feel about sex. I will also tell you a few things about lovemaking that are far from stereotyped. They may help you to introduce your man to new sexual ecstasies.

14

'Males are much more fragile sexually than women,' says Lionel Tiger, a social anthropologist. 'It is often difficult for males to perform sexually if they don't feel that the mood is just right.' Mood matters, but it is more than mood that governs a man's ability to make love. It is just about everything from whether his blue suit came back from the cleaners to whether he is coming down with a cold to how many martinis he had before dinner and whether he is taking medication for hypertension and so on and on and on.

By and large, men are far more apprehensive when it comes to sex than a woman might believe. Even if a man has shown himself as a confident and sturdy sexual performer, he worries. He worries about the size of his penis. He worries about premature ejaculation. He worries about whether he is as satisfying as his partner's previous lover. He worries about whether she will have an orgasm. He even worries if he is masturbating too much and if there might be some truth in those old beliefs that masturbating saps a man's vitality.

His very manhood is on the line every time he makes love. Women are more forgiving of a man's occasional inability to achieve an erection than a man is of himself. Just one failure and his confidence may be down the drain. Along with his performance. That is what happened with Martin.

Martin taught gymnastics in one of New York's exclusive health clubs for women. He was handsome, smoothly muscular, and graceful. All day long he was surrounded by some of New York's most beautiful women – models, young executives, journalists, television types, fashion designers, and a generous sprinkling of young society matrons, all of them lithe, active, and bright.

They found Martin attractive. He was invited to dinner and to drinks, for the weekend, here, there, and everywhere. And especially to bed. It was a great life. Martin loved women and loved sex. But sometimes he felt that enough was enough. There were nights when what he really wanted was to go home to his bachelor apartment and watch television. By himself. Drink a couple of beers. Not have to talk. Not have to be charming. But it was difficult to say no. And he did not really want to.

Then it happened. He had gone to the theatre with Jane and then back to her place. She put her arms around his neck. 'I've been waiting for this all evening,' she sighed. It was late and he was tired. He was not interested. That was the truth of it. But Jane was impatient. 'Come on,' she whispered. 'What are you waiting for?'

Martin pulled off his tie and started to unbutton his shirt. 'Half an hour,' he thought. 'With luck, I'll be home in an hour.' He began caressing Jane. She was ultra-responsive. But nothing was happening. 'Maybe I can't,' he thought in shock. He summoned up scenes from pornographic films. He ran through his favourite sexual fantasies. He pretended Jane was Brooke Shields. Nothing worked. His penis lay there like a boiled noodle.

'I'm sorry,' he mumbled. 'I don't know what's wrong. I must have had too much to drink.'

Jane wrenched herself out of his arms and began stimulating his penis vigorously. Still nothing happened. She stopped and it flopped back like a rag doll that had lost its stuffing. 'Well, you can finish me off, can't you?' she asked crossly. 'Is that asking too much?'

He shrugged. And with his tongue he gave her the orgasm she demanded. Five minutes later he was dressed and out of the door. Jane had made no attempt to delay him. He was embarrassed and ashamed.

Two nights later, the same thing happened again. It was a different young woman, but that was all that was different. Martin could not get an erection. And the following night it was the same sad story all over again.

He made an appointment to see a doctor. He had to find out what was wrong. Maybe he had some weird disease. He was too young to have this happen. The doctor listened carefully. When Martin finished, he asked, 'You never had any problem until that night. Is that right?'

'That's right,' Martin said. 'My problem has always been the opposite. All I have to do is *think* about a girl and I start to get hard. That time with Jane was the first time in my life that I ever even worried about it. And the first time that I couldn't.'

The doctor smiled. 'I think I can promise you that you'll have your old problem back again. I'll give you a physical just to be sure, but I don't think there is anything wrong with you except a bad case of panic. You've heard the old joke, haven't you? Anxiety is the first time you can't rise up to the request for sexual seconds. And Panic is the second time you can't come up for firsts.

'I think you pushed your panic button. What we have to do is get rid of the panic. If you understand what happened – and it happens to almost every male at one time or another – that's half the battle. You had a couple of things going against you that night with Jane,' the doctor said. 'You were tired and you may have had too much to drink, but I think you were resentful of the way she insisted that you had to make love. And you resisted. Without even realizing it.

'Then you got a little scared. You started worrying. About not acting like a man. About what she would think of you. About whether you would be able to get it up the next time. That kind of thing. Am I right?'

Martin nodded.

'And the next time,' the doctor said, 'it was just as you had feared. You could not perform. This is a self-fulfilling prophecy. You worry that you will not be able to do something – and then you can't do it. So you panic. When a person panics, he can't do anything right. He usually can't do anything at all.'

'There is nothing organically wrong with you,' the doctor told Martin after he had examined him. 'There is no reason why you can't go back to those "instant" erections. My prescription is for you to take the initiative. Go to bed early for a couple of nights and then ask a girl you really like out for a date, someone you have some feeling for. See what happens. But don't worry if nothing happens. Don't force it.

'And don't drink too much,' he warned. 'Alcohol is treacherous. It turns you on and at the same time it turns you off. Alcohol releases a substance that heightens sexual desire, but it also lowers the amount of testosterone your body produces and that can affect your ability to have an erection.'

Martin made a date with Carrie for Saturday night. She was one of the few women he knew who did not belong to the health club. He really liked her, but he seldom got around to calling her. He had become accustomed to women calling him.

After dinner, they went back to his apartment for a nightcap. And then to bed. Martin was eager. Carrie was even more appealing than he had thought. But in the middle of the action, the night with Jane popped into his head. His growing erection collapsed.

He started to apologize, but Carrie did not seem concerned. 'It's no big deal,' she said. 'You must be exhausted the way you work six days a week. I can tell how hard you work from these muscles.' And she stroked his biceps. 'Why don't we just lie here and watch television? It's nice being close like this.'

Fifteen minutes later, lying there with Carrie's head on his shoulder and watching an old movie, Martin was surprised and delighted. His penis was as erect as a tin soldier. He had several erections that night. His problem was no longer a problem.

It had not been a serious one in the first place. And he had done the right thing by consulting a doctor almost immediately instead of worrying and hoping the problem would go away. The longer a sexual difficulty like this exists, the harder it is to treat.

Martin was fortunate that Carrie was so understanding. She had instinctively taken the emphasis off performance and transferred it to pleasure in being close and affectionate. If Jane had had the sensitivity to do that instead of frantically trying to stimulate his penis, Martin might never have had to consult the doctor. But Jane's action had emphasized that he was not performing and that performance was what she was interested in. Not in him. That had acted as a further turn-off.

Impotence is the word for it. Doctors define impotence as a man's inability to achieve and maintain an erection. When all systems are go, achieving an erection comes as naturally as blinking an eye. The average man has three or four or five erections a night – in his sleep. Without even knowing it. Some babies are even born with erections. Doctors think that male foetuses even have erections in the womb.

A man has an erection when blood comes flooding through the penile arteries into the blood vessels in the penis. When the blood vessels are completely full, the excess blood is absorbed by the spongy tissue in the penis which stiffens the organ so that it seems to take on a life of its own and becomes erect. This rush of blood is triggered by the nervous system, which gets its signal from the sex hormones.

An erection for a man is roughly equivalent to lubrication for a woman. Both of these signify readiness for intercourse. But there is a significant difference. A man cannot have intercourse if he does not have an erection. But a woman does not have to lubricate to have intercourse. It can be uncomfortable if she does not lubricate, but there are ways around that. Saliva can substitute for her natural lubrication. Or a gynaecologist can prescribe a lubricator that resembles her own natural secretions. And her partner will not know the difference unless she tells him. But a man cannot fake an erection. Either he has one or he does not. Some men discover to their dismay that they cannot achieve one.

Some experts believe that impotency is increasing in young men. Psychiatrists have begun to call it the New Impotence and they blame it on the new female insistence on equal joy in sex. 'Women are now educated consumers of sex,' said one doctor. 'They feel entitled to sexual satisfaction and demand it. They have become more aggressive. This creates performance anxiety among men. They go into a sexual experience terrified that they won't live up to the woman's expectations. These fears can feed on themselves and cause such problems as impotence.'

It is true that women are demanding more, and more are able to compare performances. Their new insistence on orgasm may be inhibiting to some men some of the time, but I do not believe that women's desire to enjoy sex is all that inhibiting to their partners. What I think may be new about the New Impotence is women's desire for *more*. Once is not enough for most women. Or twice. But the average man is doing very well if he can do it three times. Five times is truly remarkable. Anything above that verges on the miraculous. A woman who always wants more may find her man's interest in sex disappearing along with his ability to have erections.

We are beginning to suspect that men become sexually sated rather quickly. They not only do not have the sexual endurance of women, they do not have the long-term capability for enjoyment that women do. This is definitely the case with monkeys. I grant you that there are certain differences between men and monkeys, but experiments with rhesus monkeys have opened new areas of speculation about the sexual functioning of the human male.

These monkeys have a sharply restricted sex life. It is confined to the nine or ten weeks a year when the female is in heat. The rest of the year the males might as well be in a monastery for all the sexual satisfaction they get.

All this was changed for eight monkeys – four males and four females. Psychiatric researchers at Emory University injected the females with drugs that kept them interested in sex all year round. The males took full advantage of the new situation. The laboratory was the scene of non-stop simian orgies for months. And then the males began to lose interest. The females were still eager, but when one approached a male, he would scuttle to the opposite side of their living quarters.

At this point the researchers tested the males and discovered a two-thirds drop in potency. Even if they had wanted to, they probably could not have performed.

The females were taken away and four new females brought in. The new females had also been given injections. The males perked up immediately. It was orgy time again. This went on for a month or so and then the researchers took the new females away and brought back the original four. The fun was over. The males turned their backs on their old girlfriends. They were not interested. If a female advanced, the male retreated.

The findings indicate that unlimited sex can result in

impotence – in rhesus monkeys at least. And since the impotence can be cured practically instantaneously by a change in female partners, it seems that boredom also plays a role, certainly the remembrance of past boredom.

The new impotence may indicate that men share these reactions. The female demand for more may produce less. It is important for women to understand this, because to hear men talk, you would think that they never got enough. This may be true of very young men in their late teens and early twenties, but after that the average man has a fairly limited capacity for intercourse compared to woman. Women can go on for orgasm after orgasm. It is the rare man who can keep pace with her appetite once it is awakened.

Impotence used to be considered the lot of the middle-aged and elderly, but age is not as much a factor as you might think. Statistics are understandably difficult to come by. But approximately half the men who are impotent are under fifty years old.* And above average in intelligence. Middle-aged impotence usually has more to do with boredom than anything else. Their sex lives have simmered down to humdrum and their wives no longer excite or even interest them sexually. As desire dwindles, so do their erections.

But the men who fall into this category are seldom particularly concerned about their impotence. They do not panic the way a young man like Martin does. In the first place, they do not believe in it. They are confident that they would be able to get it up without any trouble if they were presented with the right stimulus – Raquel Welch, for instance, or Angie Dickinson or Bo Derek. And the fact is that when someone new and sexy comes along, the middle-

---

* Nobody really knows how many men are impotent. One conservative estimate in the USA puts the figure at ten million. One man in six has suffered periods of impotence at one time or another.

aged husband usually can rise to the occasion. All he needed was a change. Like the rhesus monkey.

This sexual boredom is a major element in the 'twenty-year fractures', those divorces that occur after the children are grown and husband and wife find themselves alone for the first time in years. If sex got lost in the shuffle of child-rearing and career-building, and if a man meets a younger woman who finds him attractive, he is extremely vulnerable. Not only because of his boredom and the difficulty of adjusting to life as a twosome again, but also because he is in his Pivotal Decade when change for change's sake looks good to him anyway.

Too many women accept their husbands' decreasing interest in sex without stopping to think about what might be causing it. It may simply be sexual boredom but it could be something even more serious.

Doctors have always considered that impotence is 90 per cent in a man's head. Martin's difficulty certainly was. But in the past few years, responsible physicians have come to believe that the percentages may be just the reverse, that only 10 per cent is in his head and 90 per cent of the cases of impotence have a physical cause. Even some types of impotence that were formerly considered psychological have now been discovered to be physical. In any case, a man who has demonstrated little or no interest in sex over a period of time should have a thorough physical examination.

A woman can make a fairly informed guess as to whether a man's impotence is psychological or physical. If he can get an erection by masturbating or looking at pornography, if he has early morning erections, if he (and you may not be able to answer this) can have an erection with another woman, the problem may be psychological. I say 'may be', because this is a very superficial diagnosis. A careful physical checkup is of the utmost importance.

As for trying home remedies, this is not only foolish, but dangerous. You may intensify a psychological problem or neglect a serious physical condition. For centuries men have tried to bolster their sexual capabilities with a variety of powders and potions and foods. These 'aphrodisiacal' substances range from asparagus and oysters and truffles to the raw heart of a freshly killed swallow, to powdered rhinoceros horn, to the famous compound known as Spanish fly. All of them are absolutely useless. Some are harmful. Spanish fly or cantharides, for instance, an extract from the dried body of a beetle, is poisonous. But it does have one good effect. It makes dermatologists happy! Its blistering effect helps dissolve warts. But it won't do a thing for a man's penis.

Boredom, resentment, anger, grief, anxiety, depression – all can cause impotence. And there are more complicated causes that may require long-term therapy. The so-called madonna-whore complex, for instance. The saying goes that every man wants his wife to be a lady in the drawing room and a prostitute in bed. But there are men who cannot have an erection with women they love and respect. They feel that sex is dirty and she is too good. A man with this problem can pick up a girl at a singles bar and experience no difficulty in having an erection. He does not think of her as a 'nice' girl. And he can pay a call girl and have no difficulty. But with a woman he loves, he cannot function.

There is nothing a woman can do to help a man with this problem except to urge as tactfully and firmly as possible that he consult a psychologist or psychiatrist. This is not a condition that can be resolved by love or patience or tenderness. The important thing for a woman to realize is that she is not at fault. And neither is her husband. To blame a man for having this problem is like blaming a child for having chicken pox. He never asked for it.

The physical causes of impotence range from the trivial to

the serious. One of the more recent findings is that if you insist on making love in the dark and your partner is having erection troubles, it might be wise to turn on the light.

Researchers have discovered that the pineal body, a tiny organ in the brain that scientists believe may be a vestigial third eye, manufactures an anti-sex hormone. It produces more of this sex deterrent in the dark than in the light.

German researchers were able to provide additional confirmation that darkness is related to impotence. In a study of men who had been blind since puberty, who lived in constant darkness, fifty-two out of the fifty-four participants were either impotent or suffered from greatly reduced potency.

Something as simple as changing your sex timetable might make all the difference in the world in the performance of the man in your life. You can take advantage of the low production of the anti-sex hormone and of the high production of testosterone by shifting your lovemaking to the morning hours when male hormone levels are at their peak.

Some physicians believe that smoking has something to do with impotence. 'The symptoms of tobacco smoking,' says a British researcher, 'become apparent to the sufferer only after he has given it up, when he may experience an accession of high spirits, energy, and sexual potency.' It is worth trying. Giving up smoking never hurt anyone.

The same goes for marijuana. Nobody knows for sure that it causes impotence, but it has been demonstrated that constant and heavy use lowers sperm production and sex hormone levels. This probably contributes to a degree of impotence. Doctors think that if it does, the effect is probably reversible. That is, if a man stops using marijuana, his sperm and hormone levels will bounce back to normal. But they do not really know. There has not been sufficient research on this yet.

Many drugs doctors prescribe have the side effect of

inhibiting erections and ejaculation, lowering sexual desire, and changing hormone levels. Medication for high blood pressure, for instance, often causes impotence.

Intermittent impotence, which used to be considered a psychological problem, has recently been found to be caused by an endocrine imbalance. Researchers at the Harvard Medical School and Beth Israel Hospital in Boston studied 105 men who complained of intermittent impotence. They found that 36 of them had hormonal systems that were out of kilter. After treatment, 33 of the 36 were cured. Two of the men had refused treatment and one had reacted badly to the hormone therapy. This represented a 92 per cent cure rate. In psychotherapy, a success rate of 50 per cent is considered excellent. The cure rate for intermittent impotence when treated by psychotherapy had never approached the 50 per cent level. And for good reason. The cause of the problem was physical.

These endocrine problems are very sneaky. Their only symptom may be impotence. This is just one more reason why a thorough physical is the first step to be taken. And a man should ask his doctor to be sure to check his testosterone levels. These findings are so new that some doctors may not do this test automatically yet.

Impotence can also be a symptom of a number of life-threatening diseases. It is one of the symptoms of diabetes, for instance. If you remember, erections are caused by blood flooding into a man's penile blood vessels. And this flood is triggered by the nervous system. Diabetes may damage or destroy the nerves that trigger this rush of blood. Three hundred thousand men a year are discovered to have diabetes. More than half of them are or may be impotent. Diabetes-caused impotence is usually not curable, but in its early phases, if meticulous control of the diabetes is maintained for several months, reversal may be accomplished.

What happens when for one reason or another a man's

impotence cannot be reversed? Is a woman to resign herself to a lifetime of oral sex or mutual masturbation? Or no sex at all? Not necessarily. There are alternatives. Penile implants, for instance. These are out of the experimental phase now. Tens of thousands of men have benefited from them.

One procedure devised by Dr F. Brantley Scott of the Baylor College of Medicine in Houston involves inserting two hollow silicone cylinders into the penis, a liquid-filled balloon into the abdomen, and a miniature hydraulic pump into the scrotum. A man presses a valve on the pump. Fluid from the balloon fills the cylinders in the penis. And he has an erection.

Another technique is to implant two silicone rods on the underside of the penis. These act like splints to keep the organ rigid. There is no plumbing involved here – no hydraulic pump, no balloon. The drawback is that the penis is perpetually firm. A man may run the risk of embarrassing comments if he uses public urinals or open showers at the gym. Jockey shorts are enough to keep the stiffened penis under control when a man is dressed.

With both procedures there is quite a bit of pain after surgery, but it usually disappears in a couple of weeks, although some men report discomfort for almost three months.

And this is just the beginning. Doctors are working to perfect blood-vessel grafts so that the rush of blood to the penis can be duplicated. This would avoid implanting foreign materials in the body.

More men probably suffer from premature ejaculation than from impotence. Few women realize that men are subject to the law of orgasmic inevitability. There comes a time when a man cannot hold back. No matter what. He has to ejaculate. For many men that time comes much too soon. They may ejaculate as soon as their penis enters the vagina. Some even start on the way in.

This happens to all men at one time or another. Young men engaging in sexual intercourse for the first time almost always ejaculate too soon. The combination of nervousness and inexperience makes it almost inevitable. More experienced men also have periods when they come too soon, because of intense excitement, anxiety, or fatigue.

The true premature ejaculator is the man who comes too soon every time or almost every time he makes love. It is almost impossible to understand how devastating this is for a man. He is not simply embarrassed, he is humiliated. Some men try to compensate for this weakness by bringing their partner to orgasm before they enter. This is thoughtful and loving, but there is still a shadow over the couple's lovemaking.

Men try all kinds of ways to keep from coming. Most of them involve trying to keep their minds off what they are doing. Some men say the multiplication tables. One man told me that he used to close his eyes and recite nursery rhymes. 'I'd be there hoping against hope that I'd be able to last the course,' he told me. 'I'd be thrusting and saying "Jack and Jill went up a hill" or "Little Miss Muffet sat on a tuffet", but it didn't help. By the time I reached "To fetch a pail of water", I'd have come. It was like a contest. Me against my prick. And my prick always won.'

Some men keep trying, hoping that things will improve and all the time sure inside that they will not. Some stop trying. No one knows how many marriages have broken up because of this difficulty, but marriage counsellors say that it is one of the most common problems they encounter in their practice.

What every woman – and man – should know is that in most cases premature ejaculation can be cured. This is what Masters and Johnson taught the world. They treated hundreds of couples at their St Louis sex clinic. The thinking is that by involving the wife, the couple's emotional relationship will be closer, the sexual relationship better, and the cure more effective. The definition of a successful cure is when the man can stave off the moment of orgasmic inevitability until both he and his partner are satisfied – most of the time.

One does not have to go to the Masters and Johnson clinic to be cured. Other sex therapists have adopted their technique or variations of it with generally excellent results. There is nothing very complicated about it, as Colette and Sid learned when they spent two weeks at the Masters and Johnson clinic a few years ago. Their six-year marriage was on the rocks. It had been for a long time.

'If it hadn't been for our little girl, I would have left Sid two years ago,' Colette said. 'But I thought I had to stick it out for her. And Sid is a wonderful father. He's a wonderful man, too. He was just no good in bed.

'No matter what we tried, he always came the minute he got in me. It was awful. I used to cry. And he always made me lie still. "Don't move, don't move," he'd tell me. "If you move, I'll come right off." Well, I'd move. I'd rather have him come than lie there doing nothing. Feeling nothing.'

'God, it was terrible,' Sid joined in. 'Colette may not have got anything out of it, but neither did I. Just having a climax doesn't mean all that much when you're constantly feeling guilty about it. I don't think I enjoyed sex, really enjoyed it, more than two or three times all those years.'

Their sexual difficulty spilled over into every part of their life. This was literally their last resort. They were nervous and embarrassed when they had their first appointment at the Masters and Johnson clinic. And when they were told the simple technique they were to practise, they did not believe it would work. They did not believe that anything so simple could solve the problem that had brought them to the verge of divorce.

Colette described the procedure this way. 'Whenever Sid had an erection, they told me that I was to squeeze his penis hard. But not just plain squeeze it. I had to do it exactly the way they showed us on a plastic model.

'I had to put my thumb on the underneath of his penis right at the little ridge where the head starts. I had to be sure that my thumb was pressing on the vein there. Then I had to put my first two fingers on top of his penis, one on either side of that little ridge.

'I couldn't believe it when they told me to squeeze hard,' Colette said. 'I told them, "You don't know how much strength I have in my hands. I'm a tennis player." They laughed and promised me it wouldn't hurt Sid as long as I only did it when he had a full erection. If he didn't, it would really hurt him.'

'I told her "You better be careful",' Sid reported. 'I didn't like the idea at all. I was ready to pack up and go home. I figured we wouldn't get our money back, but this sounded crazy.'

'But it worked,' Colette said. 'They said that Sid could do it himself, but it was better if I did it. It showed that I cared and was taking some responsibility. It made it sexier for Sid, too. They told me that this would stop him from ejaculating. And every time I did it, then I was supposed to stimulate him and get him excited and back to a full erection again.

'Once we understood what we had to do,' she said, 'they told us to go back to our motel room and practise. We were supposed to do it a couple of times that afternoon. And we had to take at least twenty minutes each time. We could do it more and we could do it longer, but we had to do it twice for sure.

'So we went back and got undressed and had a stiff drink and then we started,' she said. 'Whenever Sid had a strong erection so that his penis stood up, I'd squeeze hard. And his erection would go down. But not all the way down. It wouldn't go away. And that way he didn't have to come. He could wait. That first time when he was able to wait for twenty minutes before coming, we couldn't believe it. It was like magic.'

There is more to the Masters and Johnson treatment, but this is the essence. It is important to remember every man is different. Every couple is different. The support and counsel of a therapist can be very important in the cure. A long-standing problem like this is nothing to try to cure yourself. What a woman should know is that it usually can be cured in a fairly short time if there is good will and caring on both sides.

Your family doctor has probably made it his business to learn about this technique. If he has not, ask him to suggest a sex therapist. Do not under any circumstances go to a sex therapist who has not been recommended by a physician whom you trust completely.

Impotence and premature ejaculation are the Big Two of men's sexual fears and problems. But other worries nag at them. Worries that have little or nothing to do with performance but that can undermine a man's sexual confidence. And women should know about them.

Men worry about masturbation. Two or three generations ago, boys used to be told that they would go crazy if they masturbated, that their penises would shrivel up and fall off – and that adults could tell just by looking at them that they were masturbators. Things have relaxed considerably since then.

Some boys still get the message that their parents disapprove of masturbation, but they are not usually threatened with insanity or penis-shrivelling. The majority of parents today tell their sons that there is nothing wrong with masturbation, although it is something that should be done in private. And the less said about it the better.

The fact is that every boy masturbates. It is an absolutely natural act. And they continue masturbating all through life. Even the most happily married and sexually satisfied men indulge in it. But most men and boys still worry about it. Not so much about it being wrong, but that they may be doing too much of it.

Even medically sophisticated men worry. Out of a group of forty students in their senior year at medical school, forty masturbated and most of them were ashamed of doing it. Twenty of them worried that it was physically or psychologically bad for them. Five actually believed that it could lead to insanity or homosexuality.

Almost all of them said that they thought it was all right for children and adolescents to masturbate, but they worried about themselves. 'I don't know,' said one twenty-five-year-old. 'I think after college age, it may be sick.'

The interesting thing was that it was not the erotic experience for them that it had been when they were younger. They reported that they masturbated when they were worried about their work or were so tired that they could not sleep or were bored. What they were doing was using it to release tension. And there is nothing wrong with that. It is cheaper than alcohol or drugs. And healthier.

Women masturbate, but nowhere near as frequently as men do. This is strange in a way, since most women achieve a stronger orgasm through masturbation than through intercourse, while men's orgasms are the same. It does not matter whether men reach orgasm through intercourse or masturbation. There is no difference in the intensity or duration of the orgasm. Nevertheless, men masturbate more and are more interested in it than women. For instance, it is a real turn-on for many men to watch a woman masturbate, but watching a man masturbate is not the average woman's idea of erotic fun and games.

Most women tend to be shocked at the idea that their

husbands masturbate. They think it means that their men do not find them sexually satisfying. This is rarely the case.

'Why does my husband masturbate?' one woman asked me. She was deeply embarrassed and found it hard to look at me. 'Why?' she asked. 'I never refuse him. I always thought we had a good sex life. I enjoy it. And he has never complained.

'The other night I'd been out playing bridge with some women friends. Laurence didn't hear me come in. When I walked into the bedroom there he was – looking at one of those magazines with pictures of naked girls and masturbating. I said "Excuse me" and I ran downstairs and started to cry.

'Laurence came down in a couple of minutes. He said he was sorry I was upset, but there was nothing to be upset about. He said every man did it. He said he did it a lot. I never knew that!' she exclaimed. 'I never dreamed that he did. He said that some nights when I wasn't home he'd watch television and do it or look at a girly magazine and do it. What do you think is wrong with him?' She was really distressed.

'I don't think there's anything wrong with him,' I told her gently. 'It's not so awful. It is a release for him. And a pleasure. It means that he is really a sexual man. Men enjoy the fantasies they have when they masturbate. It is not taking anything away from you. It would be if he preferred masturbating to making love to you, but that's not the case. He only does it when you're not there.'

And then there is that irrepressible worry that many men have about the size of their penis. Urologists tell me that almost every man they see in their practice wants to know if his organ measures up. Bachelors worry more than married men. College graduates worry less than non-graduates, possibly because they read more widely and are aware that there is not all that much difference in penile size.

Why do men worry about size so much? In the first place, they believe that bigger is better, and in the second, men are tremendously competitive. When they were little boys, they used to compare penises – and also compete to see who could produce the longest stream of urine. Grown men routinely steal a look at other men's equipment in public urinals or locker rooms.

A great many men whose penises are absolutely normal size are convinced that they are smaller than other men's. The reason for this is simple, but men do not seem to have figured it out for themselves. When a man looks at his own penis, he is looking down. A four-inch penis is pretty unimpressive when you are looking down at it. When you look across to another man, a four-incher appears very adequate. It is simply a matter of perspective.

What a woman should remember is that when a man mentions the size of his penis, he really wants reassurance. One woman who has had perhaps a little more sexual experience than most – or at least more sexual partners – told me that every man she went to bed with said something about the size of his penis.

'You know what I tell them?' she asked me.

I shook my head.

'I tell them that it's bigger than a gorilla's. That really makes them feel good,' she said. 'You know how big a gorilla's prick is?'

I had to confess that I didn't.

'It's teentsy,' she giggled. 'About the size of my little finger.' I did not ask her where she had done her research on gorilla penises, but she was probably right. The human male has the longest penis of all the primates.

Incidentally, there is practically no correlation between a man's height and the size of his penis. His feet, hands, and ears are usually in proportion to his height and build, but not his penis. A six-foot-five-inch-tall man may have a smaller penis than a five-foot-six-inch man. You just cannot tell until you see it for yourself.

Except for a tiny minority of men who are under-developed for one reason or another, most men have a perfectly adequate penis. The average penis is three-and-three-quarters to four inches long and grows to six inches or so in erection. The circumference of the erect penis – and this is really more important than the length – may be four-and-a-half or five inches. When it comes to a woman's pleasure, the circumference of the penis is more important than its length. The thicker it is, the more it will stimulate the clitoris and the lower third of the vagina during intercourse. And this is where the great sensations come from.

A woman who wants her man to feel that he is cock of the walk might surprise and please him by taking a tape measure to bed with her one night. Tell him 'I've got to measure you. I think you're way over average, verging on the enormous.' Take his limp measurements – length and width – and finish your measuring when he gets an erection, which should be almost immediately. If it turns out that he is slightly larger than average, you can expect a great performance that night. If he is a trifle below average, you don't have to say so. There is no reason for you to let on that you know anything about penile statistics. Just say something like 'Do you realize that your penis almost doubles in length when you get hard!' That will make him feel good.

But what if he has a really small penis? Well, in that event you certainly would never suggest the measuring game. After all, women are sensitive and tactful. Remember?

And men are terrible worriers.

15

Now that we know about men's sexual difficulties, what else is there to know about men and sex?

Women should really know more about men's sexual organs. To many women, a penis is a penis is a penis. But did you know that it is nothing more nor less than an overgrown clitoris? When medical students learn about the Eve Principle (Chapter Two), their physician instructors cite the penis as part of the telltale evidence. It develops from the group of cells that would have formed a female clitoris if his sex hormones had not intervened.

Most men are not aware of this. The truth is that they do not know all that much about themselves. Take that dark line on the underside of the penis, for instance. This is another reminder of the male's earliest days in the womb before his masculinity was established. The line marks the fusing of the right and left labia minora. The labia minora are the inner fleshy lips that guard the entrance to the vagina. If you separate the outer hair-covered genital lips and examine yourself with a hand mirror, you will see that there is a band of darker skin along the edge of these inner lips. In the male, these dark cells exist as that dark line on the underside of the penis.

One of New York City's top urologists told me that he gets at least one panicky call a week from someone who has suddenly started to worry about that line.

'I didn't think it was cancer,' one patient said, 'but I wasn't sure. I thought perhaps it was some crazy kind of long skinny mole. And then I started worrying that a mole that looked crazy might be malignant. I used to sneak looks

at the guys I play tennis with when we were in the showers.
But you know how it is. You just don't see the flip side of
another guy's prick. And I certainly was not going to ask
one of them.'

The urologist was able to put the patient's mind at rest.
He reassured him that the line was completely normal.
When the man left the doctor's office, he said, 'I'm going
straight home to tell my little boy what you just told me. I
wouldn't ever want him to be worried sick the way I've been
all these weeks.'

Some men are circumcised, some are not. It is a very
simple surgical procedure consisting of cutting off the
foreskin that covers the tip of the penis. How does this affect
a man's sexual enjoyment? And yours? Men who have been
circumcised as adults say that there is a certain loss in sensitivity, but that it does not impair their pleasure. Most say
that they get used to it and never think about it. It may,
however, increase a woman's pleasure because the
decreased sensitivity allows some men to postpone ejaculation for a longer period.

Why circumcision? It is considered to be a health
measure. When the foreskin is removed, it is easier to keep
the penis clean. A white secretion called smegma tends to
build up under the foreskin. If a man is not scrupulously
clean, it can produce an unpleasant odour. If a man is
circumcised, there is no place for smegma to accumulate.
Some medical men also believe that smegma may be a
factor in cancer of the penis and cancer of the cervix.

Circumcision is usually performed very shortly after
birth. Grown men who were not circumcised as infants
occasionally have to undergo this surgery because the
foreskin becomes so tight that it prevents a man from
attaining an erection.

And then there is the scrotum, that loose bag of skin that
contains the testicles. There is a thin line dividing the

scrotum that looks very much like a scar. It marks the fusing of what would have been the labia majora if the foetus had gone on its female way. The labia majora are the hair-covered genital folds that protect the clitoris and the labia minora.

When a man feels warm and relaxed, his scrotum is saggy and baggy. When he is cold or tense, it tightens up like a pair of Siamese prunes – slightly lopsides prunes, since one testicle hangs lower than the other, a fact of male anatomy that tailors have to take into account when cutting patterns for men's trousers.

Each testicle has a tiny bump on it that is excruciatingly sensitive. It is called the epididymis and it is very important. This is where the sperm cells are stored in tubes that are coiled round and round on each other. If the tubes were straightened out, each would extend for almost seven yards.

Ejaculation marks a boy's entrance into manhood just as menstruation marks a girl's becoming a woman. And just the way every woman can remember her first menstrual period and the circumstances surrounding it, every man remembers his first ejaculation, even if it happened while he was asleep. And it often does.

One man recalls that he thought he was bleeding to death. 'It took all the courage I had in me to turn on the light,' he says. 'I was sure I would find the sheets covered with blood.' Another man remembers that he woke up in a panic because he thought he had wet the bed. It is common for boys to think they are having a heart attack because of the way their hearts pound during ejaculation.

Boys have orgasms before they reach ejaculatory age, which is around thirteen on the average. Kinsey, the grandfather of modern sex researchers, discovered that almost half of the five-year-olds he studied had had an orgasm. And 80 per cent of the pre-ejaculatory pre-adolescents in the study also had had orgasms.

Not only do men start having orgasms earlier, they have
more of them. One study revealed that the average man has
some 1,500 orgasms before marriage, the average woman no
more than 250. Does this six-to-one proportion hold true
after marriage? It does not seem to. According to some
researchers, women attain orgasm about a third of the time.
Others say it is closer to half the time. But these statistics
should not be taken as more than indications. There is too
much variation in the female population. A woman in her
twenties, for instance, is more orgasmic than a woman in
her seventies. And women in their late thirties and early
forties are at their orgasmic peak.* But so much depends on
a woman's mood, health, environment, feeling for her
partner, and a host of other factors that no woman should
try to measure herself against these findings. If you enjoy an
orgasm more than half the time you have sex, however, you
are a member of a happy minority.

There is a difference in the quality as well as in the
quantity of male orgasms. The quality does not vary as
much as that of a woman's orgasm. Fatigue and health and
anxiety can affect the quality of a man's orgasm. If he is
very tired or getting over the flu or has just lost his job, he
may have a minimal orgasm, what one man describes as 'a
jerk and a dribble', instead of a strongly pulsing ejaculation.
But on the average men have ten or twelve contractions and
one orgasm is much like another. This is an average figure,
remember. Some men may have only five contractions,
others as many as fifteen or sixteen.†

* Men's sexual drive and orgasmic capability peak during the late teens
and early twenties, a fact some cite as a reason for women's marrying men
younger than themselves.
† While a man is en route to orgasm, his pulse rate increases. It may go
as high as 150 beats per minute. And his blood pressure and temperature
go up. He is totally involved by what he is doing. A woman's thoughts may
stray, but a man, as he comes close to the moment of ejaculatory
inevitability, is possessed by the drive to completion.

The first contraction is the strongest, so strong that the ejaculate containing the semen would spurt almost three feet if the penis were not contained in the vagina. About five hundred million sperm are ejaculated in the course of a single orgasm. The contractions are spaced at intervals of .8 second, which happens to be exactly the rate of a woman's orgasmic contractions. So if you have simultaneous orgasms, it can be a very powerful experience.

Men have the strongest and longest orgasms after a period of abstinence. Two days will do it for a man in his twenties or thirties. Add a day or two for each decade after that. This is probably why men think that if women do not have sex on a regular basis, they will be ravenous for it – and humbly grateful. The result is quite the opposite. For most women, the longer they go without sex, the easier it is to go without. And they do not have stronger or longer orgasms once they engage in sex again.

Most men do not understand that there is a wide variation in women's orgasms – all the way from what I think of as Will-o'-the-wisps to Blockbusters. The Will-o'-the-wisp is the orgasm you are not quite sure you had. It consists of a faint shudder or two, a contraction, but not a strong one. Next comes the Everyday or Good Enough – a pleasant three to five contractions. Then the Weekend Special, a very satisfying six to eight. And finally the Blockbuster, eight and up. Anything above twelve contractions should be thought of as a Megablockbuster. And they do occur. More often than you might think.

Women should talk to men about their orgasmic scale and make them understand that a Will-o'-the-wisp is no reflection on the man's sexual prowess. When you are not slamming your hips against the mattress and breathing hard, men find it difficult to believe that you came. If your man is aware of the orgasmic scale, you will not have to exaggerate your orgasms to protect his feelings.

And while we are on the subject of orgasms, women should stop worrying about the vaginal orgasm. It does not exist. It is just one of those bits of semi-scientific sexlore that created a temporary stir. I would like to put an end to this one once and for all, because it has made so many couples worry that something is wrong in their sexual relationship because the woman does not experience this mythical vaginal orgasm.

'It was not enough for me to have an orgasm,' Fay complained. 'Walter always wanted to know if it had been a vaginal orgasm. He had read about them in a magazine article. He knew that they were the best.

'I always told him that I had. I knew I was lying, but I didn't want to hurt his feelings A vaginal orgasm, I thought, had to be really great. Mine were good, even though I didn't feel the earth move or anything like that. But I couldn't tell Walter that. It would have made him feel inadequate. It was bad enough that I was feeling inadequate. But I can't go on lying. How do I get one? What am I doing wrong? Or is it Walter?'

'Fay, there is no vaginal orgasm,' I said. 'All orgasms are the same.'

'They can't be,' she said. 'I've read about vaginal orgasms. They're stronger. Deeper.'

'Some orgasms are stronger and deeper,' I agreed. I told her about the orgasmic scale. 'But that doesn't mean they are vaginal orgasms. A woman's orgasm, weak or strong, short or long, involves the clitoris, which is almost as exquisitely sensitive as a man's penis, and the lower third of the vagina.'

'You're sure?' Fay asked.

'I'm sure. Every orgasm involves both of them. Not one or the other.'

'What about the top two thirds of the vagina?'

'That area has practically no nerve endings,' I explained.

'There's not all that much feeling there. There will be contractions. But that marvellous feeling comes from the lower third of the vagina and from the clitoris.'

Fay sighed in relief. 'Wait until Walter asks me tonight what kind of orgasm I had. He's going to be surprised.'

'What are you going to tell him?'

She laughed. 'I'm going to tell him I had a total orgasm. The whole works. I'm not going to tell him he is all wrong about VO's. It might make him feel foolish. All he needs to know is that he's doing everything right – and so am I.'

That was Fay's way of handling it. And not a bad way. In general, however, I think that when a woman picks up a bit of knowledge like this she should share it with her husband. In a loving way.

One orgasm is usually not enough for a man until he reaches his forties.* And it is usually never enough for a woman. We women can go on and on, enjoying orgasm after orgasm until we are exhausted. But even with the best intentions and the strongest desire in the world, your man cannot do anything for you until his sexual system has had time to pull itself together. He needs a refractory period.

What exactly is a refractory period? I like the way Webster's defines it: 'The brief period immediately following the response of a muscle, nerve or other irritable element before it recovers its capacity to make a second response.'

That 'irritable element' of his, the penis, cannot do anything until it has that brief period of recovery. And the period may not be all that brief. A very young man may have a second erection within two or three minutes. But a man in his twenties may need anywhere from ten minutes to half an hour. It can take as long as twenty-four hours for older men and sometimes longer.

---

* A man's sexual vigour and stamina are very individual. Some men may never desire more than a single orgasm. Some may find their sexual vigour dwindling in their late twenties. Don't expect your man to represent the average. After all, none of us married the average man.

A woman should not try to hasten the refractory period by stimulating her man's penis. It won't help. His body has work to do. He has just emptied seventeen glands. And it *will* hurt. The penis is extremely sensitive after lovemaking. It is more of an 'irritated' element then than an 'irritable' element. Even the tenderest caress may cause discomfort. So relax and let him recuperate.

This refractory period has nothing to do with the tendency most men have to roll over and go to sleep immediately after making love. During lovemaking a chemical is released that makes a man feel overpoweringly sleepy. Sleepy, mind you. Not tired. He does not have to give in to the feeling. If he will just make an effort to talk to you, to whisper all those sweet nothings you like to hear for thirty to forty-five seconds after love-making, the urge to sleep will disappear. If he is not aware of this, I suggest that you tell him in your own self-interest. Afterplay is as delicious in its way as foreplay.

If a man fakes his orgasm, he will have no refractory period, but if he has faked it, there is very little likelihood that he will be interested in a second go-round.

'Men fake orgasms!' Shirley exclaimed. 'I don't believe it. It's impossible!'

'No, it isn't,' I told her. 'Men don't fake as much as women do, but they fake.'

'Impossible,' she repeated.

'All right,' I said, 'just how can you be sure that a man has had an orgasm?'

She looked at me and shook her head. 'If I hadn't known you, Joyce, ever since we went to Cornell, I'd have to believe you'd spent your life in a convent. Asking a question like that. In the first place, there's the way he starts thrusting and panting. And in the second, afterwards I'm all wet inside. It comes dripping out of me!'

'Thrusting and panting is easy to fake,' I said. 'And as for being wet inside, it is not necessarily from the ejaculate. A woman lubricates when she is sexually aroused. And if you use a cream or jelly as part of your birth control, you are even wetter inside. The amount of ejaculate is not all that much, you know. A teaspoon or so. Even less.'

'But why would a man fake?' Shirley asked.

'Men have their problems too,' I told her. 'Some kinds of medication can inhibit orgasm. The man can pump away forever and never come. So he fakes. It is a terrible blow to a man's ego to admit that he can't come.

'Sometimes there is an element of hostility involved. If a man feels resentful about something his wife has done or said, he may fake an orgasm just to get the whole thing over with in a hurry.

'One man told me that he faked because he didn't want his new girlfriend to know that he could not make it the second time. He pretended to be so excited he had to come almost immediately. There are a million reasons,' I told Shirley. 'A therapist told me about a man who was having an affair. He always faked with his wife. "I want to save myself for my girlfriend," he explained to the therapist. Some men fake because they lose their erection after penetration and don't want their partner to know.

'But most of the time, it is because a man is tired and wants to go to sleep. He thinks faking is kinder to his wife than telling her how he feels.'

'I don't get it,' Shirley said. 'If a man has an erection, doesn't he have to come?'

'Of course not. Think of all the times a man gets hard and does not ejaculate. The erection just subsides all by itself. Men often get an erection watching a sexy movie or when they are dancing. But men do feel under pressure to perform. What women must know is that sometimes they can't. The woman who is truly attuned to her man and understands the physical limits of his sexuality will sense when he needs a respite from sex. Lovemaking should not be a chore for him any more than for her.

'And remember, a little abstinence makes the orgasms stronger. For him, at least.'

'Well, I don't know how my husband will feel about abstinence,' Shirley said, 'but I get your message. There'll be no pressure to perform in our bedroom.'

16

Sex is not a matter of ejaculation alone for men. At its best, it is a communion. Not every time. And not every other time. But there are those blue moon occasions when sex is so delicious, when love and physical pleasure blend into such ecstasy that he feels part of you. This is what makes sex really special. Not orgasms alone. A man can have as strong and satisfying an orgasm with a perfect stranger as he can with the woman he loves. But he can never have one of those heart-stirring, blue moon peaks with a woman he does not love. And that is something every woman should know, because it is Mother Nature's way of keeping a man around the house.

Anthropologists and other scientists have recently come to believe that it is our sexiness as much as our intelligence that distinguishes us from the rest of the animal kingdom. Human beings are the most erotic of all mammals. Our sexuality tops even that of the monkey. We put rabbits to shame.

With most animals sex is restricted to the periods when the female is in heat. Over a lifetime, those periods do not add up to all that much. Men and women, however, can be sexually engaged with each other fifty-two weeks of the year.

It is as if way back in prehistory Mother Nature had searched for the most effective way of protecting mothers and children. Without someone to provide food for and defend the mother and child, they were at the mercy of wild beasts and predatory males. The mother would have to abandon her infant when she foraged for food. The interesting species might not survive. The obvious source of protection and provisions was the male. But how to keep him around?

Mother Nature's solution was sex. Sex on tap, so to speak. The day-in, day-out sexual availability of the human female created what scientists call a pair bond and most of us call love. The nuclear family was born.

But just as the male rhesus monkeys became weary of sex when it was constantly offered to them, modern men also tend to become bored. According to one survey, 52 per cent of married men think that marital sex is boring. And more than 60 per cent of married men have had at least one extramarital affair. Boredom spells the end of good sex – and often of the relationship.

Most men are not going to stray because their domestic sex life is more like tapioca pudding than cherries jubilee. But some will. And more would, given a little encouragement and the courage to take advantage of the encouragement. So to mix a couple of old sayings, an ounce of prevention is better than locking the barn door after the horse is gone. And the ounce of prevention can be a lot of fun.

Every woman should realize that she can usually transform that male ennui into renewed eagerness. The answer does not have to be a change of partners as with the monkeys, but a change of the sex act itself, more correctly, in her approach to it.

The worst thing you can do, however, is to revamp your whole sexual routine as if it had suddenly gone out of fashion. That way lies disaster. All you need to do, all you *should* do is introduce change little by little. You will discover that each change seems to trigger another. This is the ripple effect that I mentioned earlier. Remember that you do not want to make waves. Just ripples.

Having cautioned against drastic change, I am going to turn around and insist that you make one drastic change in your own sexual behaviour immediately. If you don't make this change, nothing else I suggest is going to work for you. There is no point in accumulating all this know-how about men if it is not going to make your life better. I consider this change so crucial that I have devoted the following chapter to it.

17

There is one change that every woman should make in her sex life. If not tonight, then tomorrow night. And that is to stop lying. Diogenes, the ancient Greek philosopher, used to roam the streets of Athens carrying a lantern and looking for an honest man. He searched in vain. I sometimes wonder, if he were to roam the streets of American towns and cities today, would he find an honest woman? A sexually active woman who has never faked an orgasm?

I carried out a little survey of my own recently. I asked forty women three questions.*

'Have you ever faked an orgasm?'

Forty women answered yes.

'How often?'

Forty women answered that they faked about half the time.

And then I asked 'Why?'

The two most frequent answers went something like 'I didn't want to hurt his feelings' and 'He thinks that if I don't have an orgasm he's a failure'. And then there were about a dozen answers that went like 'I knew I wasn't going to come and he would have been pumping away all night if I didn't fake it.'

This was not a scientific sampling. But I am convinced that it is at least indicative. One hundred per-cent of the

---

* Ten of the women worked in television. Ten were full-time wives and mothers. Ten worked as saleswomen in department stores. And the other ten were a shampooer in a beauty salon, a manicurist, a reservations clerk for an airline, a stockbroker, a taxi driver, the owner of an answering service, a checkout clerk at a supermarket, a florist's assistant, a lawyer, and a cloakroom attendant.

women I asked said that they faked orgasms approximately half the time! Another group of forty might not be quite so unanimous, but I would be surprised if the majority of their answers did not reflect those of my first group.

How do my findings stand up against your own experience? Are your answers similar to those of these forty women? If they are, there is no doubt about what the first change in your sex life should be.

Faking an orgasm is just about the stupidest sexual mistake a woman can make. You are the one who is getting sexually short-changed. And the more you fake, the shorter you are changed. And telling the man whom you love that you faked may be the most destructive of sexual mistakes.

Jeannie found this out the hard way. I have know Jeannie – and that is not her real name – almost all her life. She and my daughter, Lisa, went to school together. Milt and I went to her wedding. We thought Doug was almost as bright and attractive as our own son-in-law.

One day Jeannie told me that Doug had moved out of their apartment. 'I don't understand why he got so upset about it,' she said. Her eyes were red and swollen from crying.

'About what?'

'About what I said.' She swallowed and looked at the floor. 'You know, I don't usually come when we have sex. I always fake. Doug never knew the difference. But last week, I was furious with him about something. And I was kind of upset about sex being such a drag for me. Anyway, I blurted it out.'

Doug had asked 'Did you come?' He always asked after they had made love.

Jeannie usually replied, 'Sure I did. It was really good. Couldn't you tell?' But to herself she would be thinking 'You ought to have been able to tell. I put on a good act.' But this night, she gritted her teeth and said, 'Of course not, I never do.'

Doug did not believe her at first. He thought it was some kind of sick joke. 'It's no joke,' she said angrily. 'I hardly ever come. Haven't for years.'

Doug got out of bed and started to dress.

'Where are you going?'

'Out,' he said grimly. 'I need some fresh air. I've got to think about this. We've been married almost three years and you've been faking all this time. Some marriage. One big lie.'

Jeannie's angry admission rocked their marriage. All these years Doug had thought they had a pretty good sex life. And now – now it seemed that the whole thing had been a disaster as far as Jeannie was concerned.

'How would you feel,' I asked, 'if Doug had said that he only made love with you because it was his duty as a husband? And if he told you that he did not find it particularly enjoyable?'

'I guess I'd feel as if the ground had disappeared from beneath my feet. I'd think he didn't love me. Or want me.' She started crying again.

'Doug feels even worse than that,' I told her. 'His male pride is hurt. You shattered his sexual self-confidence. Not all men react this way,' I explained. 'Many men place the blame squarely on the woman. They accuse her of being frigid, which is just another way of saying it is her own fault she did not reach orgasm.

'Others develop a terrible guilt. They don't talk about it. They tell themselves that they will try to do better the next time. But the next time is often a long way off. Their guilt often makes them impotent. And some men just don't care. These are the strongly macho men who believe that men get the fun and women get the babies.'

Jeannie didn't care about how other men reacted. 'It's Doug's own fault I lied,' she exclaimed. 'If he hadn't always had to ask me if I'd come, I wouldn't have had to lie. But every time, that same dumb question. It drove me up the wall.'

'It can be irritating,' I agreed, 'but most men need that seal of approval. Besides, I think Doug *had* to ask you. What every woman should understand is that a man probably would not ask that question if he was really sure that you had come. The question shows that doubt exists. The man who keeps asking it knows that his partner has faked. He does not want to admit it. But deep down he knows. And so he keeps asking "Did you come?"'

Doug was still bitter and hurt a week later when they came to me to try to talk things out. But he said he still loved Jeannie. She was feeling both guilty and resentful, but she said she loved him, too. The important thing was that both of them wanted to get back together. 'But we have to have a rule,' Doug said. 'No more lying.'

Jeannie agreed to that. 'And we need another rule,' she said. 'Better sex. I don't know how we're going to manage that one, though.'

'You've already started working on it,' I said. 'You've got to be honest with each other.'

Neither Jeannie nor Doug really knew very much about sex. Jeannie had read a few magazine articles and Doug had picked up scraps of information here and there. But neither of them had ever read a book about sex or talked with a gynaecologist or any other adviser.

'It's a natural act. What's there to read about?' Doug asked.

'It's a natural act,' I said, 'but we humans seem to have a lot of trouble being natural. It may be that we expect too much. I am sure that Theodora Bear does not turn over in her cave bed and complain to her mate, Teddy, "That's the tenth night in a row that I didn't come." Bears don't care. People do. And people can learn to make the most of sex simply by learning more about each other's response to stimulation.'

What every woman should know is that very few men know how women respond sexually. Most have heard that women have a slower rate of arousal, but they don't quite believe it. It is hard for them to understand that they can be ready for intercourse in minutes, even seconds, and their partner is still ten minutes away from that point. Sex researcher Wardell Pomeroy put it well. 'Once aroused,' he said, 'the human male wants to rush towards intercourse by the shortest possible route and when sex begins he moves rapidly towards its culmination. A female's attitude on the other hand is best described by that old advertising phrase, "Getting there is half the fun."' The only way a man is ever going to be able to grasp that it takes a woman longer to get there is if she tells him and tells him.

A woman should not feel guilty about being slow. Freud used to call the fooling around of foreplay the 'kindling sticks' of sex. And that is exactly what it is. Foreplay lights a woman's sexual fires. If the man does not seem to enjoy the sex play involved in arousing her, perhaps she is not giving him enough positive feedback. She should let him know what turns her on and what he is doing that excites her. Men like to know that their efforts are appreciated.

Once the fire is kindled, that is not the end of it. It takes a woman longer from lubrication to orgasm than it does a man from erection to ejaculation. Most men do not know that a woman needs constant stimulation if she is to be brought to the brink of orgasm, a point similar to a man's moment of ejaculatory inevitability. The stop-and-go kind of stimulation that many men engage in once their penis has penetrated the vagina helps them postpone their point of no return, but it makes it difficult for a woman even to approach that point. Every time he stops, all her delicious sexual tension fades away and she is back at square one.

The key to a woman's orgasm is her clitoris. Some men do not even know where this sensitive little button is, let alone what they should do to it. As one man has said, 'They don't know the difference between a clitoris and a carburettor.' If your man is one of these, it is up to you to stage a little show-and-tell session. And you do not have to worry about his resenting your instruction. Men get fantastically excited watching a woman masturbate. It is a common male sex fantasy. So you can go as far as you want in your show and tell. He may even ask for another lesson some night.

When the clitoris is stimulated, it triggers contractions of the muscles in the lower third of the vagina. And then the orgasm is off and running. These orgasmic contractions cannot be controlled. Once a woman has been brought to the trigger point, she is as inevitably orgasmic as a man. It just takes her longer.

Jeannie and Doug listened to my little lecture intently. 'So the main thing,' Doug said when I paused, 'is if I want to be sure Jeannie comes, I have to stimulate her clitoris. I thought it was the vagina that counted.'

'No, it's the clitoris.' And I explained that vaginal orgasms were simply a myth.

'Another thing that both men and women should know is that it really does not matter whether or not they come at the same time. The idea of simultaneous orgasms tyrannizes too many couples. It is true that there is something special about reaching this point together. And they can be very powerful. But I think separate orgasms are more loving.'

'More loving?' Jeannie asked. 'How's that?'

'When a man has brought a woman to orgasm, he enjoys watching and feeling her pleasure. And once the woman has been satisfied, she is much more relaxed. She enjoys embracing her partner while he climaxes. She will feel very tender towards him and rather pleased with herself for having this effect on him.

'In a simultaneous orgasm, there are none of these tender, loving feelings. Orgasms are utterly selfish. You give yourself over to them – enjoying, exulting, blindly going with them. The idea of simultaneous climaxes is great, but the reality is not as loving as separate ones. I wish people would understand this and stop feeling guilty when they don't reach the point of no return at the exact same second.'

What should a woman do if she has been faking orgasms?

The first thing you should do is stop. Immediately. And start telling the truth. The next time he asks if you came, tell him 'No, not tonight' if that is the truth. It is not necessary to blurt out that you have not had an orgasm in a month of Sundays the way Jeannie did. As I said earlier, that much honesty can be devastating.

My feeling is that you forget about retroactive honesty and start with a clean slate. If he asks and you did not come, just tell him quietly and lovingly that you did not have an orgasm this time. And then reassure him. Kiss him or snuggle up to him and say 'But it was nice just the same. And I know you came. I like to think that I make you feel that way. It makes me feel very close to you. And very loving.'

And then if the mood is right (if not, wait a day or two until you feel it is), tell him what you have learned in Chapter Fifteen about the frequency of the female orgasm. He should know that very few women climax more than half the time.

It is important that you tell him these things. The more you can tell him about yourself, the better a lover he will be for you. Dr Helen Singer Kaplan, head of the Sex Therapy and Education Program at New York's Payne Whitney Clinic, tells patients that 'trying to be an effective lover for oneself and one's partner without communication is like trying to learn target-shooting blindfolded'.

Is there ever a time when a woman can or should fake an

orgasm? I think so. If it is a one-night stand or a weekend fling, I see no real reason not to fake if you want to. It might be considered a courteous gesture. But if a meaningful relationship develops from that night or that weekend, you should stop faking. You will be sorry if you do not.

18

Once you have taken the first step and stopped faking orgasms, or if you are the exceptional woman who has never faked, you are ready to start your campaign to keep your man sexually interested and stimulated. It may help to look at your sex life as a play, a long-running romantic drama. You have your cast. You are satisfied with your leading man. So turn your attention to making improvements in the classic triumvirate – the time, the place, and the action.

Can you improve on the big three elements in your personal sex drama? The time? The place? The action? Can you make just one change in one of these? Can you make one change in each of these?

'What's the point of that?' a rather settled, middle-aged woman asked. 'Just one change isn't going to make a difference.'

'Ah, but that is where you are wrong,' I said. 'It can make a tremendous difference.'

I went over to the blackboard behind me on the lecture platform and printed A B C. 'Now, let us say that A stands for the time, B for the place, and C for the action. If you go along sexually as you have been going along night after night, month after month, all you have is A B C. But make a change in the time and you have

D B C. If you add a change in the place, you have
A E C. And you also have the possibility of
D E C. Now make a change in the action and you get
A B F and
D B F. And then you get a bonus of

A E F   and
D E F.

'You have not only tripled your choices,' I pointed out, 'you have octupled them. And if you were to make two changes in each category, well, my arithmetic is not that great, but the possible combinations would be practically limitless. So don't underestimate the power of one little change.

'And there is something else to consider. You can slip one change at a time into your love life without making a big deal about it or alarming your husband. If you make too many changes, he may suspect you have a lover who is broadening your sexual repertoire.'

Another woman stood up to ask another very good question. 'If men get so bored with marital sex,' she asked, 'why can't they take a hand in making it more interesting? Why do women have to take all the responsibility?'

'The answer is that a woman should not have to take all the responsibility for the couple's sex life,' I told her. 'Nor should a man be forced to. Sex is a joint endeavour. As they say, it takes two to tango. But in sex, it is usually the woman that calls the tune, a fact that psychologists, therapists, and family-study specialists have just begun to recognize. It is the woman who is in charge, not the man.'

A recent study of middle-class couples carried out at the University of Pittsburgh and published in the prestigious *New England Journal of Medicine* indicates that it has been a long time since man dictated the sexual relationship.

'Although it was thought that it was the man who wrote, produced and performed the sexual scenario with the wife acting the role of extra,' the authors of the Pittsburgh study wrote, 'within this better educated, more affluent population, the wife emerged as the major influence on the course of the drama.'

'Perhaps one day,' I said, 'the pendulum will stop swinging and settle squarely in the middle and we may have true equality in sex. I think we are approaching it.

'There are circumstances, however, when I believe that the woman must take the responsibility. Many women, out of inertia or because they are inhibited or lazy, resist their husband's proposals to try something new in bed or to make love on the backyard swing by the light of the moon or whatever. After a while a man stops trying. He may look elsewhere. Or he may resign himself to a lifetime of the same old thing.

'In a situation like this, a woman must absolutely make the first move and the second and the third until her husband comes to the blissful realization that things have changed. And when that happens, you will find that you no longer have to take the initiative or assume the total responsibility – unless you want to.'

What change should you make first? There is no hard and fast rule. You might consider changing the time first. It may add a little instant spontaneity to your lovemaking.

If, like the majority of the population, you confine sexual activity to the twenty minutes before you set the alarm and go to sleep, you might think of doing it in the morning instead. Once in a while. Men are at their sexual peak in the morning. Their hormone level is high and they usually wake up with an erection. You should take advantage of this. And you may be surprised. Morning sex can be just as different from evening sex as night is from day.

The very best time for sex is during the week after you ovulate. A woman's desire is highest at that time. And so is a man's. Researchers have discovered that a man's hormonal levels seem to become synchronized with his wife's menstrual cycle after a while. They have no explanation for this as yet, but they have found that a man produces significantly more testosterone, the male hormone, in this period than during the rest of the month. So for supersex, make love in the morning during the week after you ovulate.

Yes, I know there are a dozen arguments against having sex in the morning. You have the children to get up and feed and see off to school. Your husband has to leave early for work. You have to get ready for your own job. But think of weekends.

It can be difficult when you have children, but there is always a way. Will a neighbour take the children on Saturday mornings once a month? If you promise to do the same for her? Would the grandparents have the kids over for a Friday or Saturday night sleepover once in a while? Some YMCAs and churches have special sleepover programmes for school-age youngsters five or six times during the school year. The kids arrive with toothbrush and sleeping bag late Friday afternoon and parents pick them up at midday on Saturday.

I know a woman who chauffeurs her three youngsters to Sunday School every week, her raincoat over her night-gown, and speeds right back home and into bed with her husband for a precious hour of morning sex.

If it is impossible to carve out enough time for relaxed sex, there is no reason why you can't surprise him now and again with an early morning quickie. Hop out of bed, brush your teeth, comb your hair, lock the bedroom door, and pop right back in bed and snuggle up. Just in case he does not get the message, you might try caressing his nipples very lightly. This is a wildly erotic zone for most men.

Arranging a little morning privacy is only the beginning. Try rethinking your love-making schedule. Most couples fall into the Friday and/or Saturday night routine with perhaps another night during the week. And they do it right after the late news and weather. If you have fallen into this kind of rut, it is time to revise your sex timetable. Try, for a few weeks anyway, making sex dates with your husband.

'Sex dates!' exclaimed twenty-four-year-old Gina. 'That's so cut and dried. There's no spontaneity in sex dates.'

'Gina, I remember before you were married how excited you always were when you had a date with Elton. You knew the two of you were going to make love and you could hardly wait.'

'But we weren't married then.'

'Marriage doesn't have to spell the end of excitement,' I said. 'Try it. Tell Elton you'd like to make love next Thursday night or whenever. Tell him you want to keep the whole evening free for the two of you. And then plan a little. Wear something that will make him whistle. Have a bottle of white wine on ice. Have supper in the bedroom by candlelight. Flirt.'

It worked. 'It *was* exciting,' Gina admitted. 'I had forgotten how it felt to look forward to going to bed and prepare for it. I made up very carefully. And I wore the black lingerie he gave me for my birthday under a sheer black negligee. And I perfumed all the interesting places.* Elton spruced up too. It's the first time he's shaved before making love in ages. And you know what? He brought me flowers.'

Sex dates make a man feel special. Knowing that you really want to make love with him turns a man on the way nothing else does. And anticipation is – well, not quite half the fun, but it does add to the fun. It heightens his senses and gets his blood flowing a little faster. This is no figure of speech. His pulse rate will go up as he prepares for this erotic date.

And since this is a date, don't just lie there. Say some-

---

* Don't overdo the perfume. The part of the male brain that reacts sexually to odours, the rhinencephalon, is not turned on by perfumes as much as by a woman's own natural body scents. In the pursuit of daintiness, we wash away and douche away the sexy scents that attract men most.

thing. Men love it when a woman gasps and groans and squeals, when she uses four-letter words during intercourse – and when she tells them how great they are. This is a good way to let a man know what you like. When he does something that feels good, sigh or groan with pleasure. Shriek if you want. And then tell him 'That really makes me wild.' He will be eager to make you even wilder. And another suggestion – try sharing your favourite sex fantasies with him. He will probably do everything he can to make them come true.

If you don't like what he is doing, don't, for heaven's sake, tell him so. You know how easy it is to deflate a man's erection. Take a positive approach. Ask him to go slower or faster or higher or lower or easier or harder. Ask him if he will suck your breasts or pinch your buttocks. Distract him from whatever it is that you don't like, but do not attack that fragile sexual confidence of his by telling him that what he is doing doesn't do a thing for you. There is one exception to this rule. And that is if he is hurting you. In that case, speak right up. There are some individuals, both male and female, who are excited by pain, but I think it has no place in healthy sex.

It is hard for most women to say 'I want . . . I need . . . I like', but it is even harder for men. They cannot seem to bring themselves to tell women that they love to have the back of their scrotum stroked very gently or their buttocks kneaded, so don't hesitate to ask your man if he liked your nibbling his nipples or licking his ear lobes. And try not to feel crushed if he says he does not. Just ask 'What would you like instead?' You may learn something about him that you didn't know before.

So much for time. You have the general idea now of how to think about changing the time of day, the time of month, and the timetable. Now let's take a look at the place where you make love. In my opinion, there is no finer place than in

your own bedroom and your own bed – most of the time. If
you have children and do not have a lock on your bedroom
door, do please get one immediately. A lock on the door will
give you the peace of mind that is necessary for uninhibited
sex.

And then take a good look at your bedroom. Is it a room
that a man will find inviting? A half-dozen attractive and
successful bachelors in New York and Los Angeles were
kind enough to let me peek into their bedrooms. For
research purposes. I promised not to name names, but you
have seen them on television or on the movie screen. All of
them are crazy about women and women are crazy about
them. Their bedrooms reflect their ideas of what a seductive, romantic room should be.

All six bedrooms are surprisingly alike. They have either
double or king-size beds with firm mattresses. 'I've got what
they call hotel quality,' one bachelor informed me. 'They
are extra firm.'

All of them had wall-to-wall carpeting in a monotone
shade – beiges, dark greys, a navy so dark that it was almost
black. They all have heavy curtains, also in a monotone,
that could be drawn to shut out every ray of daylight. Each
of their rooms had a large mirror placed to reflect the bed
and indirect lighting, which was controlled by rheostats.

The effect was elegant, comfortable – and very seductive.
In any of these rooms, a woman would glow like a jewel.
The lighting and the subdued colour schemes were all
designed to set off a woman's skin the way black velvet sets
off a diamond.

How does your bedroom compare with these bachelor
rooms? Is it pastel and frilly? Or is it the kind of room in
which a man will feel comfortable and you will look like a
Botticelli Venus emerging from the sheets?

If frills and ruffles predominate, you might plan to work
towards a somewhat less feminine atmosphere little by

little. There is no reason to make it look like a bachelor's love nest. After all, it is your room too. But your man might find you more exciting if the bedroom whispered sex instead of sweet sixteen.

As far as changes in place are concerned, a woman does not have to initiate these unless she wants to. Your husband or lover will have a dozen suggestions – if he feels you are receptive. No matter how comfortable and seductive the bedroom is, there are times when a man wants to make love someplace else – propped up against the kitchen table, perhaps, or in the shower or in an armless rocking chair. Most men have a thing about making love on a fur rug in front of a roaring fire. If there is no fur rug, it is all right with them as long as there is a fire. And if you don't have a fireplace, he will settle for doing it on the living room sofa during the commercial breaks on the late movie.

Other men dream of making love in the sand dunes or in a sunny meadow or a clearing in the woods. They never think of the sand seeping in and little insects exploring your every crevice the way women do, but there is no reason to resist these romantic desires. The secret is to be prepared. Turn a shopping bag or a tote bag or a basket into your outdoor sex kit and stock it with an old sheet or cotton blanket, tissues, insect repellent, sun screen, and a comb. Then when he gets that gleam in his eyes and suggests sex in the pines, kiss him and reach for your kit. You might want to add a couple of cold beers. You may not be that keen on alfresco sex, but he is. And you might like it. In any event, you will be giving him a memory that he will cherish. Men are truly hopeless romantics. And you can always leave home. He will probably be delighted if you suggest a night away from the children and the telephone.

And now we come to the action, the sex act itself: What changes should a woman make, what changes must a woman make if she wants to keep her husband or lover interested in sex with her? Some women are extremely sensitive and sexually responsive. They seem to have a gift for making sex exciting. And they need no advice. But judging by the current divorce rate, at least half the population of married women needs help.

And the first thing they should understand is that men are the eternal tinkerers. If they were not always trying to see if something cannot be done better or faster, we might never have had self-cleaning garlic presses or bubble gum or atom bombs. And sex is one of their favourite fields of research. Is there a way to make it last longer? Make it more intense? Are there new thrills to be discovered? Why can't we try this or that? A man may be happy in the missionary position and pleased when his partner sits astride him. He may love sex doggy fashion. But he will still hanker for change. It is a little like the urge that makes women move the living room furniture around.

When men hanker for a little variety and don't get it, a kind of dry rot sets in. They may begin to resent being taken for granted. And then they may begin to lose confidence in themselves. As you have learned, men are amazingly insecure sexually. The result is that they begin to lose interest in marital sex. They make fewer overtures. But they don't really lose interest in sex. They may blame you for taking the excitement out of sex. And then many men begin to look outside the home.

If you love him, it makes sense to keep your husband or your lover interested. Faithfulness can no longer be taken for granted.

Caroline learned this the hard way. After the first glow of romance and excitement subsided, she found the sexual side of marriage surprisingly disappointing. She no longer responded eagerly when Thomas caressed her. She found his kisses too long and too wet. Her orgasms were infrequent. There were nights when she would have rather watched television than have sex.

Eventually Thomas got the message that the honeymoon was over. Sex became a twice-a-week routine, a service rather than a shared pleasure. Caroline lay there. Thomas pumped away and – whoosh! it was over.

Thomas's eye began to wander. Not only his eye. He often spent the hours from five to seven in another woman's bed. He told Caroline that they were piling work on him at the office and if he didn't stay late, he would get behind. Caroline noticed that the nights he worked late he came home smelling faintly of Shalimar. And when, suspicious, she called him at the office, there was no answer.

About this time Caroline attended a lecture I gave on male sexuality. In the question-and-answer period, she asked about a problem that faced a friend of hers – her friend's husband was straying.

'Dr Brothers,' Caroline asked, 'do you think that if my friend took more of an interest in sex that things might be different? Is it too late for her to change?'

'It is never too late to try,' I answered. 'It seems to me that your friend has nothing to lose and a lot to gain. Her husband probably finds making love to her about as exciting as brushing his teeth.'

Caroline came up afterwards to thank me and confided, 'That wasn't a friend I was asking about. It was me.'

A few months later, she wrote that she was planning to attend a lecture I was giving in Winnetka and asked if I could spare a few minutes to hear her story. 'It has a happy ending,' she wrote.

When we met she told me that she had started taking the initiative the day after my lecture. In bed that night, she showed Thomas a book she had bought. She opened it to a photograph of a woman whose legs were twined around her partner's neck. 'What do you think?' she asked.

He looked at her in surprise. 'What do you mean, what

do I think?'

'Do you dare to try it?'

'Darers go first,' Thomas said.

'It was not one of your great sexual experiences,' Caroline told me that afternoon over tea. 'We were laughing too much. I think it was the first time we ever laughed during sex. It was more like following a new recipe for tuna-noodle casserole than anything else. But it was fun. Afterwards we went back to my favourite flat-on-my-back position. And it was really great.'

It often happens that way. Experimentation turns into a kind of sexual warm-up for the main event. The best time to fool around like this is when you are in a light-hearted mood, laughing and tender. It should be enjoyable for both of you, so don't tense up and worry about whether you are doing it right. It does not really matter. Trying something new and having fun together is what matters

'That was just the beginning,' Caroline said. 'I kept thinking about what you had said in your lecture about those rhesus monkeys. Thomas says he never knows what I'm going to come up with next. But he likes it. The only thing he didn't like,' she added thoughtfully, 'was the time we tried to have orgasms by concentrating.'

'Concentrating? How does that work?'

'It doesn't,' she giggled. 'But everyone in our town seemed to be into meditation. It was all they talked about. I figured if it was all that great, we ought to be able to meditate ourselves into coming if we just concentrated enough. So we sat cross-legged on the bed and looked at each other and concentrated. But we couldn't pull it off.'

'I'm not surprised,' I told her. 'But I can tell you about an ancient Far Eastern technique that takes a certain amount of concentration and a lot of control. I don't think you will find it boring. But you have to allow yourselves time.'

'How much?'

'It depends. At first, you may not be able to last an hour. Or even a half hour. And the first time may be disappointing. But as you do it more often, you can work up to two or three hours. The longer the better.'

The technique that I outlined for Caroline is special because it gives a woman everything she needs to reach orgasm plus tenderness, which is not always a part of sex, and at the same time it allows a man to stop and go as he feels necessary. The woman remains in a state of arousal while the man has all the time he needs to catch his sexual breath.

There is nothing freaky about it, nothing to dismay even the most inhibited woman. The man sits cross-legged on the bed or on a blanket on the floor. The woman stands facing him, her legs spread, and then lowers herself slowly until his penis penetrates her vagina. She then settles into a sitting position with his help and locks her legs around his body. That is all there is to it.

'Concentrate on doing nothing,' I told her. 'Let the sensations build. Maintain the position. You can whisper to each other. Don't forget the four-letter words. From time to time, you can kiss, rest your head on his shoulder, rub cheeks. You can rock back and forth and sideways. You can contract your buttocks and rise up and down. But most of the time you should do nothing. Move only when you must.

'In this position, there should be a constant pressure on your clitoris even when you are still. If you do not fit together that neatly, he can stimulate it gently and very slowly with his thumb or finger.

'When either of you is on the verge of coming, remain motionless until you are in control again. And when you do move next, move very slowly. Very slightly. This kind of restraint builds a sexual tension that results in mind-blowing orgasms. If you are ever going to feel the earth move, it will be after making love like this.'

When men suggest trying something new, they usually want either oral or anal sex. They fantasize about having sex this way. Especially about fellatio. (For those who may be confused, fellatio is what you do to him and cunnilingus is what he does to you.) If they had to choose, many men would opt for fellation rather than intromission.* It is that great for them. Women are not as enthusiastic about it generally, since it does very little for them, the mouth and back of the throat not being all that erogenous.

Cunnilingus is something else. Once a woman has experienced cunnilingus, she usually becomes greedy for it. Sexually sophisticated males use it to bring the woman to climax or to the very brink, when they quickly move up and enter her.

Many men, however, are reluctant to lick a woman's genitals. Some think it is dirty or disgusting. And some refuse to do it because they consider it degrading. If your man has negative feelings about it, even after you tell him how much you like it, don't force the issue. No one should have to do anything that makes him or her uncomfortable. Sex is for pleasure and togetherness. It is a way of loving, not a command performance.

There is an age-old oral sex tradeoff that allows both partners to get exactly what they want – and may convince a man to engage in cunnilingus. It is known as 69. The number is a kind of shorthand diagram for the position. The woman fellates the man while he is caressing her genitals, especially the clitoris, with his tongue.

The one drawback to this for a woman is that a man becomes intensely absorbed in his own feelings as she

---

* Not all men, however. Some men are appalled by the very thought. Men with a high level of castration anxiety will resist fellatio. They are frightened that a woman will bite off their penis. There is nothing you can do to help such a man except urge him gently and tenderly to seek professional help.

fellates him and usually gives her even less than lip service once he becomes excited. You cannot really fault him for this. You will find that you do the same thing. Sexual excitement and the culminating orgasm are intensely selfish, sweeping everything else aside.

There is a simple, non-emotional way to handle this problem. All you have to do is agree before you start that he will bring you to orgasm and afterwards you will continue fellating him until he climaxes. Or, if he should come first, he will bring you to climax afterwards.

Many women resist all experimentation with oral sex. As I said before, there is no reason for a woman or a man to do anything that he or she finds repugnant or hurtful. But I would suggest giving it a try. It is something that men really want. And the resulting pleasure is truly intense. A woman's orgasm from cunnilingus is as strong as that resulting from masturbation.

There are a couple of other considerations. Fellatio is something nice a woman can do for her husband when she is in the last weeks of pregnancy or recovering from surgery like a hysterectomy or otherwise unable to engage in conventional sex for one reason or another. You can be sure that he will love you for it. And then there is this: no one ever got pregnant from engaging in oral sex.

Anal sex is something else again. It is popular with homosexuals for obvious reasons, but most women find it painful and unpleasant, although a few claim that they enjoy it. If the size of the penis and that of the rectal opening are disproportionate, entry can be not only painful, but damaging. The skin in this area is delicate. It splits and tears easily. There is a real risk of infection if the skin is broken.

Many men have long, involved fantasies about anal sex. It is a way of asserting male dominance and degrading the female. Men often try to blackmail a woman into agreeing to it by saying 'If you really loved me, you would.'

The answer to that is 'If you really love me, you will not insist that I do something that distresses me.'

There is a possible compromise. It may not satisfy the man who is hellbent on dominance, but the average man who would like to try anal sex and who would never force a woman into an act she found disagreeable will taste ecstasy if you treat him to this compromise. It is a technique by which you can excite a man as he has never been excited before. Men who have experienced both find this more satisfying than anal sex.

It is not at all complicated. The woman inserts her forefinger into the man's rectum. She then slides her other hand between their bodies and down until she can cup his scrotum in her hand. To bring him to his greatest possible pleasure, she moves the finger in his rectum gently but firmly while she strokes the back of his testicles equally gently. This area is exquisitely sensitive. The lighter the touch and the more carefully deliberate your finger movement, the longer he will be able to enjoy these sensations before exploding in orgasm.

A few cautions: scrupulous cleanliness is advised. You should trim your fingernail very carefully, filing it to below the flesh of the fingertip. Your cuticle should not be dry or ragged. You should wash your hands both before and after. You should also lubricate your finger before inserting it to ease the entry. Either stick it in your mouth to coat it with saliva or use petroleum jelly or baby oil.

This is what I think of as a 'treat technique' to be used with discretion when you want to surprise and delight. You want to learn to pace sex just the way you pace an exercise programme, for instance, or a child's vacation activities. There should be peak moments full of high-energy excitement separated by lower-key activities. If everything were a peak, the peaks would soon become humdrum.

There is no reason that the valleys cannot be as rewarding in their way as the peaks. And there is no reason for valley sex to become ho-hum or routine. A nice quiet technique so quiet that it is almost sneaky, that may give a man sensations he has never experienced before is the squeeze. All you do is squeeze his penis with your vagina. This exerts sideways pressure and gives his penis a three-dimensional stimulation – up, down, and sideways.

You may want to improve your muscle tone before surprising him with this one. Two or three minutes a day for a week is all that is necessary. The way to do it is each time you urinate, try to stop as soon as you start. Let the urine out in a stop-and-go pattern. This exercises the muscles that you use in the squeeze.

I want to emphasize one more time how important it is to introduce your changes gradually. If you turn back to the A B C D E F combinations at the beginning of this chapter, you will understand that if you adopted all of the suggestions in this chapter, you would be set for the next three or four years. Or more. You have to remember that for all their desire for change, men are surprisingly conservative.

Ernie, for instance, kept complaining that Margot never took the initiative. 'I'd like it if you'd suggest we make love,' he said. 'You never show me that you want me. I'm always the supplicant.' Almost all men feel this way. They want a woman to desire them as much as they desire her.

Margot was startled. She had always taken it for granted that it was up to the man to make the advances. Thinking about it, she decided Ernie was right. There should be equality in bed. 'You have raised my consciousness,' she told him. And she changed her ways. She told him when she felt sexy and wanted to make love. She made sex dates with him, telling him she craved a night of mad love just the way it used to be.

But something strange happened. Ernie began criticizing

her aggressiveness. And he began having trouble achieving erections. Most of the time when Margot proposed sex, Ernie said he was too tired or he had brought a lot of work home that he had to get through before he went to bed.

'I finally got the message,' Margot told me. 'Ernie wants me to take the initiative – but only after he has indicated that he is feeling horny. Then I'm supposed to say "Ernie, let's go to bed."'

Ernie is more typical than you might think. Men want change. They get bored with the status quo. But at the same time they are a bit leery of change, especially changes they did not initiate themselves. So the wise woman will introduce her sexual innovations the way one introduces a baby to solid food. Little by little. Remember what that Pittsburgh study revealed – women are in charge of the sexual scenario. If it is successful, you can take the credit for it. Just don't tell him.

And one more thing. Do not worry that you may be making love too much once your changes start making ripples and your man gets turned on all over again. Surveys show that the more often a couple make love, the less likely they are to end up in the divorce court.

19

We all know what sex leads to. Babies, those inestimable blessings and bothers, as Mark Twain described them to a woman friend. Unless someone takes what are euphemistically referred to as precautions. And we know who usually takes them. Not the male.

But why doesn't he? Why shouldn't he?

There are a number of reasons why he doesn't. They could probably all be summed up by saying that contraception cramps his style. There has never been a really effective male contraceptive except for the condom and that has been around for centuries.* But no one has come up with anything better or more effective.

They are popular with teenagers in their early sexual ventures, and with men who are not sure that their date uses birth control or who are concerned about contracting a venereal disease. When a man marries, he usually hands birth control over to his wife. No more condoms.

There was an upsurge of interest in these devices when it was discovered that the pill was not the perfect contraceptive. Frightened and angry when they learned about its serious side effects – high blood pressure, depression, pituitary tumours, strokes, et cetera – many women stopped using the pill. But having grown used to its convenience they were reluctant to go back to the diaphragm. It would have been like turning their vacuum cleaners in for a carpet beater, they felt.

* Condoms are supposed to have been invented in the eighteenth century by a certain Dr Condom, an English physician, although historians have traced the concept back to ancient Rome, when men used animal bladders.

The answer for some couples was for the man to go back to the condom. But men complained about it. It requires a pause in the action just when it is getting really interesting. Most men feel that no matter how thin the material of the condom, they are deprived of full sensation. The decrease in sensation is actually very slight. For an older man this slight decrease in penile sensitivity is more than offset by the tourniquet effect the sheath has on the blood vessels of the penis, which helps him maintain his erection longer.

The ultimate male contraceptive at this time is the vasectomy. Many devoted husbands rushed off to the doctor's office to have this minor surgery performed when they learned of the dangers of the pill. A surprising number of men have undergone this operation in the last decade or so, some six million in the United States alone. But unless a couple have completed their family, a vasectomy is hardly the contraceptive of choice. Some men have had their vasectomies reversed, but this is a very delicate procedure and no one can guarantee its success.

The vasectomy itself could not be simpler. The man is given a local anaesthetic, then the doctor – and it is wise to go to a urologist for this procedure – makes a small incision on each side of the scrotum. He lifts out the vas deferens – this is the tube through which the sperm leave the scrotum – through the incision on one side, cuts it and ties off the two ends of the tube. He then repeats the procedure on the other side. And that's it. The man still produces sperm, but the sperm cannot travel from the testicle into the semen. From now on the sperm he produces is absorbed into his system.

The surgery takes about half an hour and is effective. There is some pain afterwards, but it can usually be controlled by aspirin.

For the couple who have completed their family, a vasectomy seems to be the ideal way of taking the worry out of sex, but there are certain factors a woman should be aware of before urging her husband to have one.

First, the good news. The operation is physically safe. Only four out of every thousand men report any problems afterwards and doctors consider most of these problems temporary and trifling. 'The problems are usually in the guy's head, not his balls,' one urologist told me. 'If he thinks that a vasectomy will make him feel less masculine, it probably will. It's a self-fulfilling prophecy. But there is no reason for a vasectomy to make any change in a man's sexual functioning except for the better now that he no longer has to worry about his wife getting pregnant.'

John certainly found this to be true. 'Whenever we made love, and that wasn't often, Judy was terrified that she'd end up pregnant,' he reported. 'She'd gone back to work when our youngest was twelve and she loved it. If she'd had to go back to bottles and diapers, she would have been miserable. It got so I felt guilty every time I went near her.

'But now our sex is dynamite,' he said happily. 'It's the best it's been during our whole marriage.'

And now for – I won't call it bad news, but there are two worrisome factors that should be considered before a couple decides that a vasectomy is their passport to carefree sex.

There can be a destructive psychological fallout.

'To have a vasectomy without psychological consultation first is a mistake,' says Dr Ari Kiev. 'If it's the man's idea, if he really wants to take the responsibility, things usually work out. But I've run into situations where the wife has made the decision. The guy who just goes along with what his wife wants is setting himself up for a lot of marital difficulties.'

Most of the difficulties stem from the fact that many men confuse fertility with libido – emotionally if not intellectually. 'Fertility is the same as virility to my husband,' one woman said explaining why he refused to have a vasectomy. 'He thinks that if he can't make me pregnant, he is no longer a man.' In this situation a vasectomy would create more problems than it solved.

If a man has not come to emotional terms with having a vasectomy, he may become impotent or he may become very macho and demanding practically overnight. Some men think they have sacrificed something and now they want to be rewarded for their sacrifice.

This highlights a major difference between men and women. A woman does not consider her sexuality to depend upon her fertility. She knows that the time will come when she will no longer be able to become pregnant. She also knows that she will still feel sexual desire and sexual delight. Men are different. Even the man who knows very well that the ability to procreate is different from the ability to have and enjoy sex may not quite believe it. Many men tend to equate a vasectomy with castration. As the urologist said, it is in their heads, not their balls.

The other worrisome factor is the suspicion, based on experiments with two species of monkeys, that vasectomies may lead to atherosclerosis – hardening of the arteries – and eventually to strokes or heart disease.

What seems to happen with vasectomized monkeys is that when the sperm is absorbed by the body, it triggers the production of defensive antibodies that muster to fight what the body now recognizes as a foreign substance. This internal battle results in injuries to the insides of the arteries. Cholesterol deposits then build up at the site of these injuries, narrowing the channel through which the blood pulses, especially in those arteries that bring blood to the brain.

There is no hard evidence as yet that the same thing happens with men. And it may take some time to find out whether or not it does, since atherosclerosis can take ten years or more to develop. The directors of major long-term studies on the effect of diet and exercise on the heart and longevity have been asked to identify study participants who have had vasectomies and observe them over the years to see if they have a greater incidence of atherosclerosis than men who have not had vasectomies.

So what should a concerned couple do? Rule out the vasectomy solution?

Some physicians advise waiting until scientists come up with more solid findings. Others pooh-pooh the monkey research as being inconclusive and unconvincing. My advice is to rely on your own doctor's advice. If your husband has a low cholesterol count, watches his diet, and gets regular exercise, the doctor may see no harm in going ahead with a vasectomy.

Another reason to consult your doctor is that by the time this book is in print, researchers may have made a breakthrough on the subject and know for certain whether or not there is a link between vasectomies and hardening of the arteries. And your doctor will be among the first to know.

In the meantime, what about the six million-plus American men who have already had vasectomies?

At this point the risk seems minimal. A study published in the *Lancet* showed that the rate of heart attacks in five thousand men who had vasectomies did not differ significantly from the rate of twenty-four thousand men who did not. And an American physiologist points out that 'there are no studies to date that indicate that having a vasectomy is going to exacerbate or increase atherosclerosis.'

The doctors I consulted advised vasectomized men to keep their weight within the normal range for their body build, to get regular vigorous exercise, and have their cholesterol count and blood pressure checked regularly. In other words, lead a normal healthy life and forget about the monkeys.

This brings us back to the question of why no effective and safe male contraceptive has been developed. Millions of dollars were spent on developing the pill. Why did they not spend equivalent money and effort to develop a male contraceptive?

The answer is that they have been trying – not quite as hard – but it is easier to develop a female contraceptive than a male one. The female produces only one egg a month that has to be sperm-proofed in one way or another. 'You knock off ovulation and you are done for the month,' says Dr Gordon Perkins of the Ford Foundation. 'But if you stop one day's supply of sperm cells, there are tens of millions the next day in addition to the millions previously spawned, which take some seventy days to be ejaculated – and which you did not affect at all.'

Researchers thought they had made a great breakthrough with one combination of drugs. And then they discovered that one of the side effects was uncontrollable vomiting whenever the man had an alcoholic drink.

They are also looking into a contraceptive called gossypol, which was developed by the Chinese who claim that it makes 99.99 per cent of the men who take it infertile. One problem is that it is not known whether this effect is reversible or whether a man who has been on gossypol may end up forever sterile. Another problem is that it also makes users feel very tired. American scientists are looking for ways of counteracting this side effect, possibly with diet supplements.

Tests are also under way for a contraceptive based on injections of a form of testosterone, but this too presents problems. One is that men have to have injections several times a month, which makes it rather impractical. Another is that some of the men who have been testing it have developed high blood pressure and have also put on a significant amount of weight.

There are probably a dozen other approaches in the testing stage, but none of them have yet been found effective enough and safe enough to be marketed.

There is another more important question for women to consider. Is a male contraceptive really all that desirable?

What would you do and how would you feel if after lovemaking your husband said, 'Ooops! I forgot to take my pill this morning. Goddammit, I'm sorry.' My feeling is that it is better for a woman to be safe than for her and her husband to be sorry. There is also the possibility of betrayal with a male contraceptive. What if you do not want a child or another child and he does? A male contraceptive allows him to control the decision.

Every woman should realize that there are possibilities for error, purposeful or not, when contraception is up to the male. And the woman is the victim of the error, not the man. For any number of reasons, then, it makes sense for the woman to take responsibility for contraception.

And until the ideal contraceptive comes along, I recommend the good old diaphragm. It does not mess up your body chemistry and it is effective. I agree that it takes a little more effort than the pill, but you are a big girl now. And if you still grumble 'It's not fair,' let me suggest a compromise. You use the diaphragm one month and he'll use condoms the next. At least with the condom, you know for sure that he is using it.

All this may be academic in another fifty years. Researchers are discovering that men are not as fertile as they used to be. One scientist, Dr Ralph Dougherty of Florida State University, says that the sperm count of American men has decreased by almost a third in the last half century.

In 1929, the median sperm count of American males was 90 million ccs. In 1979, it was 60 million. These are median figures, which means that half the male population had a higher sperm count and half had a lower. But just recently when Dr Dougherty tested 132 college students, he found that 23 per cent of them had sperm counts of only 20 million. A man with this low a count is considered functionally sterile. The suspicion is that this is due to environmental pollution. If the trend is not reversed and the sperm count again decreases by nearly a third in the next fifty years, half the male population may be sterile.

And then the search may be on in earnest for a male pill – a fertility pill.

20

There is a side to male sexuality as darkly terrifying as our worst nightmares. And it is real. Rape is real. Physical abuse is real. Sexual degradation is real.

It is normal and healthy for men to seek the new and different to maintain their sexual excitement, but there is one source of excitement that many men tap that is less than healthy. It is their inner hostility to women, which is strongest in those men we identify as male chauvinists (see pages 41 and 111.

'Hostility, overt or hidden, generates and enhances sexual excitement,' says psychoanalyst Robert Stoller. If you think back to times when you have had sex when you were angry with each other, you will probably remember that there was a special tension in the air. The sex may have been very good, significantly above average. Men get even more keyed up by anger and hostility than women do on the average. There is a reason for this. 'At the biochemical level,' explains Dr Stoller, 'scientists have found a positive relationship between the male hormone and aggressiveness.'

It is no simple equation. Male sex hormones do not equal aggression the way two and three equal five. Some men do not appear to have an aggressive cell in their bodies, but most are significantly more aggressive than females.

Both males and females possess all three of the sex hormones – testosterone, oestrogen, and progesterone – but in different amounts. Boys get more testosterone before birth, and at adolescence this sex hormone increases at least ten times and perhaps as much as twenty-five to thirty-five times, while a girl's testosterone level merely doubles. And she had less to start with. The high testosterone levels achieved during a boy's adolescence remain stable throughout his life cycle.

'This seems unimportant,' anthropologist Lionel Tiger says, 'because the absolute amounts of these hormones are so tiny. And yet hormones are like poisons. A tiny amount can have a gross effect. Hence we see adolescent males flooded at puberty with a natural chemical which apparently stimulates marked aggressive behaviour.'

There have been tremendous arguments over the last two decades about whether aggression is part of the male genetic inheritance or stems from the way boys are brought up. Both factors are probably involved, but the argument does not need to concern us here. What does concern us is that today, in the here and now, men are demonstrably more aggressive than women. Women should know about the forms this aggression takes when it is directed towards the female.

Rape, for instance, is not a sexual act. Rape is motivated by rage, not uncontrollable sexual desire. Rapists want power over women. They want to dominate and control them, to degrade them.

In half the cases of rape, the rapist is not a stranger lurking in a dark alley, but someone the victim knows. And the rape takes place in her own home after she has let him in. It may be the man in the next apartment or the man who picks up the dry cleaning or her divorce lawyer or a respected member of the community who is collecting for a local charity.

The other 50 per cent of rapes take place almost anywhere. In a ditch by the side of the road where a woman was jogging in the early morning, in a deserted corner of the supermarket parking lot, in a lover's lane (when her date is often forced to watch), on her way home from the library in the evening.

We have all read newspaper reports of violent rapes by strangers, but the other rapes by friends or neighbours or husbands – some husbands do rape their wives – are just as common, just as violent, and even more traumatic than the more publicized episodes. More traumatic because the woman usually does not report it,* does not talk about it to anyone, and does not seek professional help in dealing with her feelings. Her pent-up fear, anger, and shame can destroy her emotional health as surely as any untreated cancer can destroy her body.

Corinne, a recent divorcee, was raped by her best friend's husband. Meg had gone home to Wisconsin to take care of her mother, who was recuperating from surgery. Meg's husband called Corinne one evening and suggested they have dinner together. 'I'm tired of my own cooking,' Al said.

They went to a neighbourhood restaurant, had a couple of drinks and a good meal. Afterwards Al walked Corinne home.

'I'm not going to ask you in for a nightcap,' she said. 'It's been a long day and I'm really tired. I hope you don't mind.'

'No problem,' he said. 'I'll just come in while you turn on the lights. I don't like the idea of your going into a dark house alone.' He came in. He locked the door behind him. He backed Corinne up against a wall, then forced her head down. She was appalled to find that his trousers were unzipped.

'Suck me,' he ordered. She shook her head. He grabbed her hair and banged her head against the wall. She did as

* This is why it is difficult to know how many rapes take place. A conservative estimate is that one occurs every two minutes. The FBI reports that rape seems to be increasing by 10 to 15 per cent every year. In 1979, there was a 13.2 per cent increase of reported rapes over 1978.

she was told. Afterwards he raped her. 'You'll keep your mouth shut if you know what's good for you,' he said as he left.

Corinne was too bruised and shaken to go to work the next day, too dazed and humiliated to tell anyone what had happened. Her friendship with Meg came to an end. It was too painful for Corinne to see her and she never wanted to see Al again. She felt guilty, as if it had been her fault in some way. Corinne never reported the rape.

Four years later, Corinne is still suffering emotionally. She has not been able to establish a relationship with a man. Every time a man shows signs of sexual interest in her, she stops seeing him.

As a psychologist, I know that rape is the penultimate violation – the ultimate violation being murder. But men do not seem to understand this. Men who would never dream of raping a woman – oh, they undoubtedly fantasize about it, just as women fantasize about being raped, but they would never do it – still feel that if a woman is raped, she must have done something to deserve it.

A group of male college students were given two stories to read. One was about a male who committed a spur-of-the-moment rape, the other about a man who had carefully planned the rape he committed. The students were asked how long a prison sentence each man should serve.

The young men decided to give the man who had not planned his rape a nine-year sentence. The man who had planned the rape would be given three years. This surprised the testers so much that they went back to the group and asked how they had arrived at these sentences.

It was simple, the students said. If the rapist had planned the assault, the woman must have done something to deserve it. Therefore that rapist should not be given as long a sentence as the man who committed the spur-of-the-moment rape.

This is only one study, but it suggests that men may make poor judges and jury members when a rape case is up for trial – especially since most rapes are planned. No matter what the students thought, no woman who has ever been raped should think for one moment that she did anything to deserve it. No one deserves to be raped. But thousands and thousands of women are. And they range from little girls* to women in their nineties.

Pornography is another form of violence against women. Some women say that they are turned on by pornography. And I am sure they are. But in most cases, when it comes to pornography, men and women are talking about two different things. Women's porn is romantic. They are swept off their feet and forced to have sex. And the men who force them are virile and strong – but tender. They are a combination of knights in armour, bandits, and father figures. Remember Clark Cable as Rhett Butler in *Gone with the Wind*? That is a woman's porn hero. But when men are absorbed in pornographic fantasies, there is nothing romantic or fatherly about their fantasy behaviour. They are purely and simply sexually excited and all-powerful.

This is what a lot of men use pornography for. Excitement. An interest in soft porn, the kind that includes a detailed study of the pictures in *Penthouse* and the centrefold in *Playboy* and an occasional X-rated picture, does not mean that a man finds his sex life boring. It just means that he finds these magazines and films titillating. His interest has very little to do with the woman in his life.

Women find this hard to understand. Nearly half the women queried in one survey reported that they felt hurt

---

* Yes, little girls. There is a frightening increase in child sexual abuse. Some experts feel that the increase may be part of a backlash against the women's movement by men who see their power threatened. 'Men who fear that women are becoming their equals are now turning their sexual powers onto the kids,' says psychoanalyst Herbert Freudenberger, 'whether it is watching a pornographic movie involving children or abusing the children themselves.'

that the men in their lives enjoyed pornography. Hurt and jealous and furious. They felt that their husbands did not consider them physically attractive. They were angry that they should take pleasure in films and pictures that reduced women to sex objects.

Men, in turn, find these female reactions hard to understand. They do not see the women in the photographs or films as real flesh-and-blood women. They are fantasy women to the men who stare at them and dream of all the things they would like to do to them, things they would never suggest to their own wives.

This kind of indulgence in soft porn is essentially harmless. Some women who share their husbands' interest, look at the pictures and films with them, and talk about them together say that it makes for a better sex life. An interesting sidelight is that both men and women are turned on by pictures of women, but pictures of nude males seldom excite women. A survey of female college students found that they were not at all interested in centrefold pictures of male nudes. Most of the young women agreed with the student who said 'I'd rather see and feel my partner's body than look at a photograph that has been published in a nationwide magazine.'

Hard porn is something else. When a man is excited by films and photographs showing men whipping and beating women, chaining them and degrading them, this is a danger signal for the woman or women in his life. Men who are deeply interested in hard porn are usually quite insecure sexually and certainly not particularly loving or tender towards women. Studies have shown that men become more aggressive and abusive to women after they have been looking at hard porn films with scenes of men hurting women.* Hard porn excites men, but not into having sex as

* Soft-core films, which emphasize eroticism rather than violence, have no such effect. In fact, studies show that the soft-porn erotic films seem to reduce male aggression.

much as into having violent sex – or simply into violence alone.

Another kind of violence against women is not quite as closely linked to the sexual act. These are the cases of men who beat their wives when their personal worlds get to be too much for them. They are usually average types of men. The wife-batterer may work for a building contractor or own the firm. He lives next door or upstairs or across the street. Maybe he lives with you. And if he does, you know just how different his public behaviour is from his private. When things don't go his way, he beats you.

The battering starts when a man has accumulated more stress than he can handle. He gets rid of it at home, the place where he is most comfortable. There is a great deal of rage involved, not directed particularly at his wife, but at life in general. The only place where he feels he is in control is at home. And he demonstrates his power by beating up his wife.

These men equate manhood with violence and dominance. When they were younger, they usually looked up to older boys or men who were physically violent. More than half the wife-abusers are men who saw their fathers beat their mothers.

Otto told a therapy group how he had become a wife-beater. His father used to knock his mother around. Once he broke her arm. Another time he hit her so hard that she had to go to the hospital and have twelve stitches in her forehead. His father also beat him and his sister.

When Otto was a sturdy sixteen, he knocked his father unconscious one night when his father had started to slap his mother around. When he came to, Otto told him that he was never to touch any of them again. If he did, Otto would call the police.

But when Otto got married, he knocked his wife around just the way his father had knocked his mother around.

Once he hit her because supper was not on the table when he got home from work. Another time he punched her until she fell on the floor unconscious because his favourite shirt had not been washed. One morning he woke up to find that she had left and taken their son with her.

She eventually agreed to come back if he promised to get professional counselling. She insisted that their son must have therapy, too. 'He told me that when he got big enough,' she said, 'he was going to kill his father. And he is only seven years old! I can't let him grow up that way. He has to learn that beating people is no way to make himself feel important or make up for things that go wrong.'

How can a woman tell what a man will be like? Few women knowingly marry a man who is the captive of the dark side of his sexual nature, a man who is prone to sexual and physical violence. There are usually telltale signs that serve as a kind of early warning of danger ahead, but women tend to disregard them. Sometimes they just don't recognize them for what they are; other times they tell themselves that once they are married, they will be able to change his attitudes and actions. This is a mistake. Whatever the attitudes or actions are, they usually become intensified after marriage, not weakened.

Men who are supermacho and put women down, men who are vehement almost to the point of violence in their disapproval of the women's movement, men who flare up in sudden anger, who get into fights when drunk, who seem to be obsessed with hardcore pornography are all men who may get their kicks and their release from the dark side of sex.

There are other clues, less obvious ones. But a woman should be able to pick them up. After all, women are extremely perceptive about people. It would be impossible to list every clue, but a woman may pick up signals of future danger if she lists the things about the man she is dating that bother her. The way he behaves to his mother, perhaps. Or his friends. Or the way he drives. All these say something about the man. Take lateness, for instance.

If you are dating a man who is consistently and persistently late, this can tell you something about him, something you may not like to admit to yourself. Habitual lateness always has a reason. It may be his way of rebelling. He may feel so constrained by the demands of his job, his finances, by what he sees as the rigidity of his family or yours or the community that he asserts himself by being late. It is a safe little rebellion, but childish.

It may also be pure arrogance. It does not bother him to keep you waiting. He knows that you will wait. It is his way of showing you that he is more important than you are, that his time is more valuable than yours.

Or, and this is even more worrying, it may be his way of venting otherwise hidden hostility. He may enjoy making you wait for him. He may get a kick out of knowing that you stood on a cold windy corner for half an hour waiting for him.

One does not have to be a psychologist or a mind reader to know which of these three describes a particular man. Once you understand the underlying reasons for habitual lateness, it is easy enough to sense why your man is always late. And if it is because of the second or third reason, I would suggest that you examine your relationship carefully. Are there any other signs of arrogance or hostility? Is this something you really want? Is he someone you really want?

PART FIVE
Men and Love and Marriage

21

'If I hadn't gone on that blind date, I never would have met my husband. I never would have got married,' a woman will say. But she is wrong. This is nothing but a romantic notion. She almost certainly would have married, married someone very like the man she did marry.

Researchers in many fields have begun to assemble chunks of evidence about who attracts whom. Right now it is like a giant jigsaw puzzle with a lot of missing pieces, but enough pieces have been fitted together for it to be possible to say 'They were meant for each other' with a fair degree of accuracy. They – or someone very much like them – *were* meant for each other. This does not necessarily mean that the couple will live happily ever after. People grow and develop in unpredictable ways. Today's perfect match may be next decade's tragic mismatch.

When I studied the ancient myths in school, one of them impressed me so much that I have never forgotten it. Long ago male and female were united in one person – or so the myth ran. But one day the gods were in a mischievous mood and they separated the two. Ever since, men and women have wandered the earth seeking their lost half, longing to be whole again.

It is not necessary to wander the world to find your other half. More than 50 per cent of marriages are between people who lived within a few miles of each other. What is important is to get out and meet people. If you spend your time in front of the television set, the only man you are going to meet will be the TV repair man.

Women who want to meet and attract men should put

themselves in situations that involve activity. That is where the men are. And I do not mean singles bars.

Join a camera club or a bird-watching group. Take a course in film-making or how to do your own electric wiring. Buy a dog and walk him frequently. Enroll the dog and yourself in an obedience class. Sign up as a volunteer on an archaeological dig for your summer vacation. Don't just sit there. Do something with people.

Suppose you do and you still don't meet the man of your dreams in your chosen activity. At least you will have learned how to do something that you have always wanted to do or gone somewhere you have always wanted to go. You will be a more interesting person for it. Chances are, though, that you will meet someone. Not *the* one perhaps, but someone who may turn into a friend.

Alicia and Bert met when they took a course on collecting postage stamps as an investment. Now they meet once a week during their lunch hour and browse through the new offerings at the stamp dealers in lower Manhattan or talk stamps over lunch. Every once in a while they go to stamp auctions together. There is no hint of romance here, but they have become friends. Friendships like this are invaluable. In the first place, a good friend is a treasure; in the second, men have men friends. Most women meet the man they marry on a blind date or through a friend.

Not long ago, Bert introduced Alicia to Calvin. 'I want you to meet her,' he told Calvin. 'She's the one I've been talking about, the one who spotted the double trimmed twopenny from Trinidad.' Now Calvin and Alicia are meeting during their lunch hours, but they are not discussing stamps. They are making plans for their wedding.

I get mailbags full of letters from women wanting to know how to attract men. I tell them that women attract men no matter what. And that men are even more concerned about attracting women.*

Scientists still know less about what attracts men than they do about what attracts mosquitoes. We do know, however, that all men want one thing. No, not sex. Beauty. They want to date and marry beautiful women. Fortunately every man has his own idea of beauty. Some like redheads, others prefer blondes. Most men, in fact, prefer blondes. Women often ask me if I think it would help if they became blonde. 'Do blondes really have more fun?' they want to know. What they mean is 'Do blondes really attract more men?'

The answer is yes. Men think of blondes as fun dates. They flirt and kid around with them more. The woman who is treated warmly and flirtatiously reacts warmly and flirtatiously. Life gets lighter and brighter with her hair.† I certainly intend to remain blonde forever.

I also point out to these women that while men prefer blondes, they tend to marry brunettes. A far better way to attract a man than changing one's hair colour is to pick a field, any field, and become an expert on it. Emeralds, poker, taxidermy, Chinese porcelain, belly dancing, car repair, nineteenth-century engravings, word processing, spiders, football statistics, whatever. Your sense of confidence will radiate out to all the other aspects of your life – and men will be attracted to you. Men are almost as

---

*A publisher who puts out books with titles like *How to Pick Up Girls* makes a couple of million dollars a year on his mail-order sales. When he tried to market a similar line of books aimed at women, he lost money. Women were not interested.

†One psychiatrist, Dr Roderic Gorney, believes he knows why men prefer blondes. 'A blonde,' he says, 'is likely to find that she is expected not so much to *have* more fun as to *be* more fun. A man will want her to have the innocent sweetness of childhood combined with a mature sexuality of which no child is capable.' He theorizes that the preference for blondes stems from prehistoric times when men were fearful of the dark and thought the light was good. Thus blonde was good.

attracted by self-confidence as they are by beauty.

Blonde, brunette, or redhead, what men really like is long hair. Remember those old Hollywood movies with the plain girl with the eyeglasses who wore her hair pulled back in a knot? They still show them on TV late at night. One day she plucks the glasses off her nose and lets her hair fall loose. Lo and behold – a knockout beauty. Cary Grant or Clark Gable doesn't have a chance. The lady gets her man.

Almost all men have fantasies about women with beautiful long hair that is pinned up in a knot or twisted around her head in a severe braid. They dream about unbraiding it or taking the hairpins out and letting the gorgeous stuff tumble down around her shoulders. The woman who makes this fantasy come true for a man almost automatically becomes the woman of his dreams.

You can tell a tremendous amount about a man by the type of female figure that he considers beautiful. We have learned through psychological testing that men who like women with large breasts and small behinds are well organized. They are extroverts. They tend to date a lot before they settle on one woman. They usually know exactly what they want to do in life.

Men who are attracted to women with medium breasts and small behinds are really nice people. They have all the good qualities. They are helpful, generous, unselfish. They work hard, although success does not mean all that much to them. On the negative side, they are usually rigidly conformist and rather puritanical.

Men who get excited by plump women with big breasts, generous thighs, and dimpled bottoms tend to be hail-fellow-well-met types. They are not particularly well organized. And they are not always great at hanging on to a job. They like to have a good time, usually spending more than they can afford. But there are exceptions. When I attend business conventions and meet successful executives and their wives, there are always a good number of well-endowed women among them. Their husbands may have a taste for voluptuous figures, but it has not stood in the way of success.

Men find so many types of women attractive that the question arises: is there any common denominator among all these different types that spells beauty? There may be, but scientists think that if it exists it is so intangible that it is just about impossible to define. One man who tried to formulate a definition, Dr Arthur Feiner, believes that 'attractiveness is the capacity to evoke fantasy. Regardless of her anatomy, her shape, hair colour, the smell and texture of her skin, her movements, her eyes or whatever, the important thing is the erotic love fantasy evoked in the male.' On the other hand, he admits that 'a girl's looks may be more important to the man's sense of prestige among men than as a source of sexual pleasure.'

A man in his mid-forties, a professor, agreed wholeheartedly with this last statement. 'I really enjoy talking to a mature intelligent woman,' he said, 'and I enjoy sex with her much more than with a young girl. But I want other men to envy me. If I'm seen around with a woman in her forties, I feel slightly ashamed. But if my colleagues see me with a beautiful young girl, I feel very good about myself. I think I must have something if a young chick like that goes out with me.'

Most men, no matter what their age, equate beauty with youth. It is easier for a man to recognize beauty in a young woman than a middle-aged or older woman. To them, beauty means smooth young skin and glistening hair. Dating services have found that men in their sixties refuse to date a woman over fifty and prefer women under forty.

Men weave a whole fantasy about the beautiful woman. They believe that beautiful women enjoy sex more and have it more often. They think that they are more intelligent and liberated than plain women. But when you ask a man what it is he looks for in a woman, he rarely comes right out and says good looks. A journalist who wrote about his dream woman said that she should be passionate, feminine, a good friend and comrade, and honest. He made no mention of beauty. A poll of more than a thousand young men revealed that personality was more important to them than beauty. Another group of men reported that the most appealing quality in a woman was her ability to show affection. A survey conducted by an advertising agency found that eight out of ten men want a woman who first of all will be a good mother. Seven out of ten said that their ideal woman is intelligent, family-orientated, and self-confident. Beauty was way down on their list of desirable qualities.

No matter what men say for the record, good looks are what they want most in a woman. You have to remember that there is quite often a difference between what people say and what they really think. Men may not think it sounds correct or intelligent or sophisticated to say that beauty is what appeals to them most, so they tell the interviewer that affection or a good personality or an independent spirit is what they are seeking.

But when the dating desires of more than six thousand men and women who had used a computerized dating service were analysed, it was found that men wanted to date women who were first of all attractive, then self-confident, then good talkers.

Psychological studies that are based on observation of behaviour and choice and not just on what people say also show that beauty is the prime factor. In one study, psychologists asked a panel to grade the looks of 588 young men and women. Then they set up blind dates for the group, matching them as evenly as possible in attractiveness. The good-looking men, who had been matched with the good-looking women, reported that on the whole they had had a great time. The good-looking women had also had a good time, but they were not quite as enthusiastic. Looks alone were not enough for them. They wanted more – personality, humour, intelligence. The less attractive couples rated their blind dates as less successful. It seems that even an unprepossessing man does not want to date an unattractive woman. However, even a relatively unattractive woman becomes beautiful in the eyes of a man as he comes to know her and ultimately to fall in love with her.

And right here I am going to digress a little and talk about blind dates. I have two valuable pieces of advice for women about blind dates.

If you like the looks of your date and find him good company and would like to see him again, I would advise against going to the movies on your first date unless you go to a horror or suspense movie. Avoid under any and all circumstances films with a ravishingly beautiful star. Men who were asked to rate how attractive an average-looking woman was after they had been watching *Charlie's Angels* on television rated her as being less attractive than she was and rated her much lower than a group of men who had not been watching the programme.

The reason a suspense or horror movie is a desirable choice is that it keeps the adrenalin flow high, and this predisposes a man to transfer some of the excitement to his date. And excitement, no matter what the source, tends to make the heart grow fonder.

The second bit of advice concerns something most men do after a blind date that has caused women more soul searching than almost anything else. After the date, he usually says, 'It was a great evening. I'll be in touch. I'll give you a call.' And he never does.

Why?

It is simply his crazy way of being polite. He does not want to hurt your feelings. It would be fine if he just said 'Well, it's late. Gotta go. It was a great evening. I enjoyed it.' But they don't know when to stop and most of them add that tagline, 'I'll give you a call.' And then you sit and wait for the call. Some women won't even go to the corner to get the newspaper because he might call when they were out. What you have to do is ignore his promise to call. Don't hang around night after night waiting by the telephone.

If you want to see him again, call him. Suggest something unthreatening and not too intimate. If he refuses or says he can't make it for one reason or another, forget about him. There will be other blind dates.

And now back to beauty. The subjects of one psychological study were completely unaware of their participation. A Florida psychologist sent teams of psychology students to parties, cocktail lounges, dance floors, the theatre, restaurants – all the places where men and women go on dates – with instructions to rate the couples they observed on their looks.

What did they find? Just what their professor had expected they would find. Eighty-five per cent of the couples were just about evenly matched in looks. Attractive people dated each other. Moderately attractive men dated moderately attractive women. Unattractive men dated unattractive women.

The male emphasis on good looks increasingly includes their own. Men who once scoffed at women who had face lifts are now lining up in the plastic surgeons' surgeries themselves. Dr Dicran Goulian, Jr, of New York Hospital–Cornell Medical Center says the number of his male patients seeking cosmetic surgery has doubled in the last five years.*

---

*Incidentally, men's facelifts present some special problems. They are not advised for many bald men, for instance, because surgery leaves scars on the scalp. It may also pull some of the beard area of the face around behind the ear, which would rule out the procedure for a man with a heavy beard. A face lift may narrow or eliminate a man's sideburns, in which case he might want to think twice before undergoing surgery. The most common form of cosmetic surgery men have is an eyelift.

This recent and intense interest in their looks, says Lionel Tiger, the anthropologist, 'has to do with courtship behaviour. Divorce puts a lot more men on the street, as it were. More men are dating at an older age when they have more money to spend on themselves. One has to look at things like cosmetics and grooming as part of the mating system. As a result of the increase in divorce rates, men are involved in the courtship phase of life more frequently and for extended periods of time.'

All this adds up to big business. Annual sales of men's colognes, lotions, and cosmetics are close to the eight-billion-dollar mark. As I said before, men want to attract women even more than women want to attract them. And they are going all-out to attract the best-looking women.

'Then why is it so many beautiful women are married to men who could never be described as handsome?' an advertising executive asked me.

'Women want more than a pretty face,' I said. 'It is all well and good to date a great-looking guy, but when it comes to marriage, women prize such qualities as tenderness, intelligence, humour, sincerity, responsibility, and ambition more than looks. Of course, if he's good-looking too, that doesn't hurt.'

It is not only the male eye that is attracted by women. His other senses are involved, particularly the sense of smell. I mentioned earlier that men find natural female body odours sexually exciting. Scientists are finding that body odours form a chemical communication network between the sexes.

Some female odours can be detected only by men and some male odours only by women. There are some that neither males nor females are aware of until they have reached puberty. These are pheromones, chemical scent signals. Earlier in this chapter, I said that women attract men no matter what. And it is true. A man may swear that he would never go out with a woman who is taller than he is, but one day he stands beside a six-foot Amazon in the elevator and suddenly finds himself searching for a way to approach her. Her sex pheromones are at work.

In the insect world, females exude pheromones that draw males from miles around to mate with them. But people are not insects. Pheromones are not instant sexual turn-ons for human beings – and thank goodness for that. What they seem to do is create an empathy between a man and a woman or in some way make one aware of the other and interested in pursuing the contact or acquaintance.

The first recorded instance of the power of pheromones seems to be in the fifteenth century when a French nobleman who had been hunting picked up the first rag that came to hand to mop his aristocratic brow when he and his mount returned to the château stables. The rag as it turned out was the discarded chemise of the daughter of the house. The nobleman was instantly seized with a passion for her.

I can't vouch for the authenticity of the incident. It may have become exaggerated over the centuries. But British researchers recently isolated a chemical component of male sweat that seems to appeal to women in somewhat the way that discarded chemise appealed to the nobleman. When purified, this essence of sweat smells much like sandalwood. Right now they are working on the possibility of marketing it as an after-shave lotion. That chemical component they isolated seems to be a sex pheromone that attracts females.

A French scientist has discovered that women also react to exaltolide, a substance found in urine – twice as much in men's urine as in women's. Women are most aware of the odour during the ovulatory period of their monthly cycle. Men have no reaction to it whatsoever. It is interesting that exaltolide is used in the manufacture of many perfumes. This may be why women associate perfume so strongly with romance.

The most luring female fragrances seem to be those given off by hair, particularly pubic and underarm hair. I do not for a moment suggest that a woman sacrifices her daily bath in the hope of attracting a man, but I do think women should be aware that highly perfumed soaps and deodorants will kill or mask those sex pheromones that send come-hither signals to the male.

Women tend to feel that many body fragrances are distasteful and may put men off. Not at all. When forty thousand men were asked what they did and did not like about women, it was discovered that men did not like hairy legs, that they did not mind menstrual odour, and that they really liked vaginal odour. In view of this, women might be wise to stop using scented douches and dabbing perfume between their legs. Let the pheromones roam.

22

What kind of man will it be whom you attract and who attracts you? In many ways, the two of you may be quite alike. You will probably share the same values and attitudes. Statistics show that most couples come from roughly similar backgrounds. The very rich tend to marry the very rich. The middle and lower income groups also tend to marry within social and economic groups – although women tend to marry up, which accounts for the fact that there are more bachelors among the lower-income men and more single women among the very rich.

The man who attracts you will also be quite different. People seldom marry carbon copies of themselves, but seek a mate who will complement them and supply the qualities they lack. The insecure marry the confident, the quick-tempered marry the meek, and so on.

There is such a glorious diversity of men that it is imposs-ible to describe more than a few broad categories here – the tall and the short, the young and the old. And the divorced, because there are so many of them.

Tall men have a lot going for them. There is something about height that carries a sense of authority and com-petence and this attracts women.* A tall man can usually pick and choose among the ladies. He may choose you. And he may be wonderful. But again he may not. It is possible that you will be disappointed as you get to know him better.

---

* Frogs are much the same. A female frog will gravitate towards the biggest male in her puddle when she looks for a mate.

He may not be as capable or masterful or intelligent as you had thought.

If this turns out to be the case, you were probably misled by the halo effect. The halo effect is based on first impressions. It can be negative or positive. And it is surprisingly strong.

Height is positive. It is considered desirable in a man. A tall man who carries himself well and is pleasant makes an excellent first impression. He has everything going for him. People tend to believe that he will be good at whatever he turns his hand to.

The halo effect affects not only the observer, it affects the man himself. The tall man who is truly competent and intelligent and authoritative is extremely sure of himself, because he keeps getting positive feedback, both from his accomplishments and from the attitude of the people around him. Tall men who do not live up to their halo effect are usually full of self-doubts and anxieties, because people consistently expect too much of them.

If the tall man is a beneficiary of the halo effect, the short man is usually its victim. He may have a keen intelligence, great warmth, a superb sense of humour. He may be very attractive. But if he is five-foot-three or under, people will tend to mention his good qualities and then add 'but he's so short'. And with that phrase they seem to dismiss all his assets.

This makes a short man very frustrated. He tends to be a little more aggressive as a way of both proving himself and making up for his lack of stature. Some women have an unreasonable prejudice against going out with a man shorter than they are, let alone marrying him. I tell them that this is ridiculous. Short men make marvellous husbands and providers. They are used to trying harder. And besides, wouldn't it be nice to have someone who would always look up to you?

Falling in love with a younger man seems to be almost fashionable these days. At least in the gossip columns. We read of couple after couple where the woman is fifteen or twenty years older than the man. It seems to be most prevalent among actresses. And psychiatrist Roger Gould says there is a reason for this. 'What actresses fear most is loneliness and the loss of male companionship as they grow older,' Dr Gould says. 'It destroys their ego, their self-image. And so they turn to younger men. If they are honest with themselves, however, they know that they are offering a man material comforts in return for his companionship and sexual favours.'

One school of thought holds that women should marry younger men. The argument runs that men are at their peak of sexual vigour in their late teens and early twenties, whereas women peak in their late thirties and early forties. This presupposes that sex is enough to base a marriage on.

The younger man may have something to gain in marrying an older woman, but the woman has very little – and she has it only temporarily in most cases. As she grows older, she finds less excitement and certainly less comfort and companionship in the relationship. And when she is in her sixties and he is in his forties, she may find herself very lonely.

One woman who lived with and supported a younger man for several years told me 'What finally brought me to my senses was the way he looked at me one day when I mentioned that I was ten years old when World War Two ended. But that was only the tip of the iceberg. He used drugs, I drank martinis. My idea of a great night out is to go to the theatre, his was to go roller-skating. I decided I did not want to share the rest of my life or even another month of it with a man who shared so few memories and values with me. No matter how good he was in bed.'

Usually the young man in one of these pairings will

belong to one of two groups. Either he has some very pronounced emotional problems or he is simply using the older woman as a means of support. Neither type is a good bet for the long run. There are exceptions, of course. A young man may fall in love with an older woman because of her sophistication and competence in dealing with the world.

The older man/younger woman combination sometimes works better. Older men have been marrying young women since the beginning of time. The older man has a lot to offer – more money, more status, more experience, and a more comfortable, sheltered life. He is more sexually experienced. As forty-five-year-old Humphrey Bogart pointed out just before he married twenty-year-old Lauren Bacall, 'The mature man has seen more of the world, read more, done more. He knows how to court a woman. He has learned the hundred little courtesies that make her happy she is a woman.'

There is another and very important consideration, one that underlines the difference between the young man/older woman relationship and the young woman/older man relationship. The older man can still give his wife children. But an older woman may not be able to give her husband a child.

What kind of man wants to marry a woman twenty or more years his junior? Usually a man who places a premium on youth and beauty. He may want to be undisputed lord and master and it is easier to assert authority over a younger woman. He may want a doll – a pretty young thing to fondle and indulge and show off. He may hope that a young wife will keep him young and help him forget his fear of old age.

These marriages have their own built-in stresses. The stress common to all of them is the knowledge that the wife can look forward to early widowhood. Her marriage will not last as long as those of her contemporaries who married men closer to their own age.

His friends may bore her. He may insist that she see less of her younger friends because they annoy him. Old movies that she thinks are quaint may arouse his memories of early romances. He may try to prove himself physically in sports or jogging to show that he is the equal of men her age. He may be jealous without justification.

No matter. Studies show that most of these marriages are stable and happy.

Divorce is perhaps even more traumatic for a man than a woman in certain respects. At first, all the divorced man really wants is someone to comfort him and say 'There, there, it's going to be all right.' But that is only temporary. He starts scanning the horizon for excitement and usually starts dating almost indiscriminately just so he won't have to go home to an empty apartment – and to convince himself that women still find him attractive. He may be a rather dreary date. Most divorced men tend to feel sorry for themselves, talk a lot about their ex-wives, worry about money – and have twice the rate of heart disease and seven times the rate of cirrhosis of the liver as married men.

At the end of the first year alone, one study showed, almost 60 per cent of the men thought they should have worked harder to make their marriage succeed. By the end of the second year, the number had dwindled to 20 per cent. During those years, 20 per cent of the divorced men reported that they had more sexual problems than they had before. And more than two-thirds said that their work had suffered. So unless you are the reason for the divorce, it might be wise not to make any permanent commitment to a divorced man until he has had at least two years of freedom to regain his emotional equilibrium.

Divorced men want to remarry. And they have a five-out-of-six chance of succeeding. They certainly work hard enough at it.

As one man-about-New-York told a woman acquaintance, 'I don't regret my divorce, but I also find that I don't much enjoy my freedom. It may sound ridiculous, but it's a real strain to take out different women all the time.' Nevertheless, he doggedly pursued his dating campaign. Any amount of strain was worth it if it resulted in his finding a wife. Another thing about the divorced man, you can be sure that he is going to try to make it work the second time around. And statistics show that 54 per cent of them succeed.

No matter what type of man it is who attracts you and is attracted by you, the key to whether the attraction will last is love. Love is the 'crazy glue' that holds a couple together and strengthens the relationship year after year. But as I will explain in the next chapter, men and women often experience love quite differently.

23

Men are almost heartbreakingly susceptible to love. Much more so than women. A man seldom contracts a mild case. He falls head over heels into raging romance. The way men and women feel and act and think about love is often completely different. To understand these differences, it is important to understand a little about love, which is still pretty much a mystery.

There is love and there is love. Romantic love and conjugal love. Being in love and loving. I think of them as first-stage love and second-stage love. One is fleeting and a bit of a fraud, the other can be forever.

First-stage or romantic love is a relative newcomer. There is a reason why women tend to think of the man of their dreams as a knight in armour. Romantic love was the creation of the Middle Ages when troubadours sang of its agonies and ecstasies and brave knights dedicated their swords and their hearts to beautiful women. It was almost exclusively a male indulgence. 'Love is a folly of the mind, an unquenchable fire, a hunger without surfeit,' wrote thirteenth-century Richard de Fournival, 'a sweet delight, a pleasing madness, a labour without repose and a repose without labour.'

In this century, psychologist Dorothy Tennov, author of a book about first-stage love, coined her own word for this 'sweet folly'. She called it *limerence*, and describes it somewhat less lyrically as an obsessive passion that makes life a kind of hell relieved by moments of bliss. Limerence, she warns, can lead to marriages so unwise that divorce is inevitable.

Another psychologist insists that romantic love, like smallpox, is practically extinct. 'The notions of agony and ecstasy traditionally associated with this kind of love have become meaningless — in fact, quaint,' claims G. Marian Kinget of Michigan State University. The death of romantic love, she believes, is a healthy development that may mean marriages will no longer be founded on passionate illusions and end in the inevitable divorces forecast by Dorothy Tennov.

Studies indicate, however, that psychologist Kinget may be indulging in wishful thinking. There are signs that romantic love may be even more widespread today than in generations past and that men still preserve their sweetly passionate illusions.

In 1959 when male students were asked if they would marry someone whom they did not love, if she were agreeable to them in all other respects, 60 per cent said they would not consider it. When a similar group of students was asked the same question twenty years later, 86 per cent of the men gave a thumbs-down answer — almost a 50 per cent increase. In another study at the University of Minnesota, half of the students who were queried said that if the romantic love disappeared from marriage, they would want a divorce.

But what is this 'folly of the mind', romantic love? Is it really an intermittent hell as well as a pleasing madness?

Researchers into the mysteries of love agree that there is a distinct physical syndrome of first-stage love. It includes palpitations of the heart, a flushing of the face, fast breathing, and sometimes a slight tremor of the hands or fingers. It is interesting to note that a person can get the same cluster of sensations after an injection of adrenalin.

There are those who claim that love and adrenalin have more than a little in common. One scientist, Dr Michael Liebowitz of the New York State Psychiatric Institute, not only thinks that love may be a chemically induced state, but that one specific chemical is responsible. This chemical cupid is phenylethylamine, which belongs to the amphetamine family. Among other qualities, amphetamines have the ability to release adrenalin into the body. 'Love brings on a giddy response comparable to an amphetamine high,' Dr Liebowitz says, 'and the crash that follows breakup is much like withdrawal.'

He has found another connection between love and phenylethylamine. In observing patients who tended to fall in and out of love rather more often than the average person, Dr Liebowitz discovered that whenever a love affair went on the rocks, these people went on chocolate binges. Chocolate contains phenylethylamine and it seems to help the broken-hearted cope with withdrawal symptoms in much the way that methadone helps wean the addict from heroin.

Another researcher maintains that love is a function of the brain. Dr John Money of Johns Hopkins has found that people who have had certain kinds of brain surgery are not able to experience romantic love, although they can experience other emotions. He believes that we will solve the mysteries of love only when we are able to pinpoint and explore what he calls the 'love pathways' of the brain.

Wherever it comes from – brain or heart or hormones – a man usually succumbs to first-stage love long before his love object does. It has been established that men fall in love faster than women. When researchers took the 'romance measurements' of 250 young men and 429 young women, all of whom were in love or recovering from being in love, they found that more than a quarter of the men had fallen seriously in love before their fourth date, but only 15 per cent of the women had. In fact, half the women reported that even after they had had twenty dates with the man they eventually decided they loved, they did not yet feel they were in love. They needed still more time.

Analysing the reasons for this striking difference in falling-in-love time, the researchers decided that men are less discriminating than women. As we know, men are attracted first and most by good looks. A man does not have to know a woman for any length of time to know whether or not her looks appeal to him. The average man makes up his mind in seven short seconds whether or not he wants to know a woman better. And he may fall into the throes of first-stage love almost immediately.

Women seldom do. Women think of love in terms of marriage and their future more than men do. They are more realistic in their appraisal of the relationship. The biggest difference between men and women when it comes to choosing a spouse is, according to a study done at Purdue University, that women are more concerned with how much money a man makes.* This is not greediness or crass materialism. Until very recently marriage was a woman's whole life. It was fine for a man to be caught up in the romantic frenzy of first-stage love, because whether or not he married a particular woman, his life would still revolve largely around his work. This has rarely been true of women. Even today the woman who works outside the home takes almost as much responsibility for the smooth running of the household and the well-being of her husband and children as does the woman who stays at home.

* This may be changing. It is too early to tell, but there are indications that men are now looking at their future wives with an eye to their earning potential. Joseph Sneed, dean of the Duke University Law School, points out that 'once employers make the assumption that most families have two breadwinners, it is very likely the salary level for men will be adjusted downward. This will cause men to look for prospective wives in terms of earning power' as well as beauty and home-making abilities. The dean sees danger in this, especially if the woman is more talented or competent in her field than the husband in his. Such a woman, he suggests, 'might be well advised, if all other things were compatible, to find a husband who would be qualified and prepared to fulfill the function of home-maker'.

When it comes to love and marriage, a woman has to make a decision that not only affects the rest of her life, but the lives of her yet-to-be-born children.

Women may also be slower to fall in love because they are more in touch with their feelings. They can distinguish between infatuation and love and rarely let themselves be carried away by mere infatuation. I do not suggest for an instant that women do not feel the delightful tremors and desires of the initial stages of sexual attraction. We do. Oh, we certainly do. But most women allow their heads to control their hearts – at least in the early days.

But once a woman has decided that this is the man for her, that she respects him, that he has the qualities she wants in the father of her children (if she decides to have children), and that she wants to share the rest of her life with him, she is more intensely emotional and romantic than any man ever was. Love is a highly euphoric state for a woman. She feels lighter. Colours are brighter. The world sparkles and sings. It is as if there were champagne in her veins instead of blood. She bubbles with happiness. She has great difficulty in concentrating on anything except the man she loves and her dreams of their love together. A woman is slow in succumbing to first-stage love, but when she does, she makes up for her initial hesitancy.

First-stage love is too intense to last. Neither men nor women can maintain this high-intensity passion forever, although they swear they will. It peters out anywhere from six months to two years after the honeymoon. Some relationships do not survive its loss. These are usually couples who were more in love with love than with each other. And when the initial passion subsides, there is nothing to build on.

When the split takes place, the man is really down in the dumps. Deeply depressed. Unbearably lonely. Some men actually die of broken hearts. German scientists have established that what they describe as 'severe love sickness' can cause hypertension leading to permanent disability and sometimes death. The victims, they report, are usually men. Men are also three times as likely to commit suicide over an unhappy love affair as women.

These hyper-reactions may seem surprising, even unbelievable, but I told you in the beginning that men were susceptible to love. And they are just as vulnerable when it comes to the loss of love. We do not always realize this because men tend to keep all their romantic feelings and emotions to themselves. Everything is bottled up inside. A woman rarely knows how intensely a man feels about her. He never tells her. And this bottling up of the emotions makes the end of a love affair extra traumatic for men. If they were able to talk about their feelings, to confide in someone about how lonely and depressed they were, it would help. The broken hearts and suicides could be prevented in most cases.

The majority of couples survive the loss of first-stage love and settle happily into second-stage or conjugal love. It sounds a little staid, a little dull compared to first-stage love, but I can assure you that it is anything but. I am not talking about passion dwindling into mild affection. I am talking about love. Love and liking are very different. You can love someone more than you like him or like him more than you love him. 'As much as she exasperates me,' one man told me, 'as much as I can't stand her half the time, I love her more than anything in the world. I couldn't live without her.' He had been married to her for thirty-seven years. That's love. Real love.

Second-stage love develops over the years, increases every year as you both stretch to expand your horizons, as you share your joys and sorrows, as you become far more than you were when you first married. It comes after you have nursed him through the flu and his gallbladder operation or whatever and discovered that he is the world's worst patient. Impossible, demanding – and scared to death. It comes after you have huddled together in the stands on bleak November Saturdays year after year to watch your son play on the school football team. It comes after he has lost his job and you have both gone through nightmare weeks before he finds another. It comes when you realize that your second honeymoon was far more exciting than your first. It comes when you stop criticizing him for being so security conscious and realize that this is one of the qualities that attracted you to him in the first place. It comes when you realize that he knows all your faults and loves you just as you are – not as some romantic ideal woman whom the real you can never measure up to.

You can disagree. You can quarrel. But it never affects that solid core of love you have accumulated over the years. The two halves have become a whole without either losing its identity.

Second-stage love is friendship, tenderness, caring, understanding, passion, steadfastness, loyalty, and the ability to rise above petty exasperations. It is more than the sum of its parts. And no one can appreciate it who has not experienced it.

24

Marriage has always been absolutely delightful for men. The husband has brought home the bacon and his wife has cooked it, served it, scoured the frying pan and, a little later, hopped into bed to satisfy his other appetite. He has basked in the married state the way a cat basks in the sun on its favourite windowsill. And why not? A man's home was his castle and he was king.

Until practically the day before yesterday, the married man was happier and healthier than anyone else. Marriage turned out to be the greatest promoter of male longevity ever discovered. Men who lived alone had a 94 per cent higher mortality rate than married men. Wives have lived longer than their husbands, but they have never enjoyed quite the same sense of happy well-being. Single women, in fact, ranked just below husbands on the happiness scale. The married woman was third. And the poor bachelors were at the bottom of the heap, down where life is lonely and ridden with anxiety.

In the past, but not all that long ago, a man married because he needed a regular, socially accepted sexual outlet. A woman married because marriage was her only means of support unless she had a rich father. Both partners knew what to expect. Happiness was not a prime consideration. It was more like the raisins in the marital loaf. And sometimes the measure was scant. Husband and wife had their ups and downs, but unless the downs were truly horrendous, the couple stayed together. They built a life together. They raised a family. And, whether or not they thought of it in these exact terms, they considered themselves a link in the long chain of civilization.

Then everything changed. Sex was almost as available as the morning paper – with no commitments involved. And women discovered that a whole world of financial and emotional independence was opening up to them. The marriage contract was no longer sex and services in return for support. It was based on emotional reciprocity. Today people marry because they want someone who cares about them and what happens to them.

Marriage has become more of a process than an institution. Only those who can adapt to change make a success of it. They are the fortunate ones. They have a partner who is here today and will be here tomorrow. And for most of us, the person we marry is the only here-today, here-tomorrow person in our lives. But divorce has become a growth industry. Almost every second marriage ends in divorce. So it seems as if that here-today, here-tomorrow partner might not be here tomorrow unless we learn to adjust. And men have a lot more adjusting to do than women. They also find it more difficult, not only because they have a lot more to lose in the present forms of marriage, but because they detest change.

Men really do hate change and I want to go into this a little because it has everything to do with their present attitude towards marriage. Men welcome some changes. A new car, for instance, or a promotion to a better job in another city. But just try moving the living room furniture around or changing your hairstyle and a man will protest.

I know a brilliant scientist who has worked for years in the field of genetic engineering, something that has the potential for changing our lives in still unforeseen ways. This man became terribly upset when his wife had his favourite chair upholstered. It was not that he did not like the new fabric. This man who was devoting himself to unlocking the secrets of creation in order to produce new forms of life drew the line at a change as simple as a re-upholstered chair. Men are like that.

Women should keep this in mind when their husbands criticize them. Many women try to change themselves to please their husbands. It is usually a mistake.

'You talk too much,' he will say. 'Why don't you try letting someone else get a word in edgeways once in a while?'

Or 'Meatloaf again? Don't you know how to make anything else?'

Or 'For God's sake! You look like a blimp. Why don't you lose some weight?'

And the wife tries to please.

The next time the neighbours come over to play cards, she throttles down her flow of conversation. When their guests leave, her husband says, 'What was wrong with you tonight? You sat there like a bump on a log.' He had fallen in love with her partly because of her non-stop chatter.

Another woman will start leafing through cookbooks looking for new dishes that will fit in her food budget. But when she starts serving them, her husband protests. 'What kind of meal is that to give a hungry man? What about some hamburger once in a while? Or a meatloaf?' He didn't really want a change in menus. He just wanted to fuss a little and throw his weight around.

The business of losing weight is probably the most loaded of all. There have been a number of studies done on this, which indicate that the woman who listens to her husband on this subject and tries to please him is going to end up on the losing side – and I don't mean just pounds.

Researchers who followed twelve couples in which the wives had lost significant amounts of weight found that two couples got divorced and one couple separated after the wife reached her weight-loss goal. Others said that their relationship had changed for the worse. Only one couple seems to have been unaffected by the wife's new slim figure.

'The women felt more self-esteem,' said Dr John Marshall, associate professor of psychiatry at the University of Wisconsin Medical School, 'but the husbands were very unhappy. They were jealous, full of anxiety and in some cases became impotent.' The men did not really want their wives to change. They wanted their plump dumplings back again.

The only change a man really feels comfortable with in his wife or his marriage is a little something new and different in their sexual routine now and then. But for the rest, they want their wives and their marriages to conform to the traditional pattern. They want their marriages – like those of their fathers and grandfathers – to be geared to their needs.

A lot of men think of their wives as replacing their mothers. 'The wife becomes a support system. She integrates him, fulfils him, provides a home for him and enables him to be out in the world and feel more secure about himself,' says Alan Shanel, a New York psychotherapist. 'Many men can function better in the world if they know they have a home behind them. And they do not feel adequate to establish that home themselves.'

But not all that many women are interested in being a support system any more. Women want a husband who will consider them an equal partner, not a kind of privileged domestic. The power struggle that ensues as women claim more rights and power from men who are understandably reluctant to relinquish them has turned many unions into little civil wars that end in mutual secession.

'Nobody knows how to be married today,' anthropologist Margaret Mead said in one of the last interviews she granted. 'Every marriage has to be rethought. It is like the New York subway. There are no maps in the station. You have to get on a train to discover that you are on the wrong one. It is the same in marriage. You often have to make a mistake before you do the right thing.'

The single greatest change in marriage may be the emergence of the dual-career marriage. There have always been marriages in which both husband and wife worked, but now they are becoming the norm. They represent almost 50 per cent of marriages in the United States. And the men involved are finding them a *terra incognita*. Unsurveyed and unmapped.

Husbands in dual-career marriages tend to feel cheated. They are not getting the care and attention that their friends and colleagues with non-working wives enjoy. (Remember, I am speaking in terms of the average husband, not necessarily yours who may be wonderful.) Dinner is not on the table when he gets home. He has to rummage through the laundry basket for his socks. The bed is never made. He misses the rapt attention his wife used to pay to his stories of what went on at the office. Now she wants equal time to talk about what went on at her office. And she expects him to do the dishes while she puts the children to bed.

The ripple effect of all this is staggeringly far-reaching. One has to think in terms of tidal waves, not ripples. It is too strong to reverse, but many men persist in fighting what has to be a losing battle. Change is irreversible.

Andrea complained that when she came home from her job as an insurance claims adjuster, she was longing to sit down and relax and chat with Kevin. But every night when she walked in the house, Kevin would be on the telephone with his mother. Telling his mother what had gone on in the office. What the boss had said when the receptionist came back from a two-hour lunch. About the new vacation schedule. When he hung up, he would make himself a drink and watch the news until Andrea had supper on the table. When she asked him about his day, he grunted. When she tried to tell him about hers, he yawned.

Finally one night Andrea said, 'You can talk to your mother by the hour, but you can't say two words to me. I put my salary in our joint account, but you never do a thing to help around the house. What's going on?'

'My mother cares about me,' Kevin said stiffly. 'And she cares about my father. He never has to come home to an empty house after a day's work. He never has to wait for more than an hour to get something to eat.'

'I don't see why you can't start supper since you get home first,' Andrea said. 'It was different for your parents. Your mother has never gone out to work.'

'You're damned tooting right she never did. Her marriage has always come first.' Andrea left the table in a fury. Kevin was trying to get even with her for not being the kind of wife his mother had been.

When the extent of his childishness registered with her, Andrea was coldly angry. And then amused. And then sad. A few days later she suggested that they see a marriage counsellor and try to work out this problem of his feeling neglected.

'We don't need a marriage counsellor. Everything would be fine if you just stayed home like other women do.'

'What other women?' she asked. 'And what would I do all day? Besides, I love my job.'

'Your job!' he said scornfully. 'You better decide which is more important to you. Your job or me.'

It turned out to be an easier decision than Andrea had expected. Kevin was punishing her for having a job. If she stayed at home, he would probably try to punish her for something else, like not polishing his shoes. He certainly was never going to try to understand how she felt. Who needed a marriage like this?

Even the men, and I am thinking of the younger men especially, who claim to support the women's movement still expected marriage to revolve around them and their interests, just as their father's marriage revolved around him and his interests. As we know, a man's job is the centre of his life. When you ask a man what he does, he usually says something like 'I'm with the Turtle Tractor Company', or 'I'm with the Sticky Wicket Stock Group', whether he is the file clerk or the comptroller.

Studies show that what a man does for a living counts twice as much as his education in the eyes of the world. The Princeton man who works as a golf pro has a lower status than the man who attended Basket Weaving U. and is president of Amalgamated Sturm und Drang. And this extends to wives, as well. Mrs Princeton may have gone to university and be a highly regarded biochemist, but she is lower in the social pecking order than Mrs Sturm und Drang, housewife, since even today social status is still keyed to the husband's job. A non-working wife, in fact, is coming to be considered something of a status symbol. Although not by many women. The 'just a housewife' tag that some women still use to describe themselves shows how much a status symbol they think they are.

The interesting thing is that Mr Princeton has more in common with Mrs Sturm und Drang than he does with her husband. And Mrs Princeton and Mr Sturm und Drang are also very much alike in significant ways. When psychologists compared single-career and dual-career couples in 189 marriages, they discovered that the dual-career husbands did not enjoy life anywhere near as much as the single-career husbands.

Husbands with working wives were worriers. They worried about their health, both physical and mental. They worried about where they were living and whether they should move. They worried that they had fallen into a rut, in their personal and business lives. They found it difficult to show affection for their wives and that worried them too.

In their eyes, their masculine self-image was tarnished. The fact that their wives worked meant that they would be pressured into taking over a certain amount of domestic chores – women's work. They loved their wives, but they felt that their marriages were lacking.

The housewives resembled the dual-career husbands in many ways. Their self-esteem was low. They were worriers too. They worried about their health and their marriage and their children. They were often seriously depressed.

The single-career husbands had their own worries, but these were of a different order from those of the men married to working wives. The single-career husbands worried about inflation, the possibility of war, racial violence, the energy crisis, the stock market. But their worries seldom kept them awake at night. They felt in robust good health. They looked forward to each new day and welcomed its challenges. And they considered themselves happily married.

The dual-career wives were much like the single-career husbands. They had plenty of confidence in themselves. They were happy and healthy. They felt good about their jobs and their marriages. And they did not worry all that much.

'The picture that emerges,' the researchers wrote, 'is one of the dual-career husband experiencing a reduction in important services, an increase in his burden of responsibilities and a loss of his special status in the family. The satisfactions and comforts that husbands come to expect when the wife functions as a kind of servant, homemaker and mother are inevitably interfered with. The husband's central position in the family is eroded and with it his former dominance and power.'

A divorce lawyer who has presided over the dissolution of many dual-career marriages comments that 'while there are undoubtedly many marriages that have been strengthened when a wife works, the ones I see in my practice are the others. It takes a monumentally self-assured man not to be intimidated by his wife's success in an area he was raised to regard as his alone.'

It is even difficult for men to come to terms with the reasons their wives work. Three out of five wives work, according to a survey by the A. C. Nielsen people, because the family needed the money or they wanted money for extras – summer camp for the kids, a second car, a new kitchen, a family vacation. Only 19 per cent of the women questioned said that they worked because they wanted to. Their husbands, however, did not see it quite the same way. Three out of five men said that their wives worked because they wanted to. Only 29 per cent said that the family needed the second income.

Several major advertising agencies did studies of dual-career marriages to ascertain just how much husbands participated in the running of the household. Should they start slanting their advertising for frozen foods, detergents, labour-saving devices, and all the rest to the man of the house as well as the woman?

All the surveys came up with the same finding. Men did a lot more talking about helping than actual helping. As one research director put it, 'The male dragon in the kitchen is a reluctant one.'

Eighty per cent of the men questioned in one survey said that even though their wife worked full time, they expected her to take full responsibility for the household, the shopping, and the children. 'Today's man may be sympathetic to the fact that this is a tough juggling act,' the Batten, Barton, Durstine and Osborne study commented, 'yet the majority are not willing to lift the traditional household responsibilities from their wives.'

Thirty-five per cent of the husbands in the Doyle, Dane, Bernbach study agreed that vacuuming was an acceptable male chore and not demeaning to the masculine image, but only 27 per cent of them had ever pushed a vacuum across the living room rug. 'It is easier for men to accept the possibility of women as brain surgeons than to release their own wives from the drudgery of laundry and cleaning the bathroom,' the researchers concluded.

Men understand very well that they have as much to lose as their wives have to gain. Women are escaping from the solitary confinement of the home into the office and the laboratory, the sales territory and the stock exchange. They dress better and feel more attractive than when they stayed at home. They meet people. They face challenges. Life becomes exciting. And they get paid for it. The only thing that has not changed is the housework. It is there waiting for them every night. Rings around the tub. Dust bath under the bed. Dishes in the sink. Even the most reluctant husband finds himself forced to take over some of the domestic chores, if only to make sure he has clean underwear for the next day. But he does the minimum – and usually grudgingly.

The working wife spends an average of twenty-six hours a week on housework; her husband spends thirty-six minutes. Nor do children make much difference in the amount of help a husband gives his wife. A three-year-long study of 1,400 dual-career marriages with children under eleven years old showed that only one father in five helped out with the youngsters.

It is not only American men who refuse to pull their weight around the house. Working wives in Denmark spend an average of three hours a day on housework; their husbands spend fifteen minutes. This finding so infuriated the Danish Minister of Labour that he announced, 'Equality for men and women in the right to work outside the home must imply equality in the duty to work inside the home.' But he admitted that he did not think his words would carry much weight with Danish husbands.

The same lopsided shouldering of the load is found in the Soviet Union, despite the fact that the Soviet constitution guarantees equality of the sexes. In this economy where the non-working wife is the oddity, a government survey found that women did all the household chores and spent long hours queueing up to buy food after work while their husbands either watched television or whiled away the time drinking with their men friends until their wives had bought dinner, cooked it, and put it on the table.

The real heroes are the blue-collar husbands of America. They do not talk much about the women's movement and when they do, they do not have much that is good to say about it, but they pitch in and help their wives more cheerfully and competently than their white-collar neighbours.

'I found that the blue-collar guys – the electricians, plumbers, bull-dozer operators – were doing twenty per cent of the household tasks,' reports Dr John De Frain, associate professor of human development and the family at the University of Nebraska. Dr De Frain interviewed forty blue-collar workers and forty professional men in Madison, Wisconsin, on what, if anything, they did around the house. He found that the professional men did only 5 per cent of the domestic chores, although they gave a lot of lip service to women's rights.

'The blue-collar guy often has less power in his job, so he tends to put on a real macho face in public. He will swagger around and boast about wearing the pants in his family. But when he gets home, he tends to let the barriers down. After driving a heavy machine all day or stamping out parts on an assembly line, taking care of children and working around the house don't seem all that bad.'

Sex in a dual-career marriage often becomes as much of a hassle as housework. The demands of a full-time job plus running the household leave many women so deeply fatigued that they have little zest for sex. 'If she were seeing another guy,' one husband complained, 'I'd have a better chance of getting her in the sack. She wouldn't want me to suspect that she was fooling around. But what chance do I have against her job? She is a success. And she's crazy about success.'

There is a story – and it is probably apocryphal – of the husband who understood the effect of fatigue on sexual desire. He volunteered to take over his working wife's household responsibilities for a week in the hope that there would be a sexual payoff at the weekend.

He shopped and cooked, did the wash and coped with the baby sitter, took his turn one morning in the nursery school car pool and shepherded his twin daughters to the dentist on his lunch hour. That Friday night after she had relaxed with a drink and enjoyed the dinner her husband had cooked, the wife said, 'I really feel like a new woman, thanks to you, darling. This is the first Friday night I can remember that I haven't felt so tired that my bones ached.'

'Well, don't expect me to make love with you tonight,' her husband said petulantly. 'I've had it. And I still have to clean the kitchen. I can't work all day and half the night and fuck too.'

The childless couple can usually avoid the housework and sex hassles because their two incomes give them more financial leeway, but this does not mean that their marriage is stress-free. When there are no children, it is often because the wife is deeply committed to her career. And this commitment often results in husband and wife competing with each other.

'It bugs me,' Frank said, 'that I feel competitive with Angela. But I do. It really eats at me that she earns more money than I do. Before we were married I felt very protective of her. I would have done anything for her. But I can't feel that way anymore. She earns so much more than I do. I'd give anything to make more than she does.'

The intra-marriage competition manifests itself in other ways as well. Women have to fight to get their husbands to take their jobs seriously. Men still assume that their own jobs come first.

Bruce, a successful lawyer in his thirties, often said how proud he was of Nora's rapid climb to the management level of a department store chain. But he complained bitterly whenever she asked him to go with her to the semi-annual executive dinners.

'I feel as if I'm one of the wives,' Bruce said. 'I can't contribute to the talk about your plans to start up more suburban stores or do more mail order, but I sure as hell don't feel that I should have to spend the evening swapping stories about children and maids with the wives – especially since we don't have any children.'

'How do you think I feel,' Nora countered, 'when we go to those deadly dinner parties with your law partners and you all talk about tax law and I have to swap stories about children and maids – and we don't have either?'

This conflict was described to a panel of fifteen hundred male executives who were asked how they thought Nora and Bruce should handle this problem. Almost 40 per cent of the men thought that Nora should go to the dinners by herself, even though it might be socially awkward. Close to 50 per cent felt that Bruce should go with her and stop making an issue of it. When it came to Nora's going to dinner with Bruce and his law partners, almost 70 per cent of the executive panel said that of course she should go. Only 17 per cent suggested that Bruce might go alone.

What is really at issue with both Bruce and Frank is power. Frank felt that he had lost power because his wife made more money than he did. Bruce felt that he had lost power because he had to attend dinners as Nora's husband.

It made him feel like a wife.

The ultimate power in a marriage is decision-making, which has always been the male prerogative. But this is changing too. One study that has been going on for some twenty years has regularly queried a group of 1,200 women to see how their thinking has changed. Over the years the largest shift has been in their responses to this statement: 'Most of the important decisions in the life of the family should be made by the man of the house.' In 1962, two-thirds of the women agreed. By 1977, two-thirds of the women disagreed. By 1987 I expect 99 per cent of the women will disagree.

The most important decision that faces a husband and wife is probably that of whether or not to have children. Many women are resisting motherhood, especially those who are intent on their careers. They know that if they stay at home with their child during those vitally important early years, they are going to fall behind and will probably never regain the momentum they have now, never reach the goals they set for themselves. And yet they are not willing to compromise the future of their child by going back to work immediately. Women today have learned how important it is to be with their child in the early years. They go through harsh soul-searching and agonizing over whether to be pregnant now or later or never.* Demographers tell us that 25 per cent of couples between twenty-five and twenty-nine will never have children and another 25 per cent of this group will settle for having one child.

---

* There has recently been an upsurge in the number of women over thirty who are having their first child. 'There is a profound baby hunger around these days,' one psychiatrist reports, 'among women who have put off having children.' No one has yet analysed it carefully, but it may be that these women have come to the decision that children are more important than success. Or they may have discovered that they are not going to reach those hoped-for peaks. So they are now going to have a child before it is too late.

The decision is easy for men. Many are pressuring their working wives to get pregnant. It is not the old story of 'keep them barefoot and pregnant'. Men have gone far beyond that primitive way of thinking. It is simply that men have less to give up than women. The responsibility for the child still falls on the mother.

We hear about young fathers who have become 'house husbands' and others who happily share half the care of the baby, but as I travel around the country and talk to young mothers, I find that these men are almost as rare as crows' teeth. The only reason we hear about them is because they are so unusual. There is also an element of wishful thinking involved. By publicizing these men, others may be induced to follow in their footsteps.

Many men who pressure their wives to have a baby end up regretting it. Children place an almost unbearable stress on marriage — all marriages, not only the dual-career marriage. The idea that children strengthen marriage 'is the joke of the century', says a Californian psychologist. Another psychologist, the late Angus Campbell, who devoted much of his professional life to the study of happiness, said that 'Raising a family seems to be one of those tasks like losing weight or waxing the car that is less fun to be doing than to have done.' Dr Campbell, who observed 2,164 parents over a generation span, found that the birth of their first child marked a plunge in the happiness quotient of a couple that lasted until their last child left home.

Ironically, when the children do leave home, it is the father who suffers more. It has always been thought that it was the mother who suffered from the 'empty nest syndrome', but sociologist Lillian B. Rubin of the University of California found in interviewing 160 women that 'all except one responded to the departure of their children with decided relief'.

Their husbands did not share this relief. The men by and large had had little time for their children when they were growing up – and not much interest in them, but when the children were ready to leave the nest, the fathers were full of regret. One man who had read up on the empty-nest syndrome said, 'Everything I read convinced me that my wife would have a really tough time when the kids left home. But she didn't. I was the one who almost cracked up.

'I had started to let up a little on the time and energy I was devoting to my job. I decided that I had cheated myself. I had not allowed myself time to enjoy my children as they were growing up. They were strangers to me in some ways. I wanted to get closer to them. But they had no desire or need to get closer to me at that time.

'When they were little, they used to wheedle me to do things with them, but I tried to avoid whatever it was they wanted. Now that I wanted to do things with them, they were too busy with their own lives.

'So I went through the empty-nest miseries by myself.'

When the children leave home, husbands and wives tend to turn to each other for comfort and companionship. They rediscover the happiness that fled when the children arrived. And the years that follow can be truly the best of their lives.

Some couples, however, find themselves miles apart emotionally and intellectually. The marriage had become a support system for the children and little else. Left alone in their empty nest, husband and wife faced each other as strangers who had little in common with each other.

At one time they might have sighed and tried to put up with each other. But no longer. Especially not men. This is one marital area in which they have welcomed change. A man in his fifties can look forward to another fifteen or twenty vigorous years. If his wife has lost her appeal, he starts looking around for someone else. In days gone by when men married later and life expectancies were shorter, he could look forward to only another five years or so of an active life. Divorce hardly seemed worthwhile. But now he has almost a generation* ahead of him.

So there we are. Marriage is changing. The married man no longer thinks of himself as being in the happiest of all situations. According to a recent Gallup Poll, there are now more happy women than happy men. Almost half the women in the USA consider themselves happy, but only about a third of the men do.

This too will change. They will be happy again. But I suspect that it will take at least another generation before men can adapt to the notion that marriage is an equal partnership. By that time there will undoubtedly be other changes to face, for there is no perfect relationship. Human beings are imperfect. Especially husbands and wives – as I will discuss in the next chapter.

* A generation is considered the span between a person's birth and the birth of her first child.

25

Not even infidelity is experienced in the same way by men and women. They approach it as differently as they approach marriage itself for reasons that go way back to prehistory.

Men have always been unfaithful. In his blockbuster sex report, Kinsey told the world that 'about half of all married males have intercourse with women other than their wives at some time while they are married'. The idea that every other husband cheated on his wife at one time or another was a shocker in 1948. Today only the most naive would be surprised.

What is surprising, considering our more relaxed sexual standards, is the relatively small increase in the number of unfaithful husbands over the years since 1948. Currently six out of ten husbands are unfaithful at some time or possibly most of the time, according to quite reliable figures. What I find particularly fascinating is a recent survey that shows 60 per cent of the male population thinks adultery is wrong. There seems to be a certain element of hypocrisy here.

Men do not stray because they do not get enough sex at home – although they may not. 'What is involved is a powerful desire for novelty,' says Dr Nathaniel Branden. 'Many men engage in outside relationships with women they perceive as less attractive and less sexually exciting than their wife in their search for variety.' Sex theorist Albert Ellis confirms this. 'Men are fed up with the monotony of marriage,' he says. 'They find it a bore. Monogamy is not for humans, it's for angels.'

There is a school of thought that insists that men cannot

help philandering. It is their genes that are to blame. 'To put it in Darwinian terms,' says psychologist Richard Hagen, 'sexual arousal in women was not as crucial to the survival of the species as it was in men, since women do not have to be aroused or have orgasms in order to reproduce.' As a result of men's hovering on the brink of arousal most of the time, these victims of their genes cannot restrain themselves from giving in when the opportunity presents herself. Or so the theory goes.

There are some men who are worried about their virility, so they keep testing it with woman after woman. And some men just plain fall in love with another woman.

So there we have it. Men want variety. They are easily aroused. They are not quite sure of their manly vigour. And they are emotionally vulnerable. Put all this together and the result, six times out of ten, is infidelity. Infidelity is a breach of the marriage contract, but many men do not seem to have understood what it was they promised when they made their wedding vows. It may be somewhat cheering for a woman to know that four men out of ten are so devoted to their wives or so timorous or so faithful to their marriage vows that they never stray.

What may cheer a woman even more is that most men do not take their extracurricular affairs seriously. To them an affair is a caper, an adventure. It is almost strictly sexual. The faithless husband rarely considers breaking up his marriage. 'I always let her know that I'm happily married,' one man of affairs said. 'And I make sure that she understands that I'm not looking for a shoulder to cry on or someone to discuss philosophy with. When I make a play for a woman, it's for one reason only. I want to fuck.'

Many men go from affair to affair or one-night stand to one-night stand. Or carry on two at the same time. It is fun for them. They disclaim any and all obligations. If a woman makes the mistake of getting serious, that is her problem.

In a tape-recorded session at which I was not present, three married men recorded their thoughts about extramarital adventures for me. They all agreed that what a man with a roving eye should look for was a wife – another man's wife.

'The unmarried woman may get serious and then things get sticky,' said the first.

'There's another thing about married women,' said the second. 'I don't suppose I should say it, but I get an extra kick out of doing it to another man's wife. It kind of makes me feel more of a man than he is.'

'And they can't make scenes,' the third contributed. 'If she sees you with another woman, she can't go into a big act about it. For all she knows it could be your wife. And she doesn't bug you about taking her out, because she has to be home nights.'

'That's right,' said the second man. 'A married woman will cook you lunch and then you make love. Or vice versa. Ten minutes later you shower and are back in the office without anyone being the wiser.'

'But you have to be careful about where you park,' the first man warned. 'You don't want the neighbours to start talking. It's not fair to her. And it could mean trouble for you.'

As I listened to the tape, I had to smile. They sounded so immature. I was not even sure how much of it was the voice of experience and how much was wishful thinking and boasting. But it was an insight into the way men feel about their affairs and their reluctance to jeopardize their marriages.

A woman can usually tell if her husband is having an affair, but many see smoke where there is no fire. They think flirting is an indication of infidelity. It is usually just the opposite. The man who flirts in the presence of his wife is not embarking on the opening stages of an affair.

However, if a woman accuses her husband of infidelity enough she will put the idea into his head. Her jealousy may create the very situation she feared.

Most men flirt to reassure themselves that they are still attractive to the opposite sex. If your husband flirts at a party where you are present, you ought to allow yourself to feel a little smug that other women find him attractive.

There are exceptions. Some men flirt to make their wives feel miserable. They are not particularly interested in the other woman; it is just that they get a sadistic satisfaction out of making their wives suffer. These women are usually insecure and do not have a very high self-esteem, and their husbands like to keep them that way.

This insecurity can breed jealousy. And here too men and women are different. A woman's jealousy has a big element of fear in it. She is afraid of being displaced. Male jealousy is more possessive and it has a large sexual component. The idea that another man attracts his wife drives him practically crazy.

The significant clues to infidelity often go unnoticed, even by the most perceptive of women. It is probably because no woman really wants to know that her husband is involved with another woman. If your husband suddenly starts giving you presents for no reason, you may be justified in being suspicious.

If he comes home from work later than usual and is as shower fresh and clean as when he left that morning, you might become suspicious. If he suddenly sports a very expensive silk tie that costs more than twice as much as the tie you got him for Christmas and he tells you that it was on sale – well, you could be suspicious.

The same thing holds true if you suddenly start getting wrong-number calls in the evening and on weekends and he jumps to answer the phone. Or if he starts moving differently when you make love, or tries some new sexual ploy.

None of these by itself means anything, but two or three may add up to something. More tangible clues include lipstick on the shirt collar, the clinging fragrance of a perfume that you do not use, a red hair on his shoulder (and you are blonde), or those little bruises made by love bites. The clincher can be if he comes home with a venereal infection – that is, if you yourself are above reproach.

Another giveaway is a pattern of euphoria followed by depression and complaints of stomach-aches, headaches, and all the rest of the roster of psychosomatic ailments. Many men feel tremendously guilty when they cheat, but not guilty enough to stop. If their wife is tender and loving while they are fooling around with someone else, they feel even more guilty. And the guilt eventually surfaces as heart palpitations or ulcers.

Once a woman knows, once she is really sure, what does she do about the situation?

Nothing.

Absolutely nothing, with two exceptions that I will discuss further on.

It is not easy to do nothing. A betrayed woman has so many emotions churning around inside her – hurt and hate, guilt and vengeance, sadness. She feels rejected. She wants to lash out in anger. She wants to cry. 'Be angry, cry your eyes out. But in private,' I tell women. The wife is not aware of the intensity of her emotional turbulence. Anything she says or does at this point is going to be overemotional and counterproductive.

It takes every bit of discipline and pride a woman can muster to do nothing, to go on with her daily routine. But this is by far the wisest course. No ostentatious moping, no nasty remarks. Her energies should go towards being as pleasant and tender as possible. This is a time to make home and home life as appealing as she knows how.

This is all a woman should do unless her hand is forced –

and I will come to that later. Play a waiting game and keep what she knows to herself. Time is on her side. She may never have to let on that she was aware her husband was seeing another woman.

The fact is that most affairs are short-term. My feeling is that a one-night stand is nothing to get all that upset about. These things happen. There is not much to be gained by making an issue of it. After all, a woman may be guilty of the same little misstep herself.

Affairs that deserve the name may last anywhere from two weeks to six months. Seldom longer. A man gets into an affair because of the novelty and the lure of romance and excitement. It is wild and wonderful at first. Its very illicitness is attractive. But this phase is short. The novelty wears off. Their meetings become routine.

All he really wants to do is have a drink, have sex, have her tell him he is wonderful, and then get dressed and go home. But the other woman begins to ask for more. Why can't they have dinner out some night? She is getting tired of preparing those intimate little suppers. Why can't he arrange to see her during the weekend? She gets so lonely. When the holidays come around, she feels neglected. And the erring husband feels that his mistress has become a drag.

One day he realizes that he isn't looking forward to seeing her that afternoon or evening. The whole thing is a bore. And expensive. He can't understand what has happened. It had been so great at first. He used to find himself smiling with pleasure as he walked down the street. But no more. And he breaks off with her.

The affair is over. But not quite. He feels guilty. What he wants to do more than anything else is confess. Confess and get it off his conscience. And whom does he want to hear his confession? His wife, of course.

'Men often ask me if they should tell their wives,' a psychiatrist told me. 'They have a lot of difficulty coping with the consequences of cheating. Even when the affair is over and finished with, it is still very much with a man. He thinks that if he can just tell his wife and get it off his conscience, everything will be all right again.'

Confessing may help the man, but what it really does is transfer the burden of infidelity from his shoulders to his wife's. It does not make him feel all that much better. It makes his wife feel terrible. They both feel miserable.

'I almost jumped off the Empire State Building,' Tekla told me. 'I can't tell you how shaken I was when Sanford confessed that he'd been having an affair. It was as if my world had come to an end. I wanted to kill myself. I lay awake all night. In the morning, I decided that I'd jump. I got dressed and got in the car and drove into New York. I left the car at a parking garage and walked a couple of blocks over to Fifth Avenue.

'I took the elevator up. And down again. And up. I must have gone up and down five times. And then I felt sick. I went to the ladies' room and I threw up. Somehow that made me feel better. I had a Coke to settle my stomach and then I got the car and drove back home. I never told Sanford about it.'

This is one of the exceptions that I mentioned earlier. If a man confesses, you can no longer pretend that you know nothing. The other exception is if he has picked up a venereal disease. You cannot ignore that either. It is not like catching the flu.

In these two situations, the wisest thing for a woman to do, in my opinion, is issue a flat ultimatum. Give him an either/or. Break the affair off immediately and forever or face separation or divorce. It is not much of a risk. His confession indicates that the affair is over. And the man who has picked up an infection is usually not going to want to see the source again.

And if your life gets emotionally out of hand in the days and weeks that follow, do not hesitate to seek therapy. Both of you. It can be immensely helpful.

After the initial shock, a woman usually comes to terms with her husband's infidelity. She does not like it, but there it is. It happened. In time she forgives, although she may never be able to forget. But let a woman be unfaithful and watch her husband's righteous indignation, his angry outrage, his horror. A wife who strays has always been considered far more culpable than a husband who cheats.

A good two hundred years ago the biographer James Boswell said flatly, 'There is a great difference between the offence of infidelity in a man and that of his wife.' And Samuel Johnson agreed. 'The difference is boundless,' Johnson said. 'The man imposes no bastards on his wife.'

In our age of birth control, this would hardly seem to be a major consideration, but it is one of those core reactions that go back to caveman days. I wrote earlier that sex was Mother Nature's way of keeping the male interested in the female so that he would feed and protect her and the child he had fathered. Today specialists in the history of human development point out that it took more than a steady supply of sex for early man to think of himself as a father.

'Confidence in paternity is required for a male parental role to evolve,' say Dr Martin Daly and Dr Margo Wilson of McMaster University in Ontario. 'Any male who expends much time and energy rearing unrelated young is at a selective disadvantage.' They are referring to gene survival. In prehistoric days a man had all he could do to take care of his woman and child. If another man had fathered the child that he was taking care of, thinking it his own, he was at a disadvantage. Life spans were short. He might die or be killed before he fathered a child with that woman who had deceived him. He would have spent his time and energy ensuring that another man's child would survive, another man's genes would be passed on to future generations – and lost his own chance of early immortality.

In almost all species, not only in humans, the male animal who helps protect and provide for the young tries to make sure that his female mates with him and him alone. Scientists see this as making sure that he does not have to nurture another male's offspring. That primitive possessiveness still bubbles up from some ancient part of the brain when a man discovers his wife has been unfaithful.

His reactions are much more violent. He takes the betrayal far more seriously than a woman takes a man's infidelity. And his ways of dealing with it are more drastic. They may account for the fact that throughout history, fewer women than men have been unfaithful. It was too difficult to conceal the consequences if a woman became pregnant and the penalties were frightening. A scarlet letter was among the mildest of punishments visited upon an adulteress. Even now, with our casual approach to sex and easily available birth control, only one out of three women is unfaithful. And that woman is usually the more independent working woman. Fewer housewives indulge in affairs.

But when a woman does have an affair, it usually involves love as well as sex. It is a mixture of heartbreak and roses. Women throw themselves into the relationship and when it is over, they grieve. Even though they themselves probably initiated the break.

A sociologist who questioned some seventy men and women who had been divorced found that a third of them had been unfaithful while they were married. Two-thirds of the women had found their love affairs highly exciting and romantic. Only 34 per cent of the men had felt deeply involved. But the women paid a price for their high-voltage romances. They felt twice as guilty as the men.

That heavy load of guilt makes women, like men, want to confess. They tend to look on confession as a great emotional bath from which they will emerge cleansed and forgiven. They are wrong. A man can confess and get away with it. But a woman? Hardly ever.

When women ask me if they should tell their husbands, I advise against it. If she is woman enough to have an affair, she must be woman enough to keep it to herself. There are times when total communication can bring a marriage crashing down around one's ears.

A wife's infidelity poses a greater threat to the marriage than a husband's. Men react with anger, jealousy, and sometimes physical violence when they learn their wife has been unfaithful. 'I'll murder the guy,' they yell. And they mean it at that moment. 'Get out of my house,' the husband may shout – and throw her clothes out after her. He may beat her, walk out on her, lock her in the bedroom. Some men simply become very depressed and withdraw from the problem. In any case, the man's ego is far more damaged than that of the woman who discovers that her husband has betrayed her. 'Psychologically and in terms of marital stability, it is much more dangerous for women to engage in extramarital sex,' warns Dr Graham Spanier of Pennsylvania State University.

Knowing all this, I have nevertheless gone on record as saying that there are times when an affair can help a woman revitalize her marriage. She must be strong enough to keep it to herself and truly intent on preserving her marriage.

A love affair gives a woman the excitement and romance that have vanished from her marriage. It makes her skin glow and her eyes glisten. This is not at all true of men who have affairs. Their emotions are not as involved as a woman's. And just plain sex does not provide the stimulus that a love affair does. A woman's whole personality seems to take on a fresh sparkle.

Do you remember the scene in *Gigi* when the jaded young aristocrat looks at his mistress and realizes that she is not thinking of him?

> She's so gay tonight.
> She's like spring tonight.
> She's a rollicking, frolicking thing tonight.
> So disarming, soft and charming.
> She is not thinking of me . . .
>
> In her eyes tonight,
> There's a glow tonight.
> They're so bright they could light Fontainebleau tonight
> She's so gracious, so vivacious.
> She is not thinking of me . . .

In real life, husbands are not so cynical. They are delighted with the effect and do not look for the cause. The womans's happier feelings, her renewed interest in sex, and that love shimmer that makes her both mysterious and desirable can rekindle her husband's romantic urges and bring her marriage back to life.

Even the guilt she feels has its role. It makes her more considerate of her husband and more anxious to please him. A woman who spent the afternoon with her lover is unlikely to tell her husband that she has a headache that night. Her guilt makes her fear he might suspect.

It all goes back to the business of love and attraction being connected with excitement. Remember that some experts believe that love is at least 50 per cent adrenalin. And what produces adrenalin? Excitement.

The double standard still prevails — at least to a man's way of thinking — in matters of infidelity. If a man has an affair, a woman is expected to understand, to forgive and forget. And it may be easier for her to do this if she understands that her husband is scared to death that she won't.

But if a woman is unfaithful, her husband is not going to forgive and forget without making her miserable first. And maybe not then. There is not much she can do about this.

Knowing that his reactions were imprinted in his brain in prehistoric times and that his modern intellect is not yet able to cope with his primitive response may help a woman understand why. It will not help her change his reaction. The lesson here is that if a woman is unfaithful, it is wiser and kinder not to let her husband know. He may not be able to handle it.

PART SIX

Tomorrow's Man

26

This is just the beginning. There is more to know about the other sex. Much more. But now you have the basic tools and understanding of how men think and feel and why. You can go on to be your own researcher and explorer, building upon what you have learned here.

You will not be alone. Scientists are studying the emotional, mental, and physical differences between men and women with an interest they have never had before. Some very sophisticated techniques are being used to tease out which differences spring from nature and which are induced by nurture.

One thing is clear already. Men are at a crossroads. They have headed our families, our governments, our businesses for centuries. They have explored our planet and the space around it. They have made our laws and fought our wars. But in less than the span of a lifetime, their authority is being eroded. They are no longer in secure command of the basic unit of civilization, the family. The world they shaped is changing. One could think of them as sorcerer's apprentices who have triggered reactions that they can no longer control. They can neither control them nor adjust to them.

As Margaret Mead said, 'Every marriage has to be rethought.' The same is true of all relationships between men and women. This is an unsurveyed and unmapped territory. I think of it as a great challenge to women. They have a very special role to play. It is in their power to make men's lives better, to make them stronger and yet more tender, to make them happy again in an ever-changing world.

Women are the creators and most often the nurturers. I hope that every mother and mother-to-be who has read this book to learn more about the men in her life will use what she has learned to help her son become even more of a man than his father, a man who will want as much for the women in his life as he wants for himself. A mother can do this. It may be her ultimate power. To shape tomorrow's man.

And in the meantime, we must cherish the men in our lives. They are fragile. They are sad. They are vulnerable – and adorable. And they need us. What more could a woman ask? Except to have someone to love who loves her in return. And men do that too. God bless them.

Oh, and why do men leave that toilet seat up? Because it's easier. You leave it down, don't you.